SUPPORTING ONLINE STUDENTS

SUPPORTING ONLINE STUDENTS

A Guide to Planning, Implementing, and Evaluating Services

Anita Crawley

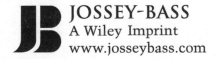

JOSSEY-BASS
A Wiley Imprint
www.josseybass.com

Published by Jossey-Bass
A Wiley Imprint
One Montgomery Street, Suite 1200, San Francisco, CA 94104-4594—www.josseybass.com

Jossey-Bass books and products are available through most bookstores. To contact Jossey-Bass directly call our Customer Care Department within the U.S. at 800-956-7739, outside the U.S. at 317-572-3986, or fax 317-572-4002.

Wiley also publishes its books in a variety of electronic formats and by print-on-demand. Some material included with standard print versions of this book may not be included in e-books or in print-on-demand. If the version of this book that you purchased references media such as CD or DVD that was not included in your purchase, you may download this material at http://booksupport.wiley.com. For more information about Wiley products, visit www.wiley.com.

Library of Congress Cataloging-in-Publication Data

Crawley, Anita, 1946–
  Supporting online students : a guide to planning, implementing, and evaluating services / Anita Crawley. – First edition.
      pages cm. – (The Jossey-Bass Higher and Adult Education Series)
  Includes bibliographical references and index.
  ISBN 978-1-118-07654-5 (hardback)
  ISBN 978-1-118-19284-9 (e-bk.)
  ISBN 978-1-118-19285-6 (e-bk.)
  ISBN 978-1-118-19286-3 (e-bk.)
 1. Web-based instruction.   2. Students–Services for–Technological innovations.   I. Title.
  LB1044.87.C75 2012
  371.33'44678–dc23

                              2011047501

Printed in the United States of America
FIRST EDITION
HB Printing   10 9 8 7 6 5 4 3 2 1

The Jossey-Bass Higher and
Adult Education Series

CONTENTS

	Foreword	xi
	Preface	xv
	About the Author	xxiii
1	Setting the Stage: The Transformation	1
2	Profile of Online Students	13
3	Supporting Online Students with Disabilities	38
4	Putting Services Online	63
5	Administrative Suite	83
6	Academic Services Suite	102
7	Personal Services Suite	129
8	Communications Suite	153
9	Planning and Implementation	178
10	Evaluation	199
	Final Thoughts	228
	References	230
	Index	245

I want to thank Tom, my husband and life partner, for always being in my corner. Together we produced two wonderful offspring, Alisha and Gregory. While the offspring are no longer physically close, they are always in my heart, as are grandchildren Juliana, Amaya, and Quentin and son-in-law Jon. Thanks for all your support.

FOREWORD

In this age of always-on, always-available uber-connectness, the value of deploying interactive web-based technologies to help more students achieve the dream of a college education may seem obvious and self-evident. Yet, the phenomenon of online learning—where a significant percentage of an academic program is delivered to students via web and online technologies—has only recently emerged from the margins of postsecondary education practice to assume its long-anticipated, mission-critical role.

Today's evidence points to increasing rates of online learning adoption, growth in the numbers and kinds of online program offerings available at colleges and universities of all kinds and sizes, and the diversification of the technological forms of instructional delivery. As the goal of increasing college graduates in the United States by more than 1 million students in less than six years has become a central part of the national postsecondary education conversation, the role of online learning takes on even more significance. The ongoing recognition that today's economies demand new skills for future workforce success has further accelerated online learning's move toward the middle of the mainstream institutional adoption.

As online learning has moved toward the mainstream, the need for services that maximize online student success has never been more pressing. Anita Crawley has written a timely and highly relevant guidebook that will come to be prized by its readers for helping them navigate the complex ecosystem of today's online learning. Crawley provides the essential framework needed to provide the full range of support services that are known to contribute to student success. As student success becomes the de facto measure of quality for online learning programs, the student services that maximize probabilities of student success become an important and integral part of the formula.

Crawley provides online learning practitioners, educational policy makers, and program managers with a comprehensive overview of today's world online learning. She makes a strong case that student services are an essential ingredient in every institutional strategy for online learning that wants to ensure student success as measured by progress, retention, and completion. She then considers how the student populations drawn to online learning need support and services that actively spark momentum and engagement while reducing barriers shown to impede progress. She provides a detailed look at essential administrative services such as online scheduling and online registration, while also walking readers through financial aid and financial planning considerations about which every online learning stakeholder should be aware. She provides a useful overview of academic services required by online students that include advising, counseling, assessment, testing, book store services, library services, and tutoring services. She helps readers understand the value of personal services for online students, such as career advising, that take on even greater significance when federal concerns for "gainful employment" continue to swirl around the discussion of online learning quality. Readers are provided with planning and implementation guidance, with particular attention paid to using Center for Transforming Student Services (CENTSS) audit tools to evaluate the delivery of online student services. Readers are also offered advice and guidance on quality measurement.

Anita brings an experienced perspective to the online student services conversation. Her writing is informed by her more than twenty years of experience in all facets of online learning. She has worked as course developer, has led faculty development efforts, has served as a director of an online learning program, and has served as a faculty member at such notable institutions as UCLA, Montgomery College, and the University of Illinois. At the heart of her experiences in postsecondary online learning is a notable dedication to ensuring that students completing online learning programs have a fair shot at securing high-quality student services.

What makes her contributions so exceptional is that she has literally helped define the field of online student services in her work with the Center for Transforming Student Services (CENTSS). Established as a collaborative effort with WCET, the Minnesota State College and Universities-Minnesota Online, and Seward, Inc., CENTSS has extended the effective practice efforts that Anita Crawley developed while working with WCET during the mid 2000s. Today, CENTSS is a virtual resource for higher education institutions interested in assessing the quality of their student services offered via the web. Since 2005, more than 200 institutions of higher education have used the CENTSS audit to assess their student services. In addition to the CENTSS audit, CENTSS offers opportunities for learning and collaboration through its workshops, webcasts, and recognition of innovations in student services online.

In these days, when the perceived value of the online learning experience is directly correlated with the quality of the online learner's academic experience, there is no doubt that high-quality online learning student support and distributed services are a key determining variable. This book fills a major gap in the professional and academic literature addressing student services because it is laser-focused on meeting the needs of online, distance, and distributed students.

The ultimate significance of the book will be determined by its ability to address the rising tide of unmet expectations that typify online student excellence. Tomorrow's student services providers will be working with online students who will not be satisfied with an online learning experience that is any less satisfying than their other online consumer experiences. Today's demands for excellence in online learning have sparked a new sensibility about the value that high-quality online student services provide. Anita Crawley's book gives us the conceptual framework we need for realizing the value that online student services offer, and provides guidance and direction for achieving excellence in providing services and support to online students.

Ellen Wagner
Partner and Senior Analyst, Sage Road Solutions LLC, and Executive Director, WICHE Cooperative for Educational Technologies (WCET)

PREFACE

The growth of online learning shows no sign of leveling off. According to the study, *Class Differences: Online Education in the United States, 2010,* 5.6 million students took at least one online course during fall 2009, an increase of 21% over the previous year. This represents the largest annual increase in the eight years of this survey and occurred at a time when overall enrollment growth in higher education was less than 2%. With 63% of the institutions participating in the study identifying online learning as a critical part of their long-term strategy, the consensus is that online learning is here to stay (Allen & Seaman, 2010).

WHY THIS BOOK NOW?

To the extent their budgets allow, institutions committed to online courses and programs are funding quality online courses, training faculty to become effective online instructors, and paying for the required technology. Yet services that support online learners are insufficiently funded, sometimes leaving students new to online learning ill-prepared to succeed in this relatively new learning environment.

For online students, their course instructor is often their prime and sometimes only point of contact. However, online instructors are frequently overwhelmed with transforming course materials for online delivery and learning new methods of teaching remotely located students. Course management tasks in the online environment become a significant responsibility that far exceeds comparable tasks required of faculty who teach in the traditional classroom. When online faculty members are the only source of support for students, the quality of support services may be compromised. Student affairs and other student service professionals with appropriate expertise are best positioned to provide academic and personal support, so that online faculty can return to what they do best: teach their courses.

During the past decade, as online learning grew from a few courses at select institutions to expansive programs on many campuses, distance learning and IT departments provided most of the support for online students. When the accepted view was that online students needed only technical support, that model may have been a reasonable approach. However, to be successful, online students require many other forms of support. In addition to the services needed by all students, online learners need to know what to expect from online learning, how to access the required technology, and what skills are needed to succeed in the online environment. The good news is that professionals who can meet these needs are found throughout the institution.

At the same time that online learning is growing exponentially, colleges and universities must do more with less. Local students who are willing to come to campus can take advantage of the already established face-to-face services. However, as online programs expand and attract remotely located audiences, institutions are rethinking their delivery of support services. Institutions have found that online students, as well as many other students, appreciate the ability to complete transactions from the convenience of their computer. They want electronically delivered services, and they may take their tuition dollars to the colleges and universities that can effectively and efficiently support them as they earn their degrees.

When institutions devote insufficient attention to the needs of online learners, the result is lower course completion and success rates of online students compared to their peers who take courses in the traditional classroom. Angelino, Williams, and Natvig (2007) combined national undergraduate attrition rates from several online learning retention studies. Using data from these studies, they found a drop rate of between 52 and 62% for online students and between 10 and 20% when comparing online and traditionally delivered courses. To succeed in the online environment, students need the support services provided for all students, along with some unique services.

PURPOSE

This book serves as a resource for the reader to review research, literature, and innovative practices for planning, implementing, and evaluating support services for online learners. Institutions planning their initial launch and institutions that already offer online courses and programs may benefit from a review of award-winning electronically delivered student services, examples of effective planning processes, and approaches for online student services evaluation. The book discusses how effective and efficiently delivered online support services may improve online student academic success and course retention and may ultimately contribute to improved rates of college certificate and degree completion. Online learning can contribute to college completion rates, but only if online students are well supported so they can achieve their academic goals. The book focuses on how to develop and deliver services that enhance the success of students taking most or all of their coursework online who cannot or will not come on campus to receive services.

SCOPE OF BOOK

The book uses the framework developed by WCET (WICHE Cooperative for Educational Technologies), which created the publication *Guidelines for Creating Online Student Services*. The guidelines grew out of a grant from the U.S. Department of Education, Fund for the Improvement of Postsecondary Education (FIPSE) through a Learning Anytime Anyplace Partnership (LAAP) program. A major contribution of this project was the creation of Student Services for Online Learners Spider Web (Figure 4.1), which illustrates the scope of online student services (Shea & Armitage, 2002). This book uses the Spider Web as a means of organizing support services for online learners. The book also uses the Spider Web framework to summarize information about retention, success factors, and standards.

CHAPTER DESCRIPTIONS

Chapter One summarizes technology's role in changing the higher education landscape, especially as technology relates to the support of online students. It also provides an overview of the growth of online learning, use of new media for communication, and current methods of supporting online students.

Chapter Two describes the demographics of online students. It also reviews the needs of student populations (adult learners, first-generation college students, students who place in developmental coursework, low-income students, and military personnel) and discusses innovative practices that may contribute to the success of online learners with one or more characteristics historically associated with a higher risk of students not completing their academic goals.

Chapter Three examines barriers that affect full participation in online learning by students with disabilities. It shows how those barriers may be overcome when institutions provide an accessible online environment where students with disabilities can learn and take advantage of remotely delivered support services. It describes the needs of students with various types of disabilities, reviews laws and standards that institutions must follow, and recommends approaches that institutions might adopt to provide accessible online student services.

Chapter Four defines online student services (services delivered electronically through college websites, learning management systems, and social networking applications) and presents the organizing framework used throughout the book: the WCET Student Services for Online Learners Spider Web. It describes the scope and benefits of online student support services. The chapter continues with a description of how institutional characteristics may either contribute or create barriers to the development of online services. It ends with a discussion of those responsible for the support of online learners and highlights the role and responsibilities of student affairs professionals.

Chapter Five discusses the Administrative Suite, online student services including Admissions, Catalog, Course Schedule, Financial Aid, Registration, and Student Accounts and Records. As students become accustomed to the ease of using these online services (applying for admission and for financial aid, registering for courses, viewing the college catalog, paying bills, and viewing their records online), they expect to access other support services from their computer or handheld Internet-connected device. Students use services throughout their enrollment at the institution.

Chapter Six describes online student services from the Academic Services Suite: Academic Advising and Counseling, Assessment and Testing, Bookstore, Library, Technical Support, and Tutoring. Each service is essential to the success of online learners.

Chapter Seven describes services that historically have required a high level of human interaction. Some institutions are concerned about whether it is appropriate to provide online, interactive activities for some services in the Personal Services Suite (Career Services, Ethical and Legal Services, Health and Wellness, Personal Counseling, and Orientation Services).

Chapter Eight describes methods of electronic communication found in the Communications Suite that student affairs and other student service professionals can use to shape online student engagement and enable students to make connections with the institution and with each other. The chapter describes how students use technology, discusses the importance of effective online communication, and briefly reviews student engagement literature in the context of supporting online students. A primer on social media, multimedia tutorials, and virtual classroom applications suggests a common language that will help the reader see the potential of these tools to deliver online student services.

Chapter Nine describes models and innovative practices for planning and implementing online student services and for making decisions about how to present student services electronically to best leverage the capabilities of college websites as a platform for delivery of online student services. This chapter includes a review of online student retention literature and explains ways institutions can prioritize development of online student services.

Chapter Ten summarizes guidelines and standards of online student services, quality indicators, approaches to measure effectiveness of online student services, and how to use results to improve services for online students.

How to Use the Book

Each chapter can be read separately, but a reader might want to start with Chapter One to understand the educational transformation brought about by online learning and Chapters Two and Three to understand online students and their issues. Chapter Four provides a broad description of student services for online learners, which serves as a basis for the services and examples described in Chapters Five, Six, and Seven. Chapter Eight describes many forms of communication, including use of emerging technologies such as social networking applications. Chapters Nine and Ten delve into general online student services planning, implementation, and evaluation; the reader can also find service-specific approaches to these processes throughout the book.

I developed a website for the book that provides links to the college websites and resources referenced in the book and links to additional materials about relevant topics. To access the website, go to http://anitacrawley.net/Resources/bookcompanion.html

Audience and Uses

This book is designed for all practitioners who support online learners: student and academic affairs deans and vice presidents, directors of career services, admissions, enrollment management, advising, counseling, student success, library, tutoring, financial aid, admissions, and distance learning at two-year and four-year, public and private, for-profit and not-for-profit colleges and universities. This book will also be useful for graduate students in leadership in higher education, student affairs administration, and distance learning degree programs.

The book provides administrators, practitioners, and graduate students with guidelines for developing online student services, an understanding of the scope of services, and a survey of electronic delivery methods that range from providing static web-based information to highly interactive, customizable, and individualized services. Readers can learn what services students need at three different times of enrollment and learn how research supports the relationship between online student retention and the delivery of effective support services. The innovative practices found throughout the book may be of particular interest to student affairs and other student service practitioners who have direct responsibilities for developing and delivering student services, as well as to online faculty.

About the Author

Anita Crawley has more than twenty years of higher education experience as a community college counselor and faculty member and, most recently, director of a distance learning program. She brings the perspectives of a student affairs practitioner, an online instructor and course developer, and an academic affairs administrator.

With an early interest in using technology to enhance the work of student service professionals, Ms. Crawley has developed seminars, online courses, and web-based tools for use with students. She has taught online since 1999, and has earned an Online Teaching Certificate from UCLA Extension, an M.A. in Educational Technology Leadership from George Washington University, and an M.A. in Counseling and Human Development from Roosevelt University. She is currently working on a Ph.D. in Instructional Design for Online Learning from Capella University.

Ms. Crawley has researched and developed online student services for various colleges and consortia since the beginning of web-based distance learning. She has presented at numerous national conferences and has consulted and written for WCET (WICHE Cooperative for Educational Technologies), an organization that, along with CENTSS (Center for Transforming Student Services), is at the forefront of developing online student services.

SUPPORTING ONLINE STUDENTS

CHAPTER ONE

SETTING THE STAGE: THE TRANSFORMATION

During the first decade of the twenty-first century, technology transformed higher education by changing how colleges and universities interact with students, from the first recruitment effort to the last request for alumni contributions. Many see distance learning as the application of technology that has done the most to revolutionize the way students earn college degrees. In the 1980s and 1990s, distance education was a combination of telecourses and correspondence courses. But once the Internet could support text, graphics, audio, and video, institutions chose web-based delivery to provide distance learning instruction. With this mode of delivery, distance education became known as online learning.

Early adopters of online learning were faculty members who typically took the "lone ranger" approach to online course development and delivery. As instructors, they taught themselves how to use the hardware and software necessary to transform their on-campus courses for online delivery. They developed and managed courses, facilitated instruction, and, equally important, they supported their online learners. These early adopters enthusiastically embraced this new way of teaching, devoting the time necessary to attend to most needs of their students. This approach was laudable but not sustainable or scalable. Online faculty who followed early adopters typically did not, and do not, have the interest, skills, or time to do it all.

Supporting online students is a collaborative effort. Faculty, student affairs, and other student service professionals work with staff from distance learning and information technology offices to design, develop, and deliver services that facilitate the success of online learners. The approach to student services may be different when delivered electronically, but the goals are remarkably similar. Professionals with expertise in specific functional areas should be involved in the planning, implementation, and evaluation of academic and personal support services for online learners.

Online learners are not the only students who are interested in receiving academic and personal support services at a distance. Today's students are comfortable with and expect to use technology whenever possible. They anticipate being able to interact with colleges and universities to accomplish many transactions whenever they need to and from wherever they are located. Many students apply to the college, register for class, apply for financial aid, access the college library, all from the convenience of their home or dorm computer. Some may be taking all of their courses online, others just a few, and some will never take an online course. But the message is clear: most students coming to colleges and universities expect the efficiency, ease, and effectiveness of using electronic means to interact with their institution.

GROWTH OF ONLINE LEARNING

Online learning has grown exponentially during the first decade of the twenty-first century. For eight years (2003–2010), the Sloan Consortium conducted a nationwide survey that tracks the growth and nature of online learning. During the fall of 2009, 5.6 million students, representing 29% of the total college and university enrollment, took at least one online course. This number of students represents an increase of 21% over the previous year, the largest annual increase in the eight years of the survey. Especially noteworthy is that this large increase occurred when overall enrollment growth in higher education was less than 2% (Allen & Seaman, 2010).

The largest colleges and universities have more online students than any other type of institution. Colleges and universities with a total enrollment of 15,000 or more students represent 14% of all institutions with online offerings. However, they educate

67% of all online students. The smallest institutions represent 18% of all institutions; however, their online offerings educate only 2% of online students. The trend is that online students are concentrated in a relatively small number of large colleges and universities (Allen & Seaman, 2010).

Most growth is from institutions that are already offering online courses and programs and that are also the largest colleges and universities. They were the first to offer online courses, have been the most invested, and have grown the fastest. A few schools, around 5% or about 250 institutions that responded to the Sloan Survey, do not currently offer online courses, but even these schools are planning to develop online courses. These tend to be the smallest schools that may view online courses as supplemental and narrowly targeted for a niche market (Allen & Seaman, 2010).

Community colleges have experienced significant growth in online courses and programs as shown by the two annual reports that track online learning growth in this sector. The Instructional Technology Council (ITC) reports a 22% online enrollment increase during fall 2009 over the previous year (*Trends in Elearning: Tracking the Impact of Elearning at Community Colleges*, 2010). In the second report, the *Survey of Community College Presidents*, 87% of participants reported gains in online student enrollment, and 54% reported gains in the number of online degree programs (Green, 2010b). Adult students returning to college are interested in enrolling at institutions that offer fully online degrees or certificates (Jaggars, 2011). Particularly significant is the growth of online degree programs at community colleges.

The greatest growth in online programs comes primarily from private, for-profit institutions. American Public University System is the largest institution, with 77,700, a 31% increase from 2009 to 2010. Bridgeport Education follows with 77,100, a 40% increase during the same period. UMassOnline, a public, not-for-profit institution, experienced a 14.5% growth to 45,800, Walden University with a 13% increase grew to 45,600, and Liberty University grew 24% to 45,000. These numbers represent full-time online enrollment. The top institutions for part-time online enrollments are University of Phoenix Online, State University of New York Learning Network, the Ohio Learning Network, Kaplan University, and DeVry (Nagel, 2011). Nonprofit public institutions feel the competition for students most keenly from for-profit institutions (Allen & Seaman, 2010). This competition factor results in online enrollment growth in both for-profit and large public institutions. From all indications, the interest in online learning will continue to grow.

Many reasons account for the increasing growth of online courses and programs. Green (2010c) states that colleges and universities are motivated to develop and grow their online programs because they can attract more students at a lower cost. Forty-two percent of the ITC Survey participants identified the economic downturn as a reason for recent growth in online learning at community colleges (*Trends in Elearning: Tracking the Impact of Elearning at Community Colleges*, 2010). From the last two Sloan surveys, 54% of the respondents in 2009 and 75% in 2010 identified the economic downturn as a reason for the increased demand for online courses and programs (Allen & Seaman, 2010). As the economy improves, some predict a possible decline in online enrollments.

Frequently, reports cite student demand as a reason for institutions to develop or increase online course and program offerings. Because of the economic downturn, students themselves are asking for more online courses. In their view, they save money when they do not drive to campus, and they are still able to maintain their work schedule while completing their educational goals (Green, 2010c). In the report *Distance Education at Degree-Granting Postsecondary Institutions: 2006–2007* (Parsad, Lewis, & Tice, 2006), 68% of the colleges and universities responded that they implemented or expanded distance learning programs to meet student demand.

Regarding community colleges in particular, 67% want to expand student access, 46% want to increase the number of course offerings, and 45% want to increase student enrollment (*Trends in Elearning: Tracking the Impact of Elearning at Community Colleges*, 2010). For community college presidents, student demand is the number one reason for increasing online offerings (Green, 2010b).

Institutions see little indication that student interest in online learning will subside, especially when the governor of Minnesota and the Minnesota State Colleges and Universities announce statewide initiatives that 25% of college credits would be offered online by 2015 to save tax dollars and to reach more students. The same announcement reported that students who earn the ACHIEVE scholarship in Minnesota would be given a $150 bonus if they complete an online course while in high school (Young, 2008).

In the *2010 Campus Computing Survey*, Green (2010c) identified two other reasons for persistent growth in online learning. Because institutions have been delivering online programs for more than a decade, newer programs can be up and running more rapidly by using established programs as models. Green also stated that technologies that support online learning are more reliable and robust than they were a decade ago. Because these enhanced technologies provide students and faculty with a smoother online teaching and learning experience, institutions are more likely to begin or expand online programs. As institutions increase their use of technology in the classroom, that increased usage may lead to growth in web-enhanced, blended, and eventually fully online courses and programs. It appears that online courses and programs will continue to grow, at least in the near future.

DEFINITIONS AND TERMINOLOGY

This section provides definitions of an online course and the electronic platforms used to deliver online instruction and student services.

WHAT IS AN ONLINE COURSE?

At the outset, writing about online learning is challenging because no current, universally accepted definition of online learning exists. However, the Sloan Consortium has identified ways of classifying types of online learning. All of Sloan's eight annual reports have used the following definitions: A *fully online course* delivers 80–100% of its content through web-based technology and typically has no face-to-face meetings, although such an online course might require on-campus orientations, labs, or testing. A *blended or hybrid course* is delivered 30–79% online. These courses use web-based technology to provide a substantial proportion of the content to students, with some reduction in the number of face-to-face meetings. A *web-enhanced course* uses web-based technology to facilitate between 1 and 29% of an essentially face-to-face course. A *traditional course* does not use web-based technology (Allen & Seaman, 2010). This book uses the Sloan Consortium's definitions to describe where learning occurs and the Higher Education Opportunity Act (HEOA) of 2008 to describe the technology and methods for delivering instruction.

The Higher Education Opportunity Act, passed by Congress on August 14, 2008, defines distance education as "education that uses one or more technologies to deliver instruction to students who are separated from the instructor and to support regular and substantive interactions between the students and the instructor, synchronously or asynchronously." The HEOA's list of technologies include the Internet, one-way and two-way transmissions through open broadcast, closed circuit, cable, microwave, broadband lines, fiber optics, satellite, wireless devices, or audio conferencing. The HEOA also includes video cassettes, DVDs, and CD-ROMs, if they are used in conjunction with the interactive media previously listed. While HEOA mentions a variety of technologies, most online courses primarily use the Internet. HEOA differentiates distance education from correspondence courses. Distance education must include substantial interactivity between students and instructor (*Final Regulations Implementing Accreditation Provisions in the Higher Education Opportunity Act of 2008*, 2009). Interactivity is equally important for engaging students both inside and outside the online classroom.

This book uses several terms interchangeably to describe instruction that is mediated by technology and delivered via the Internet where students and instructor are separated by time and place. The terms are *online learning, e-learning, web-based learning, distance learning,* and *distance education.* For purposes of this book, the key component of all terms is that the learning and services are mediated by an Internet connection.

THE PLATFORMS

The primary tools for delivering online courses and online student services are learning management systems, institutional websites, and social media applications. A learning management system (LMS) is a software application that provides a centralized location for course materials and a variety of tools for instruction, communication, assessment, and grading. The LMS is also used to deliver support services to online students.

Historically most online courses are taught asynchronously (that is, instructor and students are not online at the same time). Desktop conferencing software such as WebX or Elluminate and Wimba (now known as Blackboard Collaborate) is being used increasingly for both instruction and student services to enable students, faculty, and student service professionals to interact online synchronously (at the same time). This software includes functionalities—audio, video, whiteboard, file sharing, web tours, and others—to create a virtual classroom that most closely resembles a traditional classroom. Learning management systems that include virtual classroom software provide a dynamic platform for the delivery of instruction and student services.

Institutions frequently have well-developed external websites that include all public information. Secure internal websites, sometimes referred to as student portals, are for students and college employees. Institutional websites are discussed in context throughout the book. The following section about social media introduces how these applications are changing the way institutions communicate with their constituencies.

TRANSFORMATION OF RELATIONSHIPS VIA NEW MEDIA

Emerging technologies, including social media, may have the potential to transform the way students and higher education professionals interact with each other. Institutions are making decisions about which applications provide the best platforms for particular communication goals. Those institutions are challenged by the speed with which these applications come in and out of use: today's innovations can be tomorrow's mainstream applications, and today's mainstream applications may be overtaken by more useful products. This fluidity is exemplified by use of email, which has gone from being the only means of electronic communication to sharing the landscape with a multitude of Web 2.0 technologies: instant messaging, Facebook, Twitter, wikis, and blogs.

As this chapter was written, President Obama had a live streamed town hall meeting at Facebook; Storify was released—a web-based application that aggregates responses to local, national, and international news by contributors from several social media sites; *U.S. News and World Report* noted that leading graduate business programs at Columbia, Harvard, and Stanford were offering courses such as "The Power of Social Technology," "Competing with Social Networks," and "Social Media and Entrepreneurship"; and the Museum Special Section of the *New York Times* included the article "Is Social Media Changing Museums." The following quote from this article in the *New York Times* museum section foretells the potential social media might have not only for museums but also for the support of online students: "Talk to anyone involved with museum technology and the conversation inevitably boils down to one universal word: engagement" (Vogel, 2011, n.p.).

What guidelines will institutions use to select communication tools that best meet institutional goals and student needs? Institutions engaging students at a distance may require different methods of communication, but the goals remain the same: communication must be accurate and timely and messages must reach intended recipients and accomplish the intended goals (Sheehan & Pirani, 2009). Institutions are exploring various means of electronic communication, including the use of social media to establish a supportive virtual community for all students, especially those who do not come on campus. If an institution develops and implements virtual communities, then student affairs and other support specialist professionals have a platform from which to engage online students and facilitate their success.

In successful virtual communities, students learn about and use available resources and services, and understand how those resources and services can support their success. They are able to interact with support specialists and one another. In sum, they become part of a community that acts as an organizing agent on their behalf, resulting in improved quality of information, products, and services (Wachter, et. al. as cited in Kretovics, 2003).

Students are coming to college well versed in the use of social media and software needed for most academic courses. Here is a portrait of undergraduate student social media and other application use based on the *ECAR Study of Undergraduate Students and Information Technology:*

- 42% contribute video to websites such as YouTube.
- 90% use presentation software.
- 85% use spreadsheets.
- 40% update wikis.
- 36% contribute to blogs.
- 25% play online multiuser computer games.
- 25% use social bookmarking/tagging websites.
- 40% use Voice Over Internet Protocol such as Skype.
- 90% text message and access social networking sites (Smith & Caruso, 2010).

Many students are no longer passive consumers of electronically delivered information but are actively involved in creating online content, as illustrated by the preceding list. Students are coming to colleges and universities prepared to use technology to become actively involved in the learning process.

From these statistics, institutions may surmise that a significant portion of students know how to use these tools both for entertainment and for academic purposes. When 2010 undergraduates rated themselves in the following areas, they thought themselves expert or very skilled in the following:

- 81% in conducting Internet searches
- 51% in evaluating the reliability and credibility of online information
- 48% in understanding ethical and legal online issues (Smith & Caruso, 2010)

Although institutions may reasonably consider the possibility that these self-assessments may be somewhat inflated, they may also conclude that students have sufficient confidence in their technical skills to be successful in the online environment.

Institutions may want to consider two trends when planning new ways to communicate with students. One is the use of mobile devices and the other is the use of social media by older students. Three 2010 annual reports predict an explosion in the use of mobile devices such as smart phones and tablet PCs (Allen & Seaman, 2010; Johnson, Levine, Smith & Stone, 2010; Smith & Caruso, 2010). The *2010 Campus Computing Survey* confirms these predictions by reporting that across all sectors, institutions are planning to enhance instruction and services through the use of mobile applications (public universities, 79%; private universities, 81%; public four-year colleges, 71%; private four-year colleges, 68%; and community colleges, 68%). At the same time, fewer students are coming to college with desktops and laptops. With mobile devices, students are able to maintain continuous communication with each other and the institution. Setting aside any drawbacks from students' always being online, institutions may want to consider ways to leverage the potential for delivering online student services, knowing students are able to access information throughout the day or night.

Institutions may want to consider another trend of note: the decreasing gap of social network use between students 25 years or older and those students younger than 25 (Smith & Caruso, 2010). While social network usage among the younger group remains consistent at 95%, older students are catching up. When institutions consider the use of social media to support online learners, they may find that the age of the learner may not be as much of a consideration as it was a few years ago. For all age groups, social media applications increasingly are being used to communicate with friends and family and for entertainment. However, institutions continue to ponder whether students will also use social media in educationally meaningful ways, how to most effectively communicate electronically, and how to determine which tool to use for a particular purpose. Chapter Eight discusses these issues in the context of delivering services to online students.

RESPONSIBILITY FOR SUPPORTING ONLINE STUDENTS

The term *online student services* is used to describe all administrative, academic, and personal services that online learners need from their first institutional contact to the last interaction they have with the institution. This book focuses on those services provided by professionals throughout the institution, in addition to services provided by the online course instructor. Although many of these professionals report to deans and vice presidents of student affairs, the term *student service professionals* is used as an inclusive term that also includes professionals from such areas as enrollment management, library, and tutoring, in addition to student affairs professionals.

An institution's distance learning program typically has several components: assuming responsibility for selecting and supporting the LMS, developing online courses, training and supporting online faculty, and making a variety of policy decisions. Early programs focused most attention on developing online courses and training faculty to teach those courses. Institutions may not have considered the importance of supporting online students until someone compared retention rates for online courses with traditionally delivered instruction. When the numbers were disappointing, the institution responded.

Perhaps because these students do not come to campus and are sometimes "faceless," they may be easy to ignore. At some institutions, it is unclear which department(s) are ultimately responsible for developing and implementing the services to support their success. Staff from offices of distance learning may become the primary support personnel because they are the online student's initial point of contact and the most knowledgeable about the demands and methodology of online learning. However, distance learning staff rarely have the expertise to assist online students with a variety of decisions that accompany course registration: required placement testing, prerequisite requirements, and course selection, to name a few. Generally students are assisted with these decisions by academic advisors or student affairs professionals. Online learners might be recognized as a unique population of students with specific needs to facilitate their success. This book suggests innovative approaches for service providers throughout the institution to meet the needs of remotely located online learners.

When institutions ensure that students are prepared before starting their first online course and are supported academically and personally throughout their enrollment, institutions contribute substantially to the successful completion of online students' educational goals. However, not all institutions that offer online courses are providing adequate support for online students and, more important, it is often unclear which departments are responsible for the many support services needed by online students. This book will explore these issues.

CONCLUSION

Institutions familiar with the growth of online learning are likely to conclude that online learning is here to stay. They know that students use electronic means to take their online course and that they must provide these students effective support services via the same technology. These students fully expect that the institution will provide services that are accessible around the clock.

Given the expectations of online students and concerns with online student retention and success, institutions might consider reassessing the mission of their student service departments and rethinking their approach to supporting online students. Traditionally, student service professionals have engaged students through face-to-face relationship building that relies on interpersonal skills, nonverbal cues, voice intonation, and body language. Online communication is very different, since it is frequently conducted without the assistance of these visual cues. However, care and concern are important components for successful communications in both environments. Student service professionals must learn how to accomplish the same goals with different methods of delivery. Student affairs professionals, with a commitment to educate the whole student, will want to contribute to the support of online learners by devising ways to maintain the high-touch quality of student services, a core component no matter what the method of delivery.

CHAPTER TWO

PROFILE OF ONLINE STUDENTS

Speaking at the 2010 WCET national conference, Mark Milliron presented a picture of the changing demographics in higher education. Most institutions know that, as access to higher education increases, their campuses will receive students who never before considered continuing their education beyond high school. However, not all institutions may be aware of another salient point that he made: while increasingly diverse students are coming to college, the demographics of those who graduate is the same as it has always been. In other words, first generation students, students of color, students with disabilities, students from low-income families, adult students, and students who place in one or more developmental courses are not earning more certificates or degrees (Milliron, 2010). Some of these students are online learners. Institutions are taking proactive measures to improve graduation rates among these populations, including measures that involve technology and innovative practices for supporting online students.

This chapter references data and literature primarily from community colleges, as online enrollments and students with high-risk factors attend two-year colleges in greater numbers than they attend four-year colleges. Compared to other types of institutions, community colleges tend to have higher numbers of adults 25 years and older, underprepared students, students of color, part-time students, students receiving financial aid, low-income students, and first-generation students (Fike & Fike, 2008). Institutions also know that veterans are a growing population of college students and are developing online support services to meet their needs.

Institutions recognize that the demographics of community colleges are changing. The Achieving the Dream website contains these statistics: of 2 million community college students, 13% were Black/Non-Hispanic, 7% Asian or Pacific Islander, 15% Hispanic, 1% American Indian or Alaska Native, 57% White/Non-Hispanic, 1% Non-Resident Alien, and 6% Unknown. Institutions understand the importance of providing support services to online learners from these populations.

DEMOGRAPHICS OF ONLINE STUDENTS

The first web-based courses targeted students who could not otherwise continue their academic goals. Initially, online courses appealed to students with irregular work schedules, students with disabilities that prevented them from coming on campus, students who were living outside the country, and students whose family responsibilities prevented them from attending class on campus. This population was almost entirely returning adult students, defined by Council for Adult and Experiential Learning (CAEL) as those who are 24 years old or older.

With the growth of online courses and programs from not-for-profit colleges and universities and the expansion of for-profit colleges and universities, online offerings have become more diverse and so has the audience. With a few exceptions, students can find online general education courses and many upper division and graduate courses taught from regionally accredited institutions. The convenience and flexibility of online learning attract both traditional and nontraditional students. The expansion of online offerings has changed the landscape of who chooses to take some or all undergraduate and graduate courses and programs online. Institutions that know their student demographics and enrollment patterns will be best equipped to make decisions about developing online services that meet the needs of their audiences.

The *2010 National Online Learners Priorities Report*, which surveyed 84,000 students at 97 institutions, provides details about who is learning online. Sixty-nine percent of the population were female, and 81% of the females were age 25 and older. Eighty-three percent of the participants are primarily online students. The rest are primarily on-campus students taking a few online courses. A majority are full-time students, taking undergraduate courses while working full time. A little over half are married, and most own their own home. Returning adult students who are juggling a variety of life roles are taking traditional courses, many offered online (*National Online Learners Priorities Report*, 2010).

Nontraditional online students may need and want services different from those preferred by the traditional 18- to 22-year-old students who want a typical residential campus experience. Those traditional age learners make up only 16% of the students enrolled in public and private two-year and four-year universities (Falk & Blaylock, 2010). This trend of increasing numbers of adults returning to college is predicted to continue as adults find the need to retool for new careers. Institutions know that the characteristics, and the accompanying needs of these students, have changed over the years.

ADULT STUDENTS

Institutions understand that many adult learners are challenged to balance multiple life roles: family, work, education, and leisure activities. For adult learners, these challenges make the convenience of online learning particularly appealing. Eduventures, 2008, *The Adult Learner: An Eduventures Perspective*, reports that 53% of adults are likely or very likely to enroll in accelerated programs; 48% in fully online programs; 48% in summer session with shorter and more intensive courses; and 47% in hybrid courses/programs.

According to the Eduventures report, about half of adult prospective students used college websites to find out about programs. When adult learners visit college websites, they want to see photos of people who look like them. The information that is most important to them is cost, scheduling, reputation, and class size. Student service professionals who are developing online support services already know that adult audiences are looking for flexible and convenient online education. An institution's use of effective and efficient methods of delivering student support services is important for all populations but especially for busy adult learners.

ADULT LEARNER GROWTH PROJECTIONS

The Eduventures report of the projected enrollment growth for adult learners in higher education by age group between 2008 and 2016, based on data from the U.S. Department of Education, National Center of Educational Statistics (NCES), is as follows:

- 7% increase for 18–22-year-olds
- 20% increase for those 22–29
- 14% increase for those 30+ (*The Adult Learner: An Eduventures Perspective*, 2008)

These students include not only those who are going through a mid-career change but also learners at the beginning and end of their careers. While early baby boomers may be entering post-secondary institutions to retrain for a career change, late baby boomers are entering retirement expecting to have many active and productive years that may include a return to college. The Plus 50 Completion Strategy, an American Association of Community Colleges initiative, is funding efforts at nine community colleges to help older adults feel comfortable as they begin or resume their college education (Moltz, 2011). Adult students are not just the largest group of students represented at many colleges, but they are also a diverse group with a variety of different needs.

COHORTS OF ADULT STUDENTS

Falk and Blaylock (2010) differentiate the characteristics and expectations of three cohorts of nontraditional adult students (NS) returning to college. The NS-1 cohort is composed of non-traditional students, including veterans, who came to college after World War II and through the 1960s. Financial aid and affirmative action (informal at the time) increased the race, class, and gender diversity during the 1960s. Although institutions recognized that the NS-1 cohort had specialized needs, they expected that the

NS-1 cohort would blend in with the population of traditional students.

The NS-2 cohort began arriving on college campuses during the 1970s. Each of these adult learners has one or more of the following characteristics: delays postsecondary enrollment for at least a year after graduation from high school; attends part-time for at least one term during the year; works full-time; is financially independent from parents; has dependents other than a spouse; is a single parent; or does not have a high school diploma (Falk & Blaylock, 2010).

Compton, Cox, and Laanan (2006) provide additional characteristics that distinguish this cohort of adults:

- May be pursuing a vocational certificate or degree; hence, are more likely to enroll at two-year rather than at four-year institutions
- Have focused career goals for their education
- Consider themselves primarily workers and secondarily students, with other life roles such as family responsibilities taking precedence over educational goals
- May be enrolled in distance education courses and view acquisition of additional education as a means to an end
- May speak a language other than English
- May need developmental coursework prior to enrolling in college-level courses
- May be recipients of a GED or high school completion certificate rather than a high school diploma (Compton, Cox, & Laanan, 2006)

The NS-3 cohort began arriving in the 1990s. Oblinger (2005) reports that the group includes, "Boomers, Gen-Xers, and Millennials, each having different traits and expectations." Falk and Blaylock (2010) combined representatives from each of these groups to define a nontraditional student cohort and distinguished them from the NS-2 group. These students

- Are often foreign born or their parents were foreign born
- Speak English as a second language, and a language other than English is spoken in their house

- Have meager financial resources
- Often work minimum wage jobs and do not have access to employer-sponsored tuition assistance
- Typically have extensive need for remedial/developmental coursework

Although these students might also be a subset of the NS-2 cohort, for program planning, institutions may consider isolating these characteristics and providing services that respond to this set of needs. Institutions may find this information useful in establishing priorities for development of services to support NS-3 online students.

Professionals who develop services for online learners might be particularly interested in certain differences between the NS-2 and NS-3 cohorts, as summarized in Table 2.1.

ADULT LEARNING THEORY

While considering the diverse needs of various cohorts of adult learners, institutions may want to review the basic tenets of adult learning theory. Knowles' theory of adult learning, which may also be considered in the development of online student services, includes the following principles:

- Adults need to know why they are learning something.
- Adults need to learn experientially.
- Adults approach learning as problem solving.
- Adults learn best when the topic is of immediate value (Knowles, Holton, & Swanson, 2005).

These tenets were in play when the members of the Council for Adult and Experiential Learning (CAEL) developed the *Principles of Effectiveness for Serving Adult Learners*. These principles are part of the Adult Learning Focused Institution (ALFI) initiative. Recognizing the challenging economic times and the increasing importance of credentials in the labor market, CAEL created the ALFI initiative to help colleges and universities improve learning opportunities for adult students.

Table 2.1   Comparing the Needs of Two Cohorts of Adult Students

Programmatic Element	NS-2 Cohort	NS-3 Cohort
Extracurricular activities	Low importance	Not important
Ability to enroll full time rather than part-time	Not important	Very important
Prior coursework, perhaps from foreign institutions, evaluated and applied to domestic degrees	Important	Very important
Enroll in online or other media-based courses to minimize commuting time, trips to campus, and time to degree completion	Very important	Very important
A campus culture that permits students to quickly amass credits that will lead to degree completion	Important	Very important
Teaching and learning systems that use technology in class or offer fully online courses	Important	Very important
A setting where students and faculty members place high value on academic honesty and integrity	Low importance	Not important
An institution that accommodates varied religious traditions and customs	Low importance	Very important
An institution that has excellent "customer service" standards	Important	Very important

Source: Adapted from Falk & Blaylock (2010).

Institutions should

- Consider barriers of time, place, and tradition when conducting outreach to adult learners.
- Address adult learners' life and career goals before or at the time of enrollment in order to clarify the institution's capacity to help learners reach their goals.
- Promote an array of payment options to expand equity.

- Define and assess the knowledge, skills, and competencies already acquired by adult learners from previous college credit and life/work experience.
- Have faculty use multiple methods of instruction to connect curricular concepts to useful knowledge and skills.
- Assist adult learners by using comprehensive academic and student support systems.
- Use information technology to provide relevant and timely information and enhance the learning experience.
- Engage in strategic relationships, partnerships, and collaborations with employers and other organizations to improve educational opportunities for adult learners.
- Support transitions to and from the institution and ensure learning is relevant to adult learners' educational and career goals (*Principles of Effectiveness for Serving Adult Learners*, 2005).

The main themes are that adult learners are looking for ways to complete their degrees as efficiently as possible. They take courses at times that fit with their busy schedules. They want support services available at convenient times, frequently outside of typical business hours. Institutions may conclude they are meeting adult student needs when online learning and student services are available around the clock.

ADULT TECHNOLOGY USE

The Pew Internet and American Life Project *Generations 2010* report provides insight about how the following groups of adults are using the Internet (see Table 2.2): Millennials (born 1977–1992); Generation X (born 1965–1976); Late Baby Boomers (born 1955–1964); Early Baby Boomers (born 1946–1954); and Silent Generation (born 1937–1945). GIs who were born prior to 1937 are not included in this summary.

One general finding is that all Internet activities are becoming uniformly more popular across all age groups. The following percentages represent how many members of each group use the Internet: 79% of all American adults go online, broken down as follows: Millennials—95%, Gen X—86%, Young Boomers—81%, Older Boomers—76%, Silent Generation—58%, and GI Generation—30% (Zickuhr, 2010).

Table 2.2   Online Activities Based on Age Group

	Millennials	Gen X	Younger Boomers	Older Boomers	Silent Generation
Email	96	94	91	93	90
Search	92	87	86	87	82
Social networking sites	83	62	50	43	34
Watch videos	80	66	62	55	44
Instant messaging	66	52	35	30	29
Read blogs	43	34	27	25	23
Visit a virtual world	4	4	4	3	3

Source: Adapted from Pew Internet and American Life Project, *Generations 2010* report.

The following percentages represent the activities of Internet users in each age group.

A broadband Internet connection significantly improves the experience for online learners. The following percentages of each group have broadband connections: Millennials—81%, Gen X—73%, Younger Boomers—68%, Older Boomers—61%, and Silent Generation—44%. Although email, search, social networks, videos, blogs, and instant message all have either a moderate or great potential as platforms for delivering services to online students, Virtual World applications, such as Second Life, currently seem unlikely to be an effective mode of delivery for any group of adults.

Innovative Practices

CAEL identified a number of institutions that have been using innovative practices to educate their adult learners. Especially noteworthy is that these online services were developed with the needs of adult students in mind.

Empire State College has an Advanced Standing Through Prior Learning website that defines in general terms when a student can earn college credit for prior learning. It also provides a comprehensive student guide with detailed information about how credits are evaluated and possible ways to earn credits, including many options for credit by examination.

Athabasca University adds to their explanation of how to earn credit for prior learning with a comprehensive description of how portfolio assessment can expedite the time needed to earn a degree. The materials detail the process, fees, documents and forms, and how to begin.

The DePaul School for New Learning (SNL) provides customized programs that build on students' experiences and help adults develop skills to achieve personal and professional goals. SNL Online has links to the school's Facebook and Twitter pages that are used primarily by the institution to make announcements. SNL Online uses Wordpress, a blog tool and publishing platform, to communicate with students. The newsletter features news and events; course information; faculty, staff, and student profiles; and student resources. Newsletters are archived, students can leave comments on the articles, and links are provided to the SNL Online home page, Facebook, and Twitter.

Marylhurst University offers two accelerated online bachelor's degree programs, two accelerated master's programs, and a prior learning assessment program that allows Marylhurst students to earn up to 45 credits through prior learning assessment. These programs may be of particular interest to the newest adult student cohort, as they provide compressed time to attain degree goals.

Sinclair Community College provides a free how-to-succeed in an online course to help prospective online students decide whether online learning is right for them, familiarize themselves with the learning management system, learn what to expect from online learning, and get organized for their first online course. This self-paced course is always available to students. Another feature of Sinclair Online that is particularly helpful to online students is a transfer page that provides online degree options, including articulation (course and program transfer) agreements that facilitate completion of a bachelor's degree.

In addition to the challenges described in this section, adult online learners may have additional risk factors that may create barriers to success. The next sections of this chapter discuss characteristics and needs of students who place in developmental courses, are low-income students, and are first generation students. Although institutions recognize that the additional risk factors may not make these learners strong candidates for online or blended courses, these students are nevertheless enrolling in those options. For these reasons, student service professionals are challenged to create support mechanisms that improve these students' chances for academic success.

FIRST GENERATION STUDENTS

First generation college students are defined as children of parents who have not earned a college degree. A profile of first generation students at two- and four-year colleges has been developed based on statistics from the *First-Generation Students in Postsecondary Education* longitudinal study. The study compared the educational records of first generation and non–first generation students who were 12th grade students in 1992. First generation students entered college less prepared, got lower grades, and were more likely to drop out when compared to their peers who had college educated parents (Chen, 2005).

Fifty-five percent of first generation students, compared to 27% of their non–first generation peers, entered college needing developmental courses. The gap in credits earned begins in the first year of college, with 18 credits earned by first generation students, compared to 25 credits by non–first generation students. The first generation cohort had a 2.5 first year GPA versus 2.8. The withdrawal rate from a single course was 12% versus 7% for non–first generation students. Thirty-three percent of first generation students had not chosen a major upon entry compared to 13% of non–first generation. Those students who have a specific academic goal enhance their chances for college completion. First generation students are less likely to be white and are more likely to delay entry into postsecondary education after high school graduation and attend college part-time than their non–first generation peers (Chen, 2005).

Looking at trends over a longer period provides additional insight for program planners. *First in My Family: A Profile of First-Generation College Students at Four-Year Institutions Since 1971*, published by the Cooperative Institutional Research Program

(CIRP) at UCLA and the Foundations for Independent Higher Education, traces trends for this population from 1971 to 2005 (Saenz, Hurtado, Barrera, Wolf, & Yeung, 2007).

The following are some key findings specifically for first generation students at four-year institutions:

- The proportion of first-time, full-time, first generation entering college freshmen has declined since 1971, thus indicating an increase in the number of students whose parents have completed a bachelor's degree or more.
- Previously the thinking was that parents who did not attend college deterred their children from doing so. The CIRP research showed that first generation students are more likely than their peers to attribute their attendance to the encouragement they received from their parents.
- First generation students are working more hours and a higher percentage than ever before are working while attending college.
- More first generation students than ever before choose their college because of financial considerations and are twice as likely as their peers to be concerned about how they will finance their college education.
- Living close to home is more important to first generation students than to their peers.
- The disparity between academic preparation of first generation students and their peers has been consistent in the areas of time spent studying and average grades in high school, as well as academic self-confidence. The gap is widening in self-ratings of math and writing ability.
- First generation students have lower educational aspirations, which may be due to lack of information. The aspirations of both groups are rising, but the gap remains the same.
- All students are increasingly likely to report that they are motivated to attend college because they want to be well off financially, but the percentage is higher for first generation students.

First generation students frequently choose community colleges because of the proximity to home; the flexible course schedules with more courses being available in the evening, weekends, or online; and the ease of part-time attendance. These conveniences allow students to manage several life roles, including working more hours while attending college. Open admissions and the availability of developmental coursework make community colleges appealing to underprepared students (Fike & Fike, 2008). First generation students are at greater risk of not completing their goals, especially when they possess additional risk factors such as limited income and are academically underprepared.

STUDENTS TAKING DEVELOPMENTAL COURSES

One key to increasing graduation rates is to improve retention rates of underprepared students. Nearly 60% of community college students arrive on campus needing at least one developmental course. Only 25% of those students complete a bachelor's degree in eight years, compared to 40% who arrive on campus without needing developmental courses (Bailey, 2009). These statistics may not surprise educators working at community colleges, where offering a fresh start for students who may not have previously taken school seriously is commonplace. However, educators at four-year colleges, especially those that do not have open admissions, may be alarmed by the *Strong American Schools* report. The report shows that a significant percentage of students attending four-year institutions need remediation in either math or English or both:

- 29% of all students at public four-year institutions
- 60% of all freshman admitted to colleges in the California State University system
- 43% of high school juniors and seniors who met ACT benchmark for college math (*Diploma to Nowhere*, 2008)

BILL AND MELINDA GATES FOUNDATION

In 2010 the Bill and Melinda Gates Foundation pledged $110 million to improve community college developmental education.

Bill Gates announced this pledge during his closing speech at the 2010 American Association of Community Colleges Convention, where he stated, "Research shows that improving remediation is the single most important thing community colleges can do to increase the number of students who graduate with a certificate or degree" ("Foundation Giving $110 Million to Transform Remedial Education," 2010).

The Gates' initiative supports innovative ideas that help underprepared students spend less time and money completing developmental course requirements. Its key elements are to decrease the need for remediation at the community college level by encouraging collaboration and alignment of basic skills instructions and outcomes among middle schools and high schools; to accelerate program completion by blending career-focused credit-bearing courses with enhanced academic supports; and to develop diagnostic tools to identify specific skill deficiencies and then remediate individual deficiencies, rather than offer one-size-fits all developmental courses ("Foundation Giving $110 Million to Transform Remedial Education," 2010).

Historically, students take developmental courses in traditional classrooms with 20–30 students, wherein each student has the same curriculum and time period to complete the course. South Texas College provides the option for students enrolling in a mid-level developmental math course for the third time to enroll in a self-paced modularized format. According to *Accelerating the Academic Achievement of Students Referred to Developmental Education*, in fall 2008, 82% of students who chose this option successfully completed the course as compared to 45% of the students who selected the same course taught in a traditional classroom setting. During summer 2009, 88% in the self-paced option and 71% in the classroom passed the course. During spring 2009 the same options were offered for a developmental English course. The pass rates were 90% for the self-paced option and 75% for the traditional classroom (Edgecombe, 2011).

COMPLETION BY DESIGN RECOMMENDATIONS

The Gates Foundation is using *Completion by Design* as the framework to identify those times throughout students' enrollments when they are likely to drop out of college. Institutions are aware that students are more likely to withdraw from college after being placed in developmental courses than if they place in all college level coursework. *Completion by Design* provides examples of interventions that can support students and improve their chances of remaining enrolled as they take developmental courses (Pennington & Milliron, 2010). Many of these interventions are enhanced by the use of technology, and some can be delivered online. For example:

- Mandatory student success courses that teach study skills and help students develop career goals and academic plans that facilitate certificate or degree completion.
- Modularized developmental course content creatd using next-generation technology to accelerate the pace and compress time to completion. The modules may allow students to progress at their own pace or to contextualize the content and integrate the remediation into academic courses. An example might be to link an online developmental English and a Career Development course with career assignments to demonstrate acquisition of specific English learning outcomes.
- Early warning and early intervention systems with counselors and faculty alerted and accountable for follow-up to reengage the student.
- Tutorials and supplemental instruction that facilitate completion of gatekeeper courses (high enrollment courses, taken during early enrollment, that, if not passed, keep students from advancing).

Online Developmental Courses

Developmental English and math courses are designed to remediate the skills of students who place below college level. Students sometimes have to take one, two, or even three courses in each discipline before taking college level courses for credit. Students are frequently shocked and discouraged when they learn the results of placement tests. Institutions are trying to accelerate the process without compromising quality instruction that facilitates academic success and college completion.

Institutions rarely offer developmental courses online, expecting that many students who place in developmental courses may lack motivation and self-discipline, two important characteristics for online learning success. However, institutions might reconsider this position based on the results of the South Texas College pilot. Many professionals in developmental education recognize that, if better student outcomes are the goals, the field needs a transformation. Providing that its students are well-supported, an institution might opt for well-designed online modules, online courses, or blended learning. Online student services can be developed to provide additional supports.

While rare, online developmental courses are available. The Community College Research Center (CCRC) conducted two parallel studies of online learning throughout the states of Virginia and Washington (Jaggars & Xu, 2010; Xu & Jaggars, 2011). The Virginia study compared learning outcomes of students taking online developmental courses (online English $N = 373$, online math $N = 773$) with students taking face-to-face sections. In 2004, for English, 77% face-to-face and 53% online completed. In 2008, the percentages were 74% and 48%. In 2004, for math, 57% face-to-face and 38% online completed. In 2008, the percentages were 53% and 40%.

In the Washington study, 358 students took developmental English and 1,684 took developmental math. For English, 91% face-to-face and 79% online completed. For math, 83% face-to-face and 73% online completed. In both studies, the number of online students taking developmental courses was much smaller than those taking face-to-face courses. The total N for the three studies were 13,126, 9,295, and 28,590, respectively, with only 3–4% of those students enrolling in online developmental courses. While each case showed a statistically significant lower completion rate in online developmental courses, the numerical difference was not huge. It is interesting that the Washington success rates were significantly higher than the Virginia success rates. The researchers suggested that the higher Washington rates might be attributable to the comprehensive, around-the-clock student support services available at all of the Washington technical and community colleges.

INNOVATIVE PRACTICES

The Integrated Basic Education and Skills Training (I-BEST) program began in 2006 as an effort to educate and train adults who had not earned a high school diploma to develop literacy and work skills. As of the writing of this book, there are more than 140 approved I-BEST programs offered from Washington's 34 community and technical colleges. The I-BEST Developmental Education program extends the concepts from the original program that attracted students wanting basic literacy and work skills to students placing in developmental coursework. The four elements of the developmental program are (1) designing new curricular materials that include active learning pedagogies, (2) using instructional approaches and teacher support that advance student success, (3) providing student support that is contextualized and integrated, and (4) providing professional development tools that facilitate institutional change needed to support the program. The contextualized student support element can be used to inform the development of online student services. The student support expectations for I-BEST Developmental Education programs suggest some of the following approaches: use cohort and learning community-type models; include multiple modes, methods, and pedagogical strategies that appeal to diverse student populations; and provide clear career and educational pathways for students.

South Seattle Community College developed a collection of 36 activities to assist precollege students in mapping their educational goals and navigating their way to college success. The website has three main sections: transitions portfolio, videos and curriculum, and financial resources for college. The transition portfolio provides students with user and instructional guides along with information about education and financial planning, time management, college readiness, goal setting, scholarship, and employment planning. The videos enhance the content from the portfolio resources and add a personal touch to the materials. The financial resources section provides detailed information about financial aid and scholarships. Because these resources are delivered online, they are available around the clock.

Sinclair Community College has taken a comprehensive approach to support at-risk students, many of whom have been placed in developmental courses. Sinclair developed a web-based Student Success Plan (SSP) that includes modules available online when students are studying or wanting to communicate electronically with a counselor or tutor. Whether meeting in person or online, student, faculty, and support staff personnel all have access to the SSP. Because the SSP is connected to the student information system, it provides access to the student's academic record. Other functions include a journal tool, an action planning tool, career worksheets, attachment capabilities for such things as documentation of any disabilities, and an online self-help guide to help students map a successful plan toward degree completion. Advisors can make notes that are accessible to other advisors. There are modules for educational goals, educational plans, and assessment results such as the Myers Briggs Type Indicator and the Learning and Study Strategies Inventory.

The Community College of Baltimore County's Accelerated Learning Program allows students who place in the highest English developmental course to take English 101. The student is enrolled in a special section and attends an additional class, taught by the same instructor, immediately following the English 101 course. This approach could be taken online, with the supplemental session being taught synchronously in a virtual live classroom, providing the academic and nonacademic supports the developmental students need to successfully complete English 101 in one semester rather than two.

Supporting developmental students whether they are taking online or on-campus courses is an essential service for an increasing number of students entering higher education. This section has provided an overview of some initiatives and innovative practices that institutions might consider when developing online support services for students placing into developmental coursework.

LOW-INCOME STUDENTS

While it might be reasonable to assume that high numbers of low-income students, struggling to pay for education while working long hours, would enroll in online courses, that is not the case. Here are some of the reasons. Low-income students are looking for full degree programs in high-demand fields. As institutions create online courses, they do not always create full degree or certificate programs, but rather tend to develop high-enrollment courses because they are more confident that these online offerings will fill. Fully online degrees or certificates typically have a narrower audience; therefore enrollments are not assured. These online courses are only part of online degree programs.

Another factor working against high online enrollment of low-income students has to do with slow home computers and slow connections. Although 66% of all adults have broadband connections at home, only 45% of families with incomes below $30,000 have broadband connections at home (Smith, 2010). Slower computers and Internet connections can make completing an online course more challenging.

Jaggars (2011) makes the following recommendations to support online success for low-income learners:

- Reduce the cost of online courses.
- Provide high-speed Internet access and laptops.
- Revise financial aid structures by simplifying eligibility rules, financially supporting year-round attendance, and not reducing grants when students attend low-cost institutions for one-year or shorter certificate programs.
- Create more fully online programs with clear course scheduling guidelines for completion.
- Assess students' readiness for online learning and provide supports for deficiencies.
- Require a free computer literacy course or opportunities to demonstrate proficiency.
- Provide monetary incentives for students to become computer literate prior to initial online course enrollment.

Innovative Practices

Institutions may be aware that their students, including their low-income students, are well served when the institutions provide their students a clear web presentation of all the options for financial assistance. Harvard University has developed a Financial Aid portal with clear paths for three target audiences: prospective students, current students, and parents. It is simple, visually appealing, with current information, news, and highlights. Students are linked to Harvard's home page, the Student Employment Office, a search tool, and login to the student portal. Students admitted to Harvard whose family income is less than $60,000 attend at no cost. Harvard reduces the contributions of families with incomes between $60,000 and $80,000.

Georgia Perimeter College has added to its website a video explanation of financial planning. Creighton University created a video, "Get Your Bucks in a Row!," which is posted on YouTube to encourage students to make wise financial decisions while in college. CashCourse, a financial education course provided by the National Endowment for Financial Education, is also a good resource for low-income students. This resource is explained in more detail in Chapter Five in the section Financial Aid and Financial Planning.

Although low-income students may need additional support services, these innovative practices may create a smoother path to finding available financial resources.

MILITARY SERVICE PERSONNEL

Whether a prospective student is on active duty, a member of the reserves, or a returning veteran, online learning provides opportunities for military personnel to continue their education. Each group may need different types of support, but they benefit when an institution delivers those support services online. Military service members include military personnel who are on active duty, in the reserves, or in the National Guard. Veterans are former members of the armed services. On August 1, 2009, the Post-9/11 Veterans Assistance Act took effect, with more generous educational benefits than the previous GI Bill. The coverage is for military personnel still on active duty as well as those honorably discharged from active duty (Radford & Associates, 2009).

In its 2009 report, *From Soldier to Student: Easing the Transition of Service Members on Campus,* the American Council on Education surveyed 723 two-year and four-year postsecondary institutions to determine how prepared they were to serve the potentially two million post 9/11 veterans. Veterans have service needs similar to those of other adult students, including an interest in online education and evening and weekend courses. Almost all campuses reported offering military personnel academic support or student services; however, no campus mentioned that the services were delivered online (Cook & Kim, 2009).

Military personnel may have unique needs as they return to or begin college. Some veterans may be physically or emotionally disabled, need developmental courses, or be first generation college students. This section focuses on online services to support the learning of active military personnel or veterans.

Some of the services needed by this population are ways to earn credit for prior learning, evaluation of credit for military training or occupational specialty, and counseling for posttraumatic stress disorder, traumatic brain injuries, or physical disabilities. Veterans might like to be involved in peer networks or organizations with other veterans attending the college. They will want to be able to work with financial aid professionals who are knowledgeable not only about the new GI Bill but also about other sources of funding for veterans.

Veterans may have unique needs as they transition from the military into civilian life. They may need specialized orientation and first-year experience services. Veterans, once separated from the armed services, may look to the college website as the best source of information about all the benefits of the GI Bill. They may have had a strong support system while in the military and may be looking toward the college to replace these institutional supports.

How can colleges and universities use online services to demonstrate that the institution is a welcoming place for returning veterans and active duty military personnel? In 2009, the American Council on Education and the Wal-Mart Foundation awarded $2 million to 20 colleges and universities to develop such support services. Here are innovative online services developed by a few of the grantees.

INNOVATIVE PRACTICES

Park University created a series of five online courses. The first course, Orientation to Learning and Life Skills, is noncredit and free. The other four courses are worth three credits each and apply to a degree: Introduction to Human Communication, Personal Financial Management, First Year Writing Seminar, and Critical Thinking. In addition, Park Warrior Center offers its own service, the Success for Veterans program. Park University's website demonstrates that the school is experienced in serving active duty personnel, veterans, and their dependents. Prospective and currently enrolled students realize this institution provides the support services needed to transition from the military to higher education.

California State Polytechnic University, Pomona, veteran's website provides a profile of veterans who are attending the school. Cal Poly developed a student portal specifically for veterans, from which they can access information about admissions, enrollments, benefits/aid, academic support, student support, campus life, and community resources. Cal Poly also developed a Facebook page so students who are veterans can connect with one another. Park University and Cal Poly have each created unique online resources to support the needs of veterans and active military personnel who may or may not be able to come to campus.

SUPPORT SERVICES FOR AT-RISK ONLINE STUDENTS

Online courses are experiencing annual double-digit enrollment increases at the same time that more students with multiple risk factors are coming to college. Two factors are driving this increase in enrollment for this population. First, when unemployment rises, so do community college enrollments. Second, the Obama administration is advocating for a more educated society, with a goal to increase the number of earned college certificates and degrees by 20% before 2020. In 2010, the White House sponsored a community college summit followed by four regional meetings to discuss what community colleges can do to contribute to the development of a more educated workforce. Because the key players in this initiative are community colleges, they are receiving more attention than ever before.

Institutions, especially community colleges, are aware that nontraditional adult students have the most potential to contribute to a growth in certificates and degrees. High school graduation rates peaked in 2009 and are not projected to reach those levels again until 2016 (*The Adult Learner: An Eduventures Perspective*, 2008). Because of the complexity of their lives, at-risk adult students are tempted to enroll in online courses. For some of these students, this is not always an advisable choice, but frequently community college registration does not require approval of an advisor.

At-risk students have historically benefitted from intensive, personalized student services. In order for these students to be successful in online courses, institutions might consider delivering these services in new ways. The remainder of this section focuses on innovative approaches to supporting the needs of students with multiple risk factors.

RECOMMENDATIONS BASED ON EMPIRICALLY BASED RESEARCH

Colleges and universities, foundations, and governmental agencies are working together to research and recommend policies and practices that respond to President Obama's call for improving community college completion rates. The Community College Research Center (CCRC) is working with grant funding from the Bill and Melinda Gates and Lumina Foundations. CRRC researchers reviewed literature to determine what is known about low-income and underprepared students who enroll in online courses (Jaggars, 2011). They did not find any studies that focus specifically on low-income students and found only a few that focus on underprepared students taking online courses. Jaggars reports the literature that does exist suggests that technical difficulties, isolation, social distance, and lack of structure inherent in online courses may contribute to the lower success rates. Jaggars also suggests that high-risk students may have more difficulty utilizing on-campus support services because of time constraints, especially when offices are open only during normal business hours.

The report recommends various ways that institutions may address the needs of online students who have one or more of the risk factors. For example, institutions may provide to its online learners high-quality, easy-to-access, and round-the-clock support services. More specifically, institutions may want to consider integrating these services via the same platforms that students use for instruction, typically the learning management system. When institutions incorporate support services into course instructional materials, students are more likely to use them.

Jaggars (2011) offers three recommendations that would be best accomplished through collaboration among academic affairs, student affairs, and IT:

- Create a set of support-oriented academic activities systematically built into the curriculum of high-enrollment introductory courses taught online.
- Create automated systems that could dynamically provide key online support services without the need that they be staffed around-the-clock. Complex issues would continue to be resolved during normal business hours with the assistance of student service professionals.
- Create cost-effective support mechanisms by developing support tools that multiple institutions can use.

To respond to the issues of social distance and isolation, Jaggars recommends the following:

- Faculty development for online instructors should include course design and pedagogical strategies that incorporate interactivity, provide an encouraging online environment, and include specific activities known to improve course retention.
- Faculty development for both course design and online pedagogy should be incentivized in environments where training to be an online instructor is not required.
- Improvements in distance learning course, instruction, and program quality must be ongoing.

Institutions may recognize that, as with many support recommendations, these three suggestions improve the chances of success for all online students, not just those who are adults returning to college, the first in their family to attend college, taking developmental courses, low-income, and military personnel.

CONCLUSION

The profile of online students is no less diverse than all other college populations. Although this chapter targets the needs of specific groups of online students, the overlying message is the importance of institutions' knowing that some students who enroll in online courses and programs may be at risk and may need additional support services. Each risk factor may contribute to decreased retention rates in online courses. When students have more than one of these factors, they are at increased risk of not completing an online course. Institutions may encounter challenges as they establish support services for at-risk online populations. However, those support services are vital to their success. When institutions provide services to online students with a caring, personal tone, those students are made to feel a part of the institution even if they never come to campus.

CHAPTER THREE

SUPPORTING ONLINE STUDENTS WITH DISABILITIES

For many years, institutions have supported students with disabilities who take courses on campus. Some want to take courses online and want to access student services through the institution's websites.

Online learning has the potential to improve access to higher education for all students, especially for those students with disabilities who find it difficult to leave their home. But the promise of using the Internet to open educational opportunities has not been fulfilled. Many institutions designed their websites and online course materials and developed or purchased learning management systems that created barriers that inhibit people with disabilities from full participation in online courses and online support services.

This chapter examines some of those barriers and presents ways to overcome them by providing an accessible online environment where students with disabilities can learn and take advantage of remotely delivered support services. The chapter describes the needs of students with various types of disabilities, reviews laws and standards that institutions must follow, and recommends approaches that institutions might adopt to provide accessible online student services.

CHALLENGES AND BENEFITS OF ONLINE LEARNING

Online learning has the potential to provide access to education for people with disabilities who have been unable to achieve their educational goals. One in four Americans has a disability that interferes with their daily activities:

- 15% of American adults have serious difficulty walking or climbing stairs.
- 11% of American adults, because of a physical, mental, or emotional condition, have serious difficulty concentrating, remembering, or making decisions.
- 9% of American adults have serious difficulty hearing.
- 8% of American adults, because of a physical, mental, or emotional condition, have difficulty doing errands alone, such as visiting a doctor's office or shopping.
- 7% of American adults are blind or have serious difficulty seeing, even when wearing glasses.
- 3% of American adults have trouble dressing or bathing (Fox, 2011).

A study conducted by the PEW Institute found that 2% of American adults say their disability or illness makes using the Internet difficult or impossible (Fox, 2011).

In 2008 students with disabilities represented almost 11% of all postsecondary students. This population is growing (*Higher Education and Disability: Education Needs a Coordinated Approach to Improve Its Assistance to Schools in Supporting Students*, 2009). These students want to take online courses, access information, and complete administrative tasks and other support services online, but they cannot do so because some websites were not built to meet the needs of students with vision, hearing, cognitive, or physical disabilities. Online services use the Internet to support students, and online courses use learning management systems, documents, multimedia, and communication tools for instruction. If these products are not created to meet the needs of students with disabilities, an institution shuts the door to education for a population that sees the Internet as potentially opening so many opportunities previously considered unavailable.

BENEFICIAL IMPACT OF TECHNOLOGY

A few examples illustrate the impact of using assistive technology and developing accessible websites. Norman Coombs, a college history professor who is blind, relied on Braille, tape recordings, and the assistance of others to earn his Ph.D. and to perform the duties of his profession. In the mid-1980s his world was transformed when he got a computer with a voice synthesizer. Since then, he has been a pioneer in creating pathways to education for people with disabilities through the use of technology. When he began to use email with his students, a deaf student was similarly impressed; she noted that a particular email exchange she had with Dr. Coombs was the first time she had "talked" directly to a professor without the help of an interpreter (Coombs, 2010).

Students with motor disabilities or students with cognitive disabilities use various assistive devices, plus patience and persistence, to access the Internet. Although their perseverance allows them access to the world of information, accessible web design can make the task easier. Institutions understand that their web page design and development can either facilitate access or create substantial barriers. Ultimately, institutional decisions on these matters affect whether or not these students will continue their education and become self-supporting, productive citizens.

The number of students with disabilities seeking postsecondary education is growing. Both online and on-campus students with disabilities want to receive services from the Internet, but not all of them can use the tools that provide access to online courses and support service because they are not accessible. Currently, institutions provide accommodations such as note takers and extended time on tests when these students take courses on campus. However, when students with disabilities want to participate in the convenience and flexibility of online learning, accommodating them is more challenging.

IDENTIFYING THE ISSUES

Institutions have both the responsibility for and the challenge of developing an approach that provides access to online learning for students with disabilities. To develop effective support services for online students with disabilities, institutions might consider a three-prong approach:

1. Ensure technology, including websites, is accessible so all students can use it to access and navigate online courses and online services.
2. Provide students with disabilities the training to use assistive technology needed to successfully complete online courses.
3. Establish policies and procedures to ensure that the needs of online students with disabilities are being met.

Institutions can facilitate delivery of efficient and effective services to online students with disabilities by developing accessible online course materials and student services. Institutions may find it cost-effective to provide disabled students with the opportunity to learn independently and take advantage of online services. When accessible electronically delivered accommodations are not available, institutions are required to provide in-person accommodations, a more labor-intensive, costly endeavor that presents barriers to online students with disabilities, especially those who do not come to campus.

It is important for institutions to create or purchase accessible hardware and software, as well as develop accessible websites. Learning management systems (LMSs), the software from which most online courses are delivered, were not originally designed to meet the needs of disabled students, particularly blind students. LMSs are improving, but they still need significant additional enhancements. For example, students are sometimes required to submit assignments directly into the LMS. This creates problems for blind students that can be remedied if the assignment drop box inside the LMS is designed with accessibility in mind.

Other potential barriers to learning are blogs, live chats, polls, wikis, databases, quizzes, glossaries, grade books, email, and portfolios—all common functions found inside and outside of most learning management systems (Stenehjem, 2011). Students with disabilities may also face barriers in accessing online course and student support materials. For example, some materials are developed by using word processing or web authoring software. When they are properly designed, the course materials are accessible. Multimedia and Portable Document Format (pdf) files can be made accessible but require specific knowledge about how this is done (Stenehjem, 2011).

Students with disabilities do not always have access to assistive technologies, nor do they necessarily know how to use them to navigate online courses and student support services (Stenehjem, 2011). Training students to navigate and providing tips on how to best use the LMS, online course materials, and online support services may be a new responsibility for staff in disability student service offices, but it is important that this type of support be provided.

An institution's first steps toward solving these problems are to heighten awareness and directly and intentionally address online learning and services in order to ensure that students with disabilities are afforded the same options as all other students. Institutions are motivated to provide increased access to education for people with disabilities for various reasons. They surely want to avoid lawsuits and the resulting bad publicity and damaged reputation, but primarily they want to provide access because it is the right thing to do. Institutions traditionally provide services to students with disabilities by responding to requests for accommodations; this is a reactive model. Institutions that adopt a proactive model of support provide the success strategies students need to be successful in the online environment. A proactive approach includes the development and implementation of policies and procedures to support the needs of online students with disabilities.

Given that these students want to learn conveniently and independently through online courses, it is important for institutions to provide access to support services, using the same tools students use for learning. Institutions can facilitate these goals by developing websites and online course materials and by purchasing software and hardware with accessibility in mind.

STUDENTS AND THEIR NEEDS

Institutions commonly use the following four categories in grouping students with disabilities: visual disabilities, hearing disabilities, physical disabilities, and cognitive disabilities. Each group includes students with diverse disabilities who have different needs to be met if they are to be successful at the institution. It is important for institutions to assess the unique needs of each individual student to determine how best to support each student's college success.

FREQUENCY OF STUDENTS WITH DISABILITIES TAKING ONLINE COURSES

A study of 221 students with documented disabilities enrolled in online courses at 25 institutions that have national reputations as online education leaders reported these findings: 71.6% of the students had taken online courses, and 45% reported their disability had an impact on their ability to succeed in the online learning environment. The main reasons were difficulty concentrating, online testing (especially when timed), and difficulty reading the computer screen. Screen readers were the most commonly cited assistive technology; other technology included screen magnifiers, large monitors, speech recognition software, oversized keyboards, and special mouse technologies. Seventy-one percent of the students did not request accommodations for online courses. Forty-five percent expressed that they were either very satisfied or satisfied with the disability support services (Roberts, Crittenden, & Crittenden, 2009). These results suggest two areas of concern: one is the low percentage of online students with disabilities seeking accommodations and the other is that less than half of the students were satisfied with the support services. If institutions better understand the needs of students with disabilities, institutions may be better positioned to develop and deliver appropriate services.

Visual Disabilities

Many students with visual disabilities (blindness, low vision, and color-blindness) use a screen reader that synthesizes speech and reads a page aloud. Students listen to the screen reader as web pages are read in a linear fashion. Structural information is repeated frequently, unless each page is developed with an understanding of how a screen reader will interpret the code. Because screen readers cannot read images, it is important to supply meaningful text descriptions. Students with visual disabilities often cannot use a mouse because they cannot place the cursor appropriately on the screen. Accordingly, institutions might design websites that make all content accessible by use of keyboard strokes. Students with low vision may use screen magnifiers that zoom in on a small area of the screen. If the website is designed appropriately, the user can control the magnification of the text. Institutions should not use color alone to convey the meaning of content or use low contrast between background and text or graphics, as these design elements will create barriers for students who are color blind ("The User's Perspective," 2011). These are just some of the web design strategies that help provide accessible materials for students with visual disabilities.

Hearing Disabilities

The web has become a multimedia virtual universe. Audio presentations create barriers for students with a hearing disability (which includes hearing loss that is mild, moderate, severe, or profound). When institutions develop accessible web content for deaf students, their audio or audio portions of video presentations should include synchronous captioning or provide a text alternative. For example, University of Washington, Disabilities, Opportunities, Internetworking, and Technology (DO-IT) has a collection of accessible videos.

For some deaf students who use American Sign Language, English is their second language. For these students, using simple, clear language is particularly important. All institutions should be aware that because video on the web is not large or clear enough to make sign language understandable, video presentation of sign language is not currently an effective means of accommodating deaf students ("The User's Perspective," 2011). Although creating captioned videos is expensive, YouTube has recently found a way to caption their videos.

Physical Disabilities

Students with physical disabilities have diverse needs. These students may be unable to use a mouse, have a slow response time, or have limited fine motor control. They may need a variety of assistive technologies. Students who use a specialized mouse or keyboard may also use pointing devices to activate areas of the keyboard. Although these tools provide accessibility, the students must practice to develop the skills needed to use the tools effectively. To accommodate students with physical disabilities, institutions might design their websites with lots of white space and with code that tolerates errors. These students may need extra time to complete a task. It is important for institutions to consider all these factors to create accessible web sites for students with physical disabilities ("The User's Perspective," 2011).

Cognitive Disabilities

Institutions may want to provide web access to students with a cognitive disability (learning disabilities, distractibility, an inability to remember or focus on large amounts of information, intellectual disabilities, language and learning difficulties, head injury, stroke, Alzheimer's disease, and dementia). Some cognitive disabilities have little or no impact but others significantly affect a student's ability to access the web. These disabilities can affect memory, perception, conceptualization, problem solving, attention, concentration, executive functions, language abilities, emotion, and behavior. They also vary from person to person and can change over time (Mariger, 2005). Institutions may find this group the most challenging to accommodate through accessible website design because their needs are so diverse. Good web design for one group may create barriers for another.

As each institution endeavors to provide accessible web design for its students with cognitive disabilities, some useful and commonsense strategies are available. An institution might use standard, predictable, consistent navigation within a website; keep menus short, with meaningful labels that are easy to understand; use breadcrumbs (generally, small horizontal links at the top of a webpage) as an alternative navigation tool; provide site maps, provide prompts to let users know if they made a correct choice and help them get back if they make an error; increase the size of clickable areas; limit the number of options; and avoid simultaneous tasks.

Content should use plain language, repeat information for students with memory problems, chunk material with one idea per paragraph, use bullets, use meaningful headings, use short line lengths, provide meaningful text for images, include plenty of white space, offer a brief introduction then a link to more detail, and use a readability test to keep text at an appropriate reading level (Mariger, 2005).

The broader message of this section is that when institutions create web sites and online course materials accessible to students with disabilities, all web users benefit. For students with disabilities, the more accessible the web, the more independently can they fulfill their educational goals. Even when institutions need to make additional accommodations, their accessible web materials will save the institution money, as fewer face-to-face services may be required.

LAWS AND STANDARDS

Some, but not all institutions ensure that their websites, online course materials, and learning management systems are as accessible to students with disabilities as they are to other students. As institutions realize that the law obligates them to provide students with disabilities access to electronically delivered materials or risk losing federal funding for their noncompliance, they are likely to focus on the accessibility of these materials. It is important for institutions to establish websites and purchase learning management systems that enable students with disabilities to take online courses and receive online support services. This section surveys laws that mandate equal opportunities for all students and then discusses guidelines that assist institutions in developing accessible materials.

Legal Mandates

The Americans with Disabilities Act (ADA) was last revised in 2009. Titles II and III of ADA prohibit discrimination on the basis of disability in employment, state and local government, public accommodations, commercial facilities, transportation, and telecommunications. The ADA protects people with disabilities against discrimination and requires accommodations be provided under Title III of the same Act. When enacted, ADA did not provide specific standards for website accessibility. This is understandable, as the Internet as we now know it did not exist in 1990 when ADA was originally passed. The Civil Rights Division of the U.S. Department of Justice is revising sections of the Americans with Disabilities Act to cover website accessibility. The revisions, if approved, will establish specific standards that expand access to the Internet for people with disabilities under ADA. This will significantly affect the delivery of online services to students with disabilities.

Many government and public websites had been designed in a way that makes access to the information difficult or impossible for people with disabilities. Now that the Internet has become an essential tool for daily living, inaccessible websites create significant barriers. At the time of the writing of this book, a process is in place to remedy this situation (*Nondiscrimination on the Basis of Disability; Accessibility of Web Information and Services of State and Local Government Entities and Public Accommodations*, 2010).

Important legislation, including Sections 504 and 508, amendments to the Rehabilitation Act of 1973, provide institutions with the guidance they need to design and develop websites that are accessible to students with disabilities. Section 504 was the first civil rights law protecting people with disabilities from discrimination by institutions receiving federal financial assistance. Section 508 provides standards and performance criteria of accessibility for software applications and operating systems, web-based intranet and Internet information and systems, telecommunication products, video and multimedia products, self-contained closed products, and desktop and portable computers. This covers all technology used to design, develop, and deliver online courses and student services.

CHALLENGES TO MANDATES

The Department of Education, Office of Civil Rights (OCR) enforces Sections 504 and 508 of the Rehabilitation Act. If OCR finds that an institution has failed to comply with the requirements, the institution could lose federal funds. Typically, OCR and the institution resolve the complaint, and funding is not withdrawn. But two high-profile cases highlight issues about accessibility of hardware, software, websites, and online learning for students with disabilities. In the Arizona State University (ASU) case, the National Federation of the Blind and the American Council of the Blind charged that ASU discriminated against blind students because ASU required all students in a pilot project to use a Kindle electronic reader. The Kindle has audio options, but because it does not provide adequate navigation, students who are blind cannot find those audio options.

The Department of Justice settled with ASU and three other colleges involved in the pilot. The institutions agreed that they would not require the Kindle reader or any other similar technology until they are deemed to be accessible to students with visual or print disabilities. The Offices of Civil Rights of Departments of Justice and Education followed up with a strongly worded open letter to the presidents of colleges and universities, requesting they refrain from requiring electronic book readers or similar technology as long as the devices are inaccessible to students who are blind or have low vision (Perez & Ali, 2010).

In another case, the National Federation of the Blind (NFB) charged that Pennsylvania State University violated Title II of ADA by providing online services and information that could not be accessed by blind students. NFB claimed that numerous computer-based programs and websites at Penn State University are inaccessible to blind and print-disabled students—including websites of the Office of Disability Services. For settlement purposes, NFB has recommended that Penn State hire a full-time employee who reports to the CIO and is responsible for accessibility, write an accessibility policy statement that includes accountability for violations, conduct an accessibility audit and develop guidelines for maintaining accessibility and procuring accessible software and hardware, and develop a manual and provide training to all personnel authorized to develop websites (Goldstein, 2010).

REVISIONS TO ADA

Because of these complaints against major institutions and the likely possible passage of the 2010 ADA Web Accessibility Standards, all institutions are on notice that that web resources must be accessible to all students. These ADA revisions will significantly affect how institutions develop their websites. On September 15, 2010, the U.S. Department of Justice published and opened for public comment its 2010 Standards for Accessible Design that would revise Title II and III of the ADA. The final rules were effective March 15, 2011, and compliance is required by March 15, 2012 (Holder, 2010).

Although the ADA to date has not provided standards for accessible website development, other laws have guided public entities in providing access to people with disabilities through the Internet and other technologies. These laws are extremely important because they provide institutions with accessibility standards that are supported by the U.S. government. These laws provide compliance language and standards that can be monitored at a distance and that are binding and enforceable. They protect the rights of people with disabilities and give website designers the guidelines they need so they know what is expected for compliance (Stenehjem, 2011).

ACCESSIBILITY OF COLLEGE WEBSITES

Monitoring accessibility of college and university websites is a monumental task. Currently, many institutions might improve the monitoring of their own websites for accessibility. External agencies do no formal monitoring, and institutions have been slow to make their websites accessible. A 2009 study of 700 colleges showed only about half required that website content be accessible (Erickson, Trerise, Lee, VanLooy, & Bruyère, 2009). Another study of 100 college web pages found that only three were in compliance with Section 508 standards (Whiting, 2008). Gunderson (2010), who identified the best and worse websites for blind students, also provides examples of best practices that other institutions might follow.

PRINCIPLES OF UNIVERSAL DESIGN AND WEB CONTENT ACCESSIBILITY GUIDELINES

Some institutions have tried to create accessible websites by following evolving sets of standards: Universal Design (or Accessible Design) and Web Content Accessibility Guidelines (WCAG) version 2.0 guidelines developed by the World Wide Web Consortium (W3C). Universal Design is "the design of products and environments to be usable by all people, to the greatest extent possible, without the need for adaptation or specialized design" ("The Center for Universal Design," 2008). Universal Design standards were originally used to design physical environments that are barrier-free and accessible for everyone. The virtual world has adopted these standards to apply to the design of a variety of technologies, including websites.

Universal Design principles are that websites are equitable for everyone, flexible, simple, and intuitive, information is universally perceptible, allows a tolerance for error, and can be navigated with a minimum of effort ("The Center for Universal Design," 2008). The principles are as follows:

- *Equitable* use means the design should be appealing, useful, and marketable to people with diverse abilities rather than being targeted to a specific segment of the population.
- *Flexibility* in use means the design accommodates a wide range of individual preferences and abilities, accommodates right- and left-handed people, and lets users work at their own pace.
- *Simple and intuitive* means the user can easily understand how to use the website, regardless of the user's experience, knowledge, language skills, or current concentration level. The website should also provide effective prompting and feedback during and after task completion.

- *Perceptible* information means that the design communicates necessary information effectively to the user, regardless of ambient conditions or the users' sensory abilities. One way to do this is to use different modes (pictorial, verbal, tactile) for redundant presentation of essential information and provide adequate contrast between essential information and its surroundings.
- *Tolerance* for error means that the design minimizes the adverse consequences of accidental or unintended actions. The design should provide warnings of possible errors and provide fail-safe features.
- *Low physical effort* means the design should allow the user to use the item efficiently and comfortably with a minimum of fatigue (Coombs, 2010).

Websites developed and maintained using Universal Design principles benefit all users. Online learners with disabilities benefit by needing fewer—or no accommodations—in order to access online instructional materials and student service websites. When websites and course materials are created using Universal Design principles, the content is compatible with a wide range of assistive technologies.

The World Wide Web Consortium (W3C) has a full-time staff that works with an international community to develop protocols and guidelines that ensure the long-term growth of the web ("Help and FAQ," 2009). One of many W3C projects is the Web Accessibility Initiative (WAI). WAI develops strategies, guidelines, and resources to help make the Web accessible to people with disabilities ("WAI Resources on Introducing Web Accessibility," 2010).

One WAI project is the Web Content Accessibility Guidelines (WCAG) 2.0. These guidelines explain in detail how content, web browsers, assistive technology, users, developers, and authoring and evaluation tools contribute to the accessibility of websites for people with disabilities. WCAG provides guidelines for developers who are using web authoring and evaluation tools to create content for the web ("Essential Components of Web Accessibility," 2005). These technical standards are excellent, but student support personnel would benefit from understanding how students with disabilities actually use the web (i.e., usability standards).

Usability Standards

Usability standards require that websites be perceivable, operable, understandable, and robust. Institutions have several strategies available to make websites perceivable for students with various disabilities. People with full use of vision are able to read text, view images, understand visual cues presented by web page layout, and understand the symbolic meaning of color. People with full use of hearing are able to participate in voice chats, listen to audio presentations and video presentations with audio, and hear music. Institutions have various ways to transform online content for students who do not have full use of vision and hearing. When using audio online, the preferable way to accommodate students with hearing disabilities is to create synchronized, equivalent, and accessible captioning for audio content because it integrates presentation of visual and audio elements. Transcripts are an alternative to captioning, but separating audio from video is not as good for learning ("Constructing a Perceivable, Operable, Understandable, Robust Website," 2011).

Institutions have available common approaches to create *perceivable* online content that accommodates the needs of students with visual disabilities. Screen magnifiers assist students with low vision and are most effective when web developers use true text rather than graphical representations of text. This is also important for students who want to customize their contrast settings. Students with low vision are helped by web pages designed with high-contrast graphic, font, and backgrounds. Web pages should not require students to use a horizontal scroll bar to see a full page. This problem is remedied if the web pages are designed using percentages rather than absolute pixels.

It is important that institutions use meaningful link descriptions to tell the user what will be found if the user goes to the next location. Institutions should not use the term "click here," since this command does not tell the users what is to be found by going there. It is important to provide alternative text for nontext elements. Color-blind students have full access to web pages when color is not used as the only method of conveying important information. For instance, a graphic of a subway system should include the words "green line" and "red line" rather than only using colors to differentiate the two ("Constructing a Perceivable, Operable, Understandable, Robust Website," 2011).

Operable online content considers the assistive technology hardware some people use to access the Internet. Not everyone is able to use a standard mouse and keyboard to navigate the Web. Blind people, for example, do not use the mouse because they cannot see the screen to determine placement of the cursor. Some people may use a variety of assistive technologies to facilitate their use of the Web. Accessible web development allows use of keystrokes rather than only the mouse. Operable websites allow users to navigate through a website via multiple means.

Well-designed websites provide site scarches, site indexes, and site maps. Typically, people should have unlimited time to complete tasks. However, unlimited time limits might not be appropriate for academic testing; other accommodations may be used. Users should be able to control how fast media players, animation, and any other time-dependent content advances. Students should be able to easily recover from mistakes. Web developers can program second chances to make the web more forgiving of errors ("Constructing a Perceivable, Operable, Understandable, Robust Website," 2011).

To make a website *understandable*, institutions should use language that is simple and concise, explain background information, provide clear directions, and provide alternative representations such as graphics, videos, animations, and audio. These alternative representations may help students with some disabilities, but a possible downside is that they may hinder students with other disabilities.

An understandable website is not just technically sound but also functional. To ensure that that websites are functional, navigation should be consistent and predictable throughout the site. Interactive elements and controls should be labeled, and instruction for how to find information on the site should be clear and succinct. Institutions may consider using organization tools such as headings and lists for clarity ("Constructing a Perceivable, Operable, Understandable, Robust Website," 2011).

Robust websites support as many current and past technologies as possible. If the institution wants to develop web pages that anticipate future technology, the institution should use its current technology according to specification. When developers customize the way software is used, it lessens the chance that the site will be backward compatible with new versions. It is also important to provide links to necessary plug-ins or applets ("Constructing a Perceivable, Operable, Understandable, Robust Website," 2011).

INSTITUTIONAL LEVEL STUDENT SUPPORT STANDARDS

These Distance Learning Program (DLP) Accessibility Indicators were developed by the University of Washington in collaboration with 16 other two-year and four-year colleges and universities. Institutions can use the indicators to create a checklist against which to measure the accessibility of distance learning programs. Of the ten DLP Accessibility Indicators, the first five pertain to current and prospective online learners:

Indicator 1. The distance learning home page is accessible to individuals with disabilities (e.g., it adheres to Section 508, World Wide Web Consortium, or institutional accessible-design guidelines/standards). An example is the University of Wisconsin-Madison, Continuing Education home page.

Indicator 2. A statement about the distance learning program's commitment to accessible design for all potential students, including those with disabilities, is included prominently in appropriate publications and websites along with contact information for reporting inaccessible design features. An example is the Arizona State University, ASU Online Accessibility Statement.

Indicator 3. A statement about how distance learning students with disabilities can request accommodations is included in appropriate publications and web pages. An example is the University of South Carolina Student Guidebook: Policies and Procedures for Distance Education Classes.

Indicator 4. A statement about how people can obtain alternate formats of printed materials is included in publications. An example is the University of Minnesota Independent and Distance Learning Course Catalogue that offers students alternative forms of the catalog and lets students know how to obtain the other forms.

Indicator 5. The online and other course materials of distance learning courses are accessible to individuals with disabilities. Institutions may need to develop an additional checklist to measure this indicator.

The next two indicators pertain to the work of instructional designers:

Indicator 6. Publications and web pages for distance learners should include a statement of the program's commitment to accessibility, guidelines and standards regarding accessibility, and relevant resources.

Indicator 7. Accessibility issues are covered in regular course designer training.

The next two indicators pertain to online instructors:

Indicator 8. Publications and web pages for distance learning instructors should include a statement of the program's commitment to accessibility, guidelines and standards regarding accessibility, and relevant resources.

Indicator 9. Accessibility issues are covered in online instructor training.

The last indicator is for program evaluators:

Indicator 10. A system is in place to monitor the accessibility of courses, and based on this evaluation, the program takes action to improve accessibility of specific online courses and update information and training given to all constituencies (Burgstahler, 2006).

All students benefit when websites and online course materials and student support are developed and technology purchased with the needs of students with disabilities in mind. These laws, standards, and guidelines enhance educational opportunities for everyone.

PLANS FOR IMPROVEMENT

Institutions must ensure that their websites are ADA, 504, and 508 compliant to meet accessibility standards for all students. In many institutions, online student services are unavailable to students with disabilities who are already enrolled or who could not enroll because they could not access necessary information from the institution's website. Institutions typically use learning management systems and other technology tools for instruction of online and on-campus students, but these sometimes create significant barriers for students with disabilities.

ARE INSTITUTIONS IN COMPLIANCE?

The 2010 Managing Online Education Survey calls for a systematic planning process to bring institutions into compliance. Survey data show that many institutions do not have formal policies and procedures to ensure that their online courses and programs are compliant with ADA, 504, and 508 mandates. For example:

- 34% report that responsibility for compliance resides with individual faculty who teach an online course.
- 24% report that responsibility for compliance resides with academic programs or departments.
- 17% report no institutional policy or procedure for compliance.
- 9% report that a central campus office examines a sample of online courses to ensure compliance.
- 6% indicate their institution has a central office that examines each course for compliance (Green, 2010a).

According to Green, institutions may be vulnerable to complaints about access to online courses when the responsibility for ensuring compliance is decentralized. Institutions that are concerned about possible noncompliance might seek guidance from the WebAIM model of reform.

WEBAIM MODEL

WebAIM, an initiative of the Center for Persons with Disabilities and Utah State University, has provided web accessibility solutions since 1999. WebAIM's mission is to empower institutions to make their content accessible to people with disabilities by providing knowledge, technical skills, tools, organizational leadership strategies, and vision ("About WebAIM," 2011).

The goal of the WebAIM Model ("Eight-Step Implementation Model," 2011) is to create an institutional awareness that inaccessible websites produce barriers for students with disabilities.

The model sets out eight steps to accomplish the goal:

1. Gather baseline information
2. Gain top level support
3. Organize a web accessibility committee
4. Define standards
5. Create an implementation plan
6. Provide training and technical support
7. Monitor conformance
8. Remain flexible through the changes

The planning process requires leadership and commitment from the institution that is backed up by policy, standards, procedures, and methods for monitoring compliance ("Eight-Step Implementation Model," 2011).

Gather Baseline Information

The first step—to gather baseline information—includes defining the scope of the problem. Institutions determine whether students with disabilities can access the web pages that lead to and allow them to complete online support services. If the web pages are inaccessible, an institution has not provided access to educational opportunities; this may have significant repercussions. Students may decide not to attend the institution. Even if they are helped by others to overcome these initial barriers, they still may be worried about whether they can succeed at the institution and may not be convinced that the institution will provide appropriate accommodations to support their success.

Institutions that want to gauge the accessibility of their web pages can use an evaluation tool. Tests using the evaluation tool should be run on the home page, top level pages that link off of the home page, and the multiple layers that are subsumed under the top level pages. This evaluation can be done by someone who understands not only the technical aspects of website accessibility, but also the characteristics of usability. This evaluation may help institutions determine the scope of the problem, how many pages create barriers, who are the people responsible for these pages, and the units represented by these pages. The evaluation might also identify the decision-making methodology.

Gain Top Level Support

The second step—gain top level support within the institution—is important because it increases visibility of the issue and confirms that the institution is committed to the changes in website accessibility. Those responsible for implementing the development of accessible websites can justify the necessary expenses if top level administrators have designated this as a priority. Top level support creates a framework for ongoing monitoring and development of an accessible website.

However, making websites accessible is not a one-time event. It is important to understand the campus culture as one decides how to approach the leadership. The basic reason for the improvements that will result from this planning effort is to provide access to students with disabilities. Institutions might need additional information about the laws, perhaps case studies, the consequences of not making websites accessible, and best practices from institutions, especially those viewed as competing for the same students, in order to justify the commitment of resources ("Eight-Step Implementation Model," 2011).

Organize a Web Accessibility Committee

To organize a web accessibility committee, an institution might identify those constituencies that want to be represented at the table and, from those constituencies, key stakeholders that include respected individuals from various areas of the college who can influence their peers and have the time to commit to the project. Representatives might come from administration, faculty, students with disabilities, and disability support services and include a webmaster.

An institution might acknowledge the challenges associated with this type of process. If the institution has decentralized website maintenance, it will have a hard time gaining commitment from each component. For example, web developers may be unaware of how to create accessible websites and will need training. Web development and maintenance at postsecondary institutions may have grown organically. In some cases, the responsibility has been added to the work load of those who first learned the skills. These employees may not have the time or interests to acquire the skills needed to learn how to create accessible web pages. However, if an institution uses the model, the result might be a more organized approach to institutionwide website development ("Eight-Step Implementation Model," 2011).

Define Standards

The web accessibility committee is responsible for developing a policy that defines accessibility standards and guidelines for the institution's website. When the web accessibility committee begins drafting the institution's policy, it might derive its policy from the resources of Universal Design and WCAG guidelines and standards, as well as Sections 504 and 508 of the Rehabilitation Act, and ADA requirements. This policy might also include an implementation plan that ensures consistency across the institution and gives web developers a planning guide.

The approach taken to develop an institutionwide web accessibility policy should be inclusive. The committee might create a draft of the policy, hold public meetings to gather feedback and comments, revise the policy as appropriate based on public comments, and present the policy to the college community. When announcing the policy, the committee should explain why it is important, describe the regulations used to develop the policy, list what is included, post a list of standards and links to more detailed information about how to implement the standards, and make clear that it is a work in progress ("Eight-Step Implementation Model," 2011). The University of Wisconsin-Madison website has an example of a web accessibility policy.

Create an Implementation Plan

The next step is to develop an implementation plan to establish time lines that are realistic for the size of the institution and the complexity of the internal and external college websites. The implementation plan sets priorities and sequences that establish goals and benchmarks for accessibility changes. It might identify people or units who are responsible for overseeing each task and define work groups, their responsibilities, and mechanisms for accountability. It assigns responsibility for monitoring progress for the initial changes and ongoing upgrades. Finally, it should define a process and identify those responsible for decision making and approval of accessibility changes made to the institution's website ("Eight-Step Implementation Model," 2011).

Provide Training and Technical Support

Training and technical support is an essential component of implementing institutionwide website accessibility improvements. Website accessibility skills should be standard knowledge for all web developers. Some developers are hired with those skills, while others will need to learn them. It is important to identify everyone in the organization who has responsibility for creating and maintaining web pages, assess their skill set, and develop or purchase training resources that are appropriate for novice through experienced web developers. Training topics might include web accessibility issues, the organization's standards, and technical training ("Eight-Step Implementation Model," 2011).

Monitor Conformance

It is important to develop a plan for monitoring compliance and sustainability to ensure the ongoing accessibility of the institution's website. The plan might include a schedule for periodic (annual, biannual, quarterly) checks of all web content and ongoing monitoring. These responsibilities might be added to a job description.

Remain Flexible Through the Changes

The institution must remain flexible throughout the process, knowing that standards do change in the virtual world. Being flexible and ready to adapt to those changes provides opportunities for improvement ("Eight-Step Implementation Model," 2011). The National Center on Disability and Access to Education has developed a tool called Gaining Online Accessible Learning Through Self-Study (known as GOALS) to assist institutions in bringing websites into compliance. GOALS, a web accessibility benchmarking and planning tool, is a collection of materials and processes that have been developed specifically to help post-secondary institutions improve the accessibility of their web resources ("Gaining Online Accessible Learning Through Self-Study," 2005).

SERVICES FOR ONLINE STUDENTS WITH DISABILITIES

While planning for and implementing accessible websites and online learning technologies are essential in providing students access to online courses and services, these support services are only part of what students with disabilities need to be successful in online courses. Disabled students taking courses online need both services unique to the online environment and services provided to disabled students taking courses on campus. The disability support staff is accustomed to training students to use assistive technology for traditionally delivered courses. This staff may also be asked to help students use the technology and accommodations students need to access and succeed in their online courses. This may include learning how to overcome barriers created by inaccessible college websites, access the learning management system, navigate various functions inside the learning management system, and use online course materials.

The disability support staff might also work with online faculty and instructional designers to improve accessibility of the courses. As members of the web accessibility committee, disability support staff can help write a policy and implement plans about how online students with disabilities are to access accommodations and support services. An essential part of this plan is determining who is responsible for ADA, 504, and 508 compliance for online learning. When an institution decides to assign the responsibility to one component, that decision protects the institution and facilitates accountability. According to the Managing Online Education Survey, many institutions have not paid sufficient attention to creating access (Green, 2010a).

Disability support staff also have an advocacy role to play for online students with disabilities. They can emphasize the importance of purchasing technology that is compliant with current and emerging accessibility standards and can be responsive to students who report barriers that hinder their success in online courses. Taken together, these support services will lead to improved success for online students with disabilities.

CONCLUSION

This chapter covers a wide range of challenges that institutions may want to address in order to facilitate the learning and support of online students with disabilities. With an ever increasing number of these students wanting to take advantage of online learning, institutions might take a proactive, strategic approach to improving the design and delivery of online support services and creating accessible online courses.

While the breadth of these changes may raise concerns, the necessity of implementing accessible web content is not only legally mandated but is also the right thing to do. Institutions should take a systematic approach by using an implementation plan that might include a series of phases that reflects institutional priorities.

When institutions participate in a strategic planning process of making online student services accessible for all, one unintended benefit may be an increased awareness of the needs of students with disabilities and the barriers that can be created by inaccessible technology. That increased awareness may improve all services that institutions provide for students with disabilities.

CHAPTER FOUR

PUTTING SERVICES ONLINE

If institutions put student services online, they can develop support mechanisms that respond to the needs of online learners. Online students benefit when cross-functional teams collaborate to create comprehensive services delivered through electronic means.

THE LAUNCH PADS

Online student services are launched from four possible web applications: an institution's external website, an internal website, from inside a learning management system, or through social media applications. An institution's external website is its face to the world. Internal websites, generally password-protected portals, provide a place to deliver services that may be linked to student information systems, can be personalized, and sometimes allow students to customize the information that is presented to them.

Learning management systems are used primarily to deliver online, blended, or web-enhanced courses, but they can also be used to deliver online student services. If an institution delivers student services from inside its learning management systems, students can access the services when they are actively involved in the process of learning. If student support services are placed into coursework, that makes the support services inescapable, eliminates obstacles of time and place, and leverages the time when institutions have the best access to their students.

Moreover, when an institution integrates its support services into an online course, it creates an opportunity for students to interact with one another, as well as with support specialists, thereby nurturing relationships. Students need not feel singled out or stigmatized by being referred for help because support is just another feature for any student in a particular course (SENSE, 2010). Arguments against classroom integration cite the limited audience that benefits from this delivery method and potential added responsibility placed on the faculty.

The Scope of Online Student Services

Put simply, online student services are those services that online students need to accomplish their educational goals. Most online services are the same as those provided on campus but delivered through the Internet rather than in person. Online students may require additional services: for example, what to expect from online learning, how to navigate the learning management system, and how to access the services they need to successfully complete their educational goals.

Initially, online learning appealed to students who would otherwise be unable to complete their education goals. They were frequently returning adult students who juggled many life roles. Today, online learning is attracting a much broader, more diverse audience, whose needs are as varied as the students who come to campus. Some need intrusive student services that involve live interaction with student service professionals, while others merely want information that allows them to independently serve themselves by using resources available on the institution's websites. Some come to the college as competent, capable students whose success depends on little other than time, quality instruction, and clear paths to finding the needed resources. The reality is that the vast majority of students need a variety of support services to guide their academic success. Some students who arrive with financial, academic, and psychosocial needs may not be the best candidates for online learning, but, for many, the only way that they can continue their education is by enrolling in online courses. Unless barriers prevent them from taking online sections, they will enroll and, with sufficient support mechanisms, they may succeed.

Student Services for Online Learners Spider Web. The remainder of this book describes the services and provides examples of innovative practices to assist student service professionals plan, implement, and evaluate online student service programs. The book uses the framework developed by WCET (WICHE Cooperative for Educational Technologies) that in 2002 published the Guidelines for Creating Online Student Services (Shea & Armitage, 2002). The guidelines grew out of a U.S. Department of Education, Fund for the Improvement of Postsecondary Education (FIPSE) grant through a Learning Anytime Anyplace Partnership (LAAP) program. The project, Beyond the Administrative Core, was designed to help institutions plan and implement online student services (Shea, 2005). These guidelines are just as relevant today as they were when they were first established. *Beyond the Administrative Core* contributed significantly to the evolution of online student services. A major contribution is the graphic of the Spider Web of Services for Online Learners. This book uses a modified version of the framework to illustrate the scope of online student services. See Figure 4.1.

FIGURE 4.1 WCET STUDENT SERVICES FOR ONLINE LEARNERS SPIDER WEB

Student Services for Online Learners

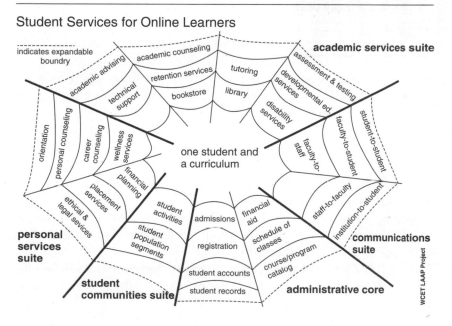

The Spider Web shows that student services for online learners are provided by a wide variety of an institution's divisions and departments. Although institutions have varied organizational structures, the Spider Web shows that student affairs, academic affairs, administrative services, information technology, and marketing all have functional responsibilities to support online learners. Working collaboratively is the key to effective online student services. The focus of this book is supporting online students, but all students benefit from online services.

Most online student services are delivered from an institution's websites. As the Spider Web illustrates, if an institution's online student services puts student needs in the center, students have an easier time finding the information that will help them achieve academic success. Online services do not have to be organized according to departmental reporting structures. Rather, online delivery can reflect the needs of students by creating a virtual one-stop student services center.

The Spider Web's perimeter (defined by dotted lines) indicates that the services listed are not all inclusive; institutions accordingly may decide to adopt additional services or they may find that they do not need some services listed on the Spider Web. This book modifies the framework as follows:

- Chapter Five includes all services from the administrative core, which in this book is labeled Administrative Suite.
- Chapter Six, Academic Services Suite, includes the following modifications: academic counseling and academic advising are combined; retention services are discussed in Chapter Nine, Planning and Implementation; disabilities services are discussed in Chapter Three, Supporting Online Students with Disabilities; and developmental education services are discussed in Chapter Two, Profile of Online Students.
- Chapter Seven, Personal Services Suite, combines career counseling and placement services into Career Services. Financial planning is combined with financial aid and can be found in Chapter Five, Administrative Suite.
- Chapter Eight, Communications Suite, does not include faculty-to-staff and staff-to-faculty services because these services only indirectly benefit students.

- From the Student Communities Suite, student populations are described in Chapter Two, Profile of Online Students; and student activities are included in Chapter Eight, Communications Suite.

CATEGORIES OF SERVICES

The next section provides an overview of the five suites of services, a framework developed by WCET. This organizing structure may help institutions understand the breadth of services needed to support the success of online students.

ADMINISTRATIVE SUITE

The Administrative Suite represents business transactions that students are accustomed to completing online. Typically, institutions first use the web to implement services such as applications to the college, applications for financial aid, student records, course registration, and catalog and course schedules. After students successfully use these online services, they both want and expect that other services are available online.

ACADEMIC SUITE

The Academic Suite includes services, some of which are typically the next to come online. Many institutions now provide online libraries, bookstore services, and technical support, services that are essential for an online learner's success. Online students are particularly dependent on technical support. Many select online learning because they are otherwise occupied during normal business hours and cannot attend classes during the day. They also need to access technical and numerous other support services at similarly convenient times. Despite these demonstrated needs, surprisingly, the 2010 Managing Online Education Survey results show that 16% of the responding colleges make technical support available only during normal business hours, 20% of the colleges add some evening hours, 32% also add some weekend hours, and only 33% provide around-the-clock technical support (Green, 2010a).

The Academic Suite also includes online academic advising, the service most desired by online learners and the one they see as essential to help them complete their academic goals (*Academic Advising Highly Important to Students*, 2009). Academic advising is substantially aided by online degree audits, reports that place courses students have taken into the requirements for a certificate or degree. However, these reports are sometimes confusing and therefore students often need to work with an academic advisor to fully understand how to complete the requirements for their degree.

For institutions that consider putting tutoring online, another service from the Academic Suite, their first issue may be to decide whether putting tutoring online is essential for student success. If they decide it is, they may next decide whether an online tutoring program should be developed internally or contracted with a vendor.

The Academic Suite also includes online assessment and testing, perhaps the service that is least ready for web-based delivery. Institutions offer local online students proctored testing services on campus and help remotely located students set up proctored tests near their homes.

PERSONAL SERVICES SUITE

The Personal Services Suite is perhaps the most controversial suite for online delivery because student service professionals are concerned with retaining the high-touch quality of these services while delivering them through high-tech mechanisms such as the web. Institutions early on placed career and placement information online, and it is currently one of the richest sources for online information. Some institutions are providing online career and personal counseling, but other institutions are opposed to online counseling. Institutions have long considered orientation an effective retention strategy. An institution might reasonably conclude that orientation to online learning is essential for student success.

Sources for Health and Wellness services have been available for quite some time. Some institutions are developing interactive self-assessments, but others are concerned that type of health and wellness service, which sometimes include psychosocial concerns, may be inappropriate for self-service delivery. Institutions with fully online programs may be concerned about how to effectively provide online ethical and legal services. Many institutions struggle with plagiarism, student authentication, and other academic honesty issues when students and faculty are separated in time and place. They note some progress but recognize that many problems remain to be solved. The Personal Services Suite includes such a wide array of services that institutions will have to decide whether the ones they place online are consistent with and appropriate to their mission.

COMMUNICATIONS SUITE

The Communications Suite includes ways of using emerging technologies to support online learners in the context of faculty-to-student, institution-to-student, and student-to-student engagement and relationship building. Social networking and other Web 2.0 technologies have altered the way institutions communicate with all stakeholders. When an institution is considering adopting emerging technologies to facilitate communication with students, the institution first must determine what it is trying to accomplish before deciding what tools to use. While an institution may be tempted to experiment with the newest technology, it may ultimately decide that the best approach is matching the technology to the intended purpose.

STUDENT COMMUNITIES SUITE

The Student Communities Suite contains student activities, an essential component of the college experience for many traditional students and population segments. One question is how student activities can be brought online. Students are designing creative ways of using the Internet for clubs, student government, and college newspapers. These areas are just beginning to be explored for online delivery as a means of connecting students to the institution. Chapter Eight offers some examples.

Chapter Two discusses the support needs of various populations: online students who are adult learners, first generation college students, students enrolled in developmental courses, low-income students, and students currently or formerly in the military.

BENEFITS OF PROVIDING ONLINE STUDENT SERVICES

Putting student services online benefits both students and the institution. When institutions leverage their websites to engage students and support their learning, the payoffs are many. Students appreciate the convenience, institutions see potential cost savings, and relationships begin to develop as students become engaged with the institution.

All stakeholders benefit when institutions make a commitment to high-quality, accurate, and easy to find information on the web. College websites may have evolved organically and sometimes rather chaotically, thus making information difficult to find. Some institutions are now taking a more strategic approach to website development, maintenance, and updating. Recognizing that their websites are a powerful tool for communicating with a variety of audiences, institutions are investing significant resources to improve them.

CONVENIENCE

When institutions decide to put student services online, they typically focus on how online services benefit students. Online services meet the support needs of remotely located students and the just-in-time support needs of local students. Most students decide to take online courses primarily because of the convenience of being able to learn when they have time and from wherever they are located. These students want support services to be delivered as conveniently as are their online courses.

Being able to easily find online information is important for everyone, especially online students for whom college websites may be their primary source of information. Whether users of online services are prospective students exploring the site to determine college fit or registering for class or current students conducting research via the online library or getting information from their academic advisor, nothing is more important to them than being able to quickly find information and successfully completing transactions. Students learning at a distance are studying around the clock. Many are no longer willing to wait for normal business hours to complete their tasks. When convenience is the most important factor for completing educational goals, institutions that provide quality services at a distance will be well-positioned to compete for students.

Both online and on campus students are interested in using web-based resources. Because so much important information is now available on college websites, students are empowered to take the initiative for finding that information, even before they meet with a student service professional. Students who use on-campus services can be encouraged to use web resources for concrete information; when they meet with academic advisors, career counselors, or orientation professionals, they have the knowledge to become actively involved in making their own decisions. With both blended and fully online approaches to student services, students can assume more responsibility for their own learning both inside and outside the classroom.

An institution's websites are only the beginning of delivering online student services. These websites are no longer limited to presenting static information. Institutions now offer dynamic websites that allow students to complete a variety of transactions with the college. Institutions are developing secure portals, internal websites that enable students to conduct numerous business transactions: applying to the college, registering for classes, applying for financial aid, and paying bills.

Institutions have developed or have contracted with vendors to provide enterprise-wide student information systems. The student information systems connect with other services available behind the student portal. As these connections become more sophisticated, institutions will be able to offer even more comprehensive online student services. For example, student information systems provide always-available, permanent records of student transactions. When students lose their class schedule, another can be printed in minutes, without the student having to find the appropriate campus office to stand in line and have someone else print it. Self-service transactions save both students and the institution time and resources.

COST SAVINGS

Another benefit of online student services is cost savings. Given today's tight budgets, institutions benefit when their online services support students but use fewer dollars. Facing lower budgets, increasing student enrollments, and declining rates of retention, institutions may be motivated to put more services online. As some services become automated, institutions may better utilize staff who no longer need to perform repetitive functions that can now be accomplished by technology. Online student services have the potential to make the interactions students have with professionals at the college more meaningful.

STUDENT ENGAGEMENT

Online student services can foster student engagement. An institution's websites can serve users with different needs by creating navigation paths for specific audiences. An institution's home page commonly links to these audiences: prospective students, currently enrolled students, parents and families, alumni, faculty and staff, and visitors. When websites anticipate the needs of specific audiences and organize information accordingly, they personalize the user experience. As students are directed to information that is most relevant to them, they begin to believe that the institution will meet their needs and care about their success. A relationship is beginning to form.

Students are no longer passive consumers of information. They want to take control of what they see and create content, as they have been doing through YouTube, Facebook, blogs, and wikis. Institutions can respond to these desires by allowing students to customize their views of college website content from inside the student portal. The most sophisticated websites use artificial intelligence to anticipate what an individual student needs based on a variety of metrics. Those systems deliver content relevant to an individual student in their personal web space. Although these applications are far from commonplace, they do point to a future direction for online student services that facilitate student engagement even for students who do not come to campus to receive services.

The benefits of effectively developed and delivered online student services are many. However, some student service personnel are concerned that excessive use of technology to deliver services may result in a loss of the personal touch so characteristic of higher education. To address this reasonable concern, those who do the planning and management of online support services might keep focused on the balance between efficiencies afforded by the use of technology and the personal touch so necessary for relationship building between the institution and its constituencies.

DEVELOPMENT OF DYNAMIC ONLINE SERVICES

In addition to the Online Student Services Spider Web (Figure 4.1), another contribution from the *Beyond the Administrative Core* project is the concept that the development of online student services could be described in "Generations" based on the degree of interactivity associated with each service. Generation 1 signifies a service that is not available through the institution's website. Generation 2 describes online services that are presented according to the organizational structure of the institution. Generation 3 describes audience-focused presentation of online services. For example, information is organized that is particularly relevant to prospective students, currently enrolled students, and alumni. Users from each of these groups can find relevant information without navigating through information targeted at the other audiences. Generation 4 services are generally found behind a student portal, within a learning management system, or in some other secure online environment sponsored by the institution. Generation 4 services can be customized and personalized either by the student or by the institution. Generation 5 services use virtual mentors, artificial intelligence, and other advanced technologies to enable students to make decisions and complete complex processes ("Overview of the CENTSS Online Student Services Audit," 2011).

To illustrate how services can evolve, an institution's external website might provide a description of academic advising services, information about the advisors, including a link that students can use to send an email, and hours of operation. That may be considered a Generation 3 online academic advising service. If the site adds a live chat option, that moves the service to Generation 4 because the site now provides an opportunity for personalized interaction between the student and someone from the institution. A Generation 5 academic advising site might include a degree audit tool that allows students to request audits for different programs to determine which major would lead to the shortest time to graduation. Institutions will make individual decisions about each service and how many transactions can be completed virtually. There are several common characteristics that are found in all services at each level of development.

GENERATION 2

Using Generation 2 online student services, students should be able to easily find general information about online student services from the institution's home page. The initial or landing page for each service might include, or provide a clear path to, basic information such as location and hours of operation for campus-based service, expected turnaround time for asynchronous communication such as email, and descriptions of the service, target audience, pertinent policies and procedures, and relevant FAQs.

The site might also include contact information for staff, a list of staff specialties, and a means of sending an email to all staff. Photographs might be used to personalize the presentation of personnel within that department. The site might also include a description of the process for making an appointment with a student service professional, how to reschedule a missed appointment, and consequences for not showing up for an appointment. A key theme for Generation 2 services is that the information is presented in a way that resembles a printed brochure.

GENERATION 3

Generation 3 services provide clear paths for students to follow through the website to find relevant information. This might be based on audience (prospective students, currently enrolled students, alumni, community members). Students can sign up for individual appointments or group sessions and receive confirmation that the appointment has been scheduled through online forms for such services as academic advising and tutoring.

Linkages between the external and internal college websites should provide students with a seamless online student services experience. *Seamless* also refers to the connections between related services. For example, the financial aid page might have a link to a book store and registration, and the bookstore page might have a link to financial aid. Another example of a seamless service is when students can access tutoring from inside their online course site.

Generation 3 sites use various ways to communicate with students. One example is an online calendar that the institution updates with events in each of the service areas. Other communication tools may be used to inform students of events. Generation 3 sites may have online multimedia tutorials explaining the services and relevant and searchable frequently asked questions that are service specific. Generation 3 services might include opportunities for student to interact with professionals via live chat.

Generation 3 sites are developed to allow students to bookmark not only pages on the external institution's website (these can easily be done by using common browser functionality), but also to bookmark pages visited from inside the student portal. This makes it easy for students to return to frequently visited pages inside the portal. Upon selecting the bookmarked page behind a password-protected site, a student is first provided the authentication screen and then taken directly to the bookmarked page. This procedure preserves security and provides convenience. A key difference between Generation 2 and 3 services is that Generation 3 is targeted to specific populations.

GENERATIONS 4 AND 5

Generations 4 and 5 services move from developing information that targets specific populations to information and transactions that meet the needs of individual students. These services are frequently located behind a password-protected student portal. Students can access records of transactions with the institution through MyAccount or an ePortfolio application. Students can keep records of self-initiated online service transactions, such as appointments with tutors and advisors and bookstore purchases. Both students and professionals have access to records kept by student information system or other institution-based systems, such as degree audits or registration history. Using ePortfolios, students can make personal information visible to specific service providers.

Some MyAccount systems track all services received by a particular student, including date, service provider, contact person and email, description of the service, and outcome of the service. Students can sort the list according to each category. For example, if a student participated in several library tutorials about how to do academic research and an academic advising tutorial about how to develop an academic plan, the student could save all tutorials in MyAccount and sort them by service provider or by date and be provided a link to easily return to each tutorial.

What distinguishes Generation 5 from 4 is that the transactions become progressively more interactive, personalized, and customizable. A service is personalized when students receive responses by name to inquiries or their name appears when they sign into the student portal. An example of a customizable service is when a student is able to sort grades by using different views such as by term, major, or general education requirements. Generation 5 online services allow students to make decisions, create "what if" scenarios, and see the consequences of various decisions.

Another example of interactive, customizable, and personal online student services is an interactive, dynamic, calendar attached to a searchable database that allows students to make appointments for services. The calendar allows students to indicate the service needed, see when service providers such as advisors or tutors are available, select a time slot, receive a confirmation of the appointment, and set a time for an appointment reminder. Both students and the institution are able to populate the calendar. The institution pushes to everyone certain calendar events (registration and financial aid application deadlines), whereas other notifications are determined by student enrollment status, demographic information, or student-identified preferences and areas of interest. Students can subscribe to relevant notifications and can keep a record of all communications and transactions with the institution in their MyAccount or ePortfolio.

Other Generation 5 services include allowing students to make grade predictions or create "what if" scenarios to anticipate graduation based on a selected major, and allowing students to subscribe via RSS (Really Simple Syndication) feed to institution-sponsored wikis, blogs, and social networks focused on specific services that interest the students.

Institutions are not yet making extensive use of Generation 5 services, but many are moving from Generation 2 to Generation 3 delivery, which significantly improves the audience experience. Very few institutions have developed all services at the Generation 4 level (Steele & Thurmond, 2009). Whether an institution develops Generation 4 or 5 online student services may be determined by its mission, institutional type, and culture.

INSTITUTIONAL CHARACTERISTICS

Institutional type and campus culture may be factors that drive decisions about the depth and breadth of online student services. These factors, closely tied to the mission and vision, may inform the planning and development of services to support online students.

INSTITUTIONAL TYPE

A single-purpose, fully online institution without a campus must provide all student support services at a distance. These institutions have a strong incentive to provide comprehensive online student support services around the clock. Their existence depends on students' continuing their enrollment.

Dual-purpose institutions—colleges and universities that offer traditionally delivered instruction and distance learning courses— also offer on-campus and online student support services. When these institutions serve remotely located students, they may want to consider making all support services available at a distance to better serve their online learners.

Remotely located online students may be dependent on electronically delivered student services, but residential students can take advantage of a blending of online and on-campus services. For example, local students may gather some information from the college website before coming to campus for face-to-face meetings with student service professionals. The students who have prepared themselves may gain more from the face-to-face meeting than if they had met with the professional without obtaining the online information. When students have obtained information from the institution's website, student service professionals may not have to repeat the same information, thereby giving these professionals additional time to spend with students on in-depth interactions or to accomplish more in a shorter time than otherwise possible. In an ideal world, this would also create time for student service professionals to be able to focus on students who are most in need of intensive assistance. In any event, online student services have the potential to improve effectiveness and efficiencies of support services for all students.

Dual-purpose institutions must decide which services are best delivered online and which are best delivered face-to-face. Institutions that enroll only online students have been delivering all services at a distance for quite some time. Dual-purpose institutions may be able to learn from the experiences of those institutions.

INSTITUTIONAL CULTURE

The culture of an institution may influence its decision about what services to make remotely available. Manning and Munoz (2011) categorized student affairs practices based on the dominant characteristics of campus cultures. They describe the following types of campus cultures: virtual, tangible, collegial, managerial, developmental, and advocacy. The *virtual culture* typifies institutions that are most open to transformation through the use of technology. The Internet and electronic devices are integrated into educational experiences both inside and outside the classroom. These tools have become commonplace on campuses with a virtual culture. These institutions leverage the capability of technology to communicate with multiple audiences and thereby create a more open educational environment not just within the institution but also well beyond. This type of institution has a dynamic web presence that allows it to deliver a variety of online student services.

An institution with a *tangible culture* might be the least likely to adopt the technologies needed to deliver comprehensive online student services. Tangible cultures strictly follow practices to maintain the revered history and customs that preserve the reputation, status, and hierarchy within the institution. Those traditions are not always easy to implement in the online environment. Tangible culture institutions may choose to use the college website for information only and encourage students to interact with one another and with college personnel primarily in person.

The other cultures are the *collegial culture*, in which research and scholarship are highly valued; the *managerial culture*, in which teaching is central and students are viewed as customers; the *developmental culture*, in which the organizational priority is a student's personal growth; and the *advocacy culture*, in which fairness, equity, and justice influence institutional decisions. Each of these campus cultures may be more or less inclined to provide dynamic online student services. When cross-functional teams are aware of their own campus culture, the teams better understand the struggles they may face as they ponder decisions about what student services to put online.

Campus culture, institutional type, the needs of remotely located students, and the demands of all students are factors that inform decisions about the development and delivery of online student support services. Institutions of higher education, both for-profit and nonprofit, are pondering issues of consumerism. Students thinking of their education as a product and wanting to get what they pay for are expecting the convenience of remotely delivered services to support their educational goals. Although the issues of consumerism are highly controversial in academic affairs, the issues may not be as contentious within student affairs and student services. Student services are typically driven by a desire to meet the needs of students. While the culture of the institution may contribute to the depth and breadth of which services are put online, the ultimate goal is to meet the students where they are—both literally and figuratively—and provide the services they need to succeed.

STUDENT AFFAIRS AND SUPPORT OF ONLINE STUDENTS

Current literature and recent national studies provide little if any information about what departments are taking the lead for supporting online learners. Frequently the key players in the development of online student services are the departments of distance education, information technology (IT), student affairs, and other student services offices, but high-level oversight of online student support services is rarely mentioned. The 2010 Managing Online Education Survey did not collect data on which position in the institution was responsible for the support of online students. Many early journal articles argued for increased involvement from student affairs professionals (Dale & Drake, 2005; Dare, Zapata, & Thomas, 2005; Floyd & Casey-Powell, 2004; Kendall, 2005; Kretovics, 2003; Shea, 2005). Kleemann (2005) emphasized that student affairs professionals have skills and experience that make them natural leaders in the development and delivery of online student support services. Student affairs professionals understand students, have experience with relationship management, and know how to build community. One mission of student affairs professionals is to "develop the whole person."

Student affairs professionals bring to the support of online students an educational and experiential expertise to facilitate the intellectual and personal growth of college students. Student affairs professionals understand and advocate for the needs of all students, including target populations: adult learners, students with disabilities, students of color, low-income students, commuter students, first generation students, and military personnel. Online students from these groups may need unique services in addition to the services needed by all students.

Realizing that online students have specific needs, institutions are assessing answers to important questions. Who is developing orientations to online learning, assessing readiness for online learning, remediating readiness deficiencies, and supporting students throughout their online enrollments? Are offices of distance learning developing some services and student affairs developing others? If institutions decide to develop separate support services for online learners, they not only confuse their students but they also incur unnecessary costs when duplication occurs.

Institutions are looking at online course retention rates and are seeking expert advice from student affairs and other student service professionals to help improve online student success. In order to respond to the call for improved retention rates in online courses, these professionals will need to be involved in the planning and delivery of retention efforts. Many institutions may want to more clearly define the role of student affairs in the support of online learners.

Student affairs departments have worked with instructional technology departments on many initiatives. Professionals from these departments have helped develop online applications such as bill paying, registration, and other functions of the student information system, to name just a few. However, student affairs departments are not always included in discussions and decisions about how to support online students. Student affairs professionals have used technology extensively to deliver on-campus services. That expertise, along with an understanding of college student development, makes them well positioned to lead the development and delivery of services to online learners.

The formal relationship between student affairs and IT may be changing as some institutions are identifying a person or team that has responsibilities for student affairs technology services. Dare (2011) identified twenty-six universities with designated Student Affairs Technology Services. However, these services appear to be primarily focused on web design and development, student affairs technical support and professional development, and student affairs application and solution development. Although these efforts are essential to the improvement of online student services, with the exception of North Carolina State University, none of the institutions mentioned the support of online students as part of their mission, goals, or responsibilities.

Conclusion

This chapter provides an overview of the breadth of support services that can be put online. Although the benefits of online delivery are many, institutions still have concerns to resolve. Institutions have to make individual decisions about how best to support online students. They may want to make decisions about both the content and how to present each service. These decisions may become more complex as emerging technologies allow for increasingly dynamic delivery of online services. While organizational structures might differ, many institutions may decide to rely on an inclusive and collaborative approach to plan for and then implement online student services. The goal of such an effort is to deliver seamless online services so that online students receive appropriate support throughout their enrollment at the institution.

CHAPTER FIVE

ADMINISTRATIVE SUITE

The Administration Suite includes Admissions, Catalog, Course Schedule, Financial Aid, Registration, and Student Accounts and Records. As students become accustomed to the ease of using online services (applying for admission and for financial aid, registering for courses, viewing the college catalog, paying bills, and viewing their records online), they expect to access other support services from their computer or handheld Internet-connected device. Students use services from the Administrative Suite throughout their enrollment at the institution. When institutions focus on establishing engaging online services from the Administrative Suite, they establish an excellent foundation for ongoing relationships with prospective and currently enrolled students, as well as alumni (P. A. Shea, 2005).

The services from the Administrative Suite are closely tied to the student information system (SIS) that serves as a database of all student records. Institutions can elect to purchase or develop the SIS. A study by the American Association of Collegiate Registrars and Admissions Officers (AACRAO) found that only 11% of the 447 respondents were using internally developed systems. Most institutions use one of several vendor products: 35% use Sungard/Banner, 19% use Jenzabar, and 17% use Datatel (*Student Information Systems, Collection of Grades, Application for Degree, and Degree Audit Function*, 2007).

The SIS forms the electronic backbone that integrates all services and provides an interface for seamless delivery. The SIS can handle the admissions process and inquiries from prospective students, enroll new students, create class and teaching schedules, maintain grades and academic progress, record communication with students, and provide statistical reports and accounting and budgeting services. The SIS has various modules (e.g., financial aid, human resources, assessment, transportation, food service, library, finance modules) that institutions may decide to implement. The AACRAO study found in 2007 that 18% used an electronic process to collect grade changes, 16% to change majors and minors, 23% to collect applications for a degree, 76% to collect course grades, 60% to produce a degree audit, and 41% for "what if" scenarios to review their courses in relation to particular programs. These percentages undoubtedly have increased since 2007.

To a great extent, the breadth of online student services available at an institution depends on the institution's decisions about what functions to make available to students through the student information system. This chapter reviews online services from the Administrative Suite based on what online students need in order to complete transactions without coming to campus.

ADMISSIONS

While student information systems and student portals are primary tools for students who have already established a connection with the institution, external websites are the primary means for prospective students to learn about the institution. Websites are powerful tools for recruiting students, developing relationships, and promoting the institutional brand. At the outset, an institution wants to convince students that it is a good fit for them. An institution wants its admissions website to persuade prospective students to complete an application and, if accepted, enroll for their first semester.

In order to help students connect immediately, an institution might develop a prospective student portal. A portal serves as a place for the institution to post relevant information and a platform for students to submit forms required to complete their application to the college using a password-protected website. In addition to websites, institutions are using a variety of social networking communication tools to engage prospective students.

This section uses Noel-Levitz research to identify the rate at which institutions are putting admissions services online and what students are looking for in online admissions services.

IMPORTANCE

An institution cannot overestimate the importance of presenting online admission services that are current, accurate, relevant, and engaging. Students are seeking information that is both detailed and easy to find. A Noel-Levitz 2010 study, *Focusing Your E-Recruitment Efforts to Meet the Expectations of College-Bound Students,* found that 92% of prospective students would be disappointed or drop a school from their search if the website did not have relevant information or its information was out-of-date, incorrect, or unhelpful. This study found that general principles of good web design that discourage creating long web pages that require users to use the vertical scroll bar to read all the information does not apply to admissions websites. In the case of students seeking a college, 74% of the respondents were willing to read detailed admissions information, even if it meant reading a great deal of text.

The admissions website should blend marketing and recruiting information along with answers to questions that encourage visitors to return and look for new content. Interestingly, the study also found 80% of the respondents said content is more important than the look of the website. If an institution intends for its website to start a potentially long relationship between the institution and the student, then the website should be student-centric and provide easy ways to find information.

CONTENT AND PRESENTATION

Institutions recognize that the two main elements of website design are content and presentation. They also know that unless website audiences can quickly find relevant information, they will go elsewhere. Visitors can find information easily if navigation throughout the website is consistent, predictable, and logical. Many institutions use a simple approach for organizing information.

The admissions home page is an entry to the information needed by most prospective students. The institution then provides paths that lead various target audiences to unique information relevant to them. These are but a few of the many elements of good presentation.

Presentation is important, but content is what brings users back to an institution's website. An admission website might include admission requirements, the admission process, what materials to include with the application, deadlines, and cost of application and of attendance. Specific information may include how to schedule an in-person campus visit or to take a virtual tour of the campus. Visitors may be given options to choose various paths. For example, one path may be for recent high school graduates and another for returning adult students. Perhaps an institution might create a path for transfer students and another for students with disabilities. Online students may need specialized information about what to expect from online learning. Because the admissions home page may be one of the first pages visited by prospective online students, institutions may want to include a prominent link to additional information about online learning. These paths to audience-targeted information should be readily apparent either from the institution's home page or by selecting a link to the admission landing page.

Your Audience

Institutions may choose to conduct their own student needs assessments or use vendors to ascertain the needs of their particular populations. Noel-Levitz, in *Focusing Your E-Recruitment Efforts to Meet the Expectations of College-Bound Students* (2010), examined what admissions content was most important to 1000 college-bound high school seniors: 54% of the respondents identified academic-related material (a list of academic programs or degrees, academic program details, and school rankings or reputation) as the most important information; 30% ranked cost-related information (cost/tuition/fees, financial aid, and scholarships) as the most important information. The next two items in order of importance were criteria for admission to the institution and student life information.

Special populations of students may need additional information. Adults returning to school may be looking for resources to help them manage school with the many roles they are already juggling. They may be looking for information about accelerated programs and ways to earn credit by exam or from experience. Students transferring into the institution may need to understand the guidelines the institution uses to accept previously earned college credits. Students interested in eventually transferring out to other institutions will be interested in articulation agreements. Both groups of transfer students will be interested in the steps in each process and the time lines for completing the required tasks.

Student with disabilities may want to understand how the institution will provide accommodations, what documentation they will need to produce, and the steps required to begin the process of receiving accommodations. Online students may be interested in learning more about what it is like to take courses at a distance and how to complete the admissions process when they cannot come to campus. The key is to use concise, concrete, and clear language to explain what students need to apply to the institution.

INTERACTIVITY

While admissions websites are becoming increasingly interactive, they are but one method of communicating with prospective students. The survey *Focusing Your E-Recruitment Efforts to Meet the Expectations of College-Bound Students* (2009) indicates what communication methods prospective students prefer:

- Online—completing an application (70%), communicating with current students (60%), communicating with faculty (50%)
- Mail—sending a deposit (42%), transcript delivery (43%), financial aid award (52%), acceptance (70%)
- Online, in-person, and by phone were fairly evenly split about getting answers to questions (34%, 30%, 30%)

The survey *Focusing Your E-Recruitment Efforts to Meet the Expectations of College-Bound Students* (2010) identified what interactive website features are most important to prospective students. Respondents indicated the following are either extremely valuable or have a lot of value:

- Online application (81%)
- Campus visit request form (77%)
- Cost calculator (68%)
- Online course catalog (67%)
- RSS (Really Simple Syndication) feed (64%)
- Site personalization (59%)
- Virtual tours (48%)

An ever-increasing number of traditional age students are using social media:

- 76% use Facebook
- 59% use YouTube
- 33% use MySpace
- 20% use other social media applications

Thirty-three percent use social media sites to search for college information. Students also have preferences about how an institution should use social media.

- 74% think schools should have a social media presence
- 67% think it appropriate for admissions counselors to contact them through social media
- 42% watch college videos on the college website
- 10% watch college videos on You Tube

Students are most interested in videos about student life, academics, locations around campus, athletic events, and details about programs and faculty. The majority are interested in seeing videos made by the college and by students. These data from the 2009 and 2010 E-expectation surveys provide insight institutions might consider when using social networking applications for engaging prospective students. A number of institution's websites have innovative features that may respond to the preferred content and delivery methods.

Communication with Prospective Students

Institutions have a number of ways to answer student questions. Admission websites sometimes include a list of answers to frequently asked questions. Facebook and Twitter provide additional ways that allow students to communicate with admissions counselors and other students. Students are comfortable accessing the static information on the college's website and using interactive social media applications, but they are still interested in talking to admissions representatives either in person or by phone. Many schools provide daytime live chat hours, along with links to email for after-hours communication. Students who can come to campus will want to know how to make an appointment for a tour or to speak with an admissions representative. Many variables, such as the complexity of the question and the immediacy of the need for a response, determine which means of communication a particular student will choose.

The admission website is an extremely important component of an institution's web presence. Many institutions prioritize the development of this area above all others. Recruitment is a key service, and the institution's website has become the prime means of communicating with prospective students. The overarching point is that an institution's admission website provides the students' first impression of the college and ultimately is an important factor in a student's college selection.

Innovative Practices

The University of Illinois Admissions website uses a Mashup (a web page or application that combines two or more sources to create a new service) of several Web 2.0 tools to engage and communicate with prospective students. It has a series of YouTube videos, a Facebook page for the incoming class, an admissions blog with pictures and participation from admissions counselors, student bloggers identified by graduating class and major, guest bloggers representing areas of the college that may be of interest to new students, and pictures of alumni bloggers identified by graduating class and major. Blog entries are categorized into 17 topics. Students ask substantive questions and get thoughtful answers. The Flickr page has pictures from around campus, a campus event, and student portraits. Visitors have an option to follow Illinois Admissions on Twitter.

The Worcester Polytechnic Institute Admissions website has a series of campus videos and a variety of information provided by students. These videos are unique as they allow the user to drag and drop just those videos that interest them or to select videos for one topic to create a personalized play list. The videos then play automatically.

The University of Texas at Austin Admissions website targets information for the following groups of students: first-time freshmen, transfer students, former UT students, summer transients, international undergrads, coordinated admission program, counselors, graduate students, and law school students. They also have a specific section of the website called "Do Stuff Online." From a single page, UT Austin provides links with short explanations that cover most things a student applying to the college would need to do.

Catalog

Students have come to expect easy access to a digital version of the college catalog. As with all online information, a digital college catalog can be brochure information that is an exact duplication of the print copy of the catalog. Or it can provide users with interactive tools to search the catalog, links to related information for those looking for in-depth information, and the capability to bookmark specific pages. Many students assume that the digital catalog will have at least all information found in the print catalog. They use the digital version of the catalog because they can conveniently access it from a computer and easily find information, providing the catalog has good techniques for indexing, a table of contents, site maps, and search capabilities.

Students typically want information from the catalog of the year they enter the institution, but they may also want to consult an archive of past catalogs. Students can find past catalogs at Collegesource.org, which has 57,906 digital college catalogs, institution profiles, and other related resources.

INNOVATIVE PRACTICES

University of California, Berkeley online catalog shows how an institution can organize information in an innovative way. Its catalog has these categories: Undergraduate/Graduate Education, Courses/Curricula by Department, Course Search, Related Sites, and Printing a Catalog. Users can easily follow the clear and concise directions about how to use the online catalog. Undergraduate and Graduate Education areas provide broad overviews of policies and regulations, along with links to relevant department websites for in-depth information. In the Courses/Curricula by Department areas, students can read information typically found in a print version of a college catalog. They can then go to links to departmental websites for in-depth information. If students want to understand how academic programs are structured, they can go to links for each of the 14 colleges and schools within which are organized the 350 degree programs. Students also have links to profiles of instructors who have won distinguished faculty awards.

The course search function provides an easy way to find information about all courses offered by the institution. Students can search by department name, abbreviation, course title, course number, instructor name, units, terms, course description, and prerequisite. A schedule of classes for three semesters is linked from the search page where students can browse all offerings. The catalog includes links to the admissions home page, the university's home page, the A-Z list of websites, and a link to an email for questions. The catalog is easy to navigate and presents content in a manner that makes it efficient to use. The online college catalog is an essential tool that facilitates a successful college experience.

COURSE SCHEDULE

Some students want guidance in scheduling courses to complete their college degree or certificate, and others can accomplish this task alone if provided comprehensive and updated information. Online course schedules serve students who have confirmed their academic goals as well as those who are exploring options.

An institution's course schedule website may include the following: the ability to search or browse courses offered for the current and at least one of the following semesters, the ability to search open courses, a wait list for closed classes, an explanation about how to read the course schedule, a final exam calendar, a printable version of the undergraduate and graduate schedule, other relevant deadlines that might be linked from the registration page, a link to a syllabus for the course that can be viewed prior to registration, information about the instructor, and the capacity to identify appropriate courses needed to complete specific degrees.

Institutions use various tools that might be linked on the course schedule website to assist students in creating plans for degree completion and identifying which courses they will take each semester. Some institutions create curriculum checklists that are populated with catalog information. Students may make copies of these documents and manually enter passed courses, current enrollment, and plan future semesters. Other degree plans are dynamic forms, allowing students to electronically enter courses into a four- or eight-semester plan. Students can project the semester each course will be taken as long as the institution provides advance notice about the availability of courses during future semesters.

Some schools use degree audits connected to student information systems to automate course placement into various degree requirements. Online degree audits need specific instructions about how to read the degree audit report. Because the systems rarely take into account a variety of exceptions, students are sometimes confused and can make mistakes unless they ask for guidance from an advisor. It is important to place email links to academic advisors on the course schedule website so students will know whom to contact if they have questions.

INNOVATIVE PRACTICES

North Carolina State University distance learning website provides a list of courses offered for each term for an entire year. The course schedule entry page for each term lists courses by discipline. Upon entering the discipline link, students find a link to the courses. At the top of each page are the course description and the instructor's picture, email address, and phone number. Each course includes information about on-campus requirements, testing information, course requirements, and a message from the instructor.

Under the Course Materials tab, students find information about the learning managements system, additional technology requirements, and information about textbooks and instructional materials. The Tuition and Fees tab lists cost information and any messages from the Distance Education Department with information unique to a particular section. Some courses have a course syllabus, a link to the faculty website, and any restrictions about who can register for the course. Other courses have links to course lectures that have been captured using MediaSite software. From the course information page, students can immediately apply to the college, register for the course, or get help. This comprehensive information greatly assists students in making informed course selections.

FINANCIAL AID AND FINANCIAL PLANNING

With the skyrocketing cost of higher education, a faltering economy, and a high unemployment rate, many students who want to continue their education beyond high school are facing greater challenges than ever before. Students must deal with these negative factors at a time when a postsecondary certificate or degree is even more important for entry into an increasing number of careers. Fortunately, many students can rely on financial aid as a source of support to access higher education and in particular online courses. Prior to 2006, students taking more than 50% of their courses at a distance did not qualify for financial aid. *The Higher Education Act Reform Amendments of 2005* ended a limit on the amount of distance education courses an institution can offer and still provide opportunities for students to pay for the courses using financial aid (*The Higher Education Act Reform Amendments of 2005*, 2006).

GENERAL FINANCIAL AID INFORMATION

Most institutions' basic financial aid websites contain a description of the application process, eligibility guidelines, including institutional policies, and application deadlines. The websites may also contain general information, such as the different types of financial aid, terminology, specific costs associated with attending the institution, links to other forms of financial assistance (which includes a comprehensive lists of scholarships), and how to get assistance throughout the process of application and an eventual award.

Institutions have various approaches to conveying online financial aid information. For example, distance learners can access the SUNY Learning Network (SLN) Tuition and Financial Aid FAQ page. They can find answers to commonly asked questions and links to information about scholarships, grants and loans, tax credits and deductions, and military aid for online education. This centrally located financial aid page provides general information for all prospective and currently enrolled SLN students. Online students can obtain additional information by accessing the financial aid website of the school they are or will be attending. The website has a secure portal that provides personalized information where students can complete transactions such as applying for financial aid, finding out the status of the application, and gathering ongoing information about financial aid standing throughout their enrollment.

Institution-based financial aid information is often complemented by the many high-quality websites developed outside of individual institutions. Examples include Free Application for Federal Student Aid (FAFSA), Student Aid on the Web, FinAid, FastWeb, FedMoney, The College Board, College.net, and College Navigator for cost comparisons between colleges. Many institutions provide easy access to this information by linking to these sites. Institutions also provide information about college-specific scholarships and community-based scholarships. Many institutions link to these resources rather than create and maintain extensive aid and scholarship information. Financial aid information becomes especially meaningful when students are able to apply to their own situation the various ways to finance their education. With easy access to this financial information, students can predict whether they will qualify for financial aid and how much their package might be.

All postsecondary institutions receiving federal Title IV funds must meet the 2008 Higher Education Opportunity Act requirements to have a net price calculator posted on their website by October 2011. The U.S. Department of Education has provided a template, but institutions can build their own calculator or purchase a vendor product (Whorley, 2010). Duke University uses a video to explain how financial aid packages are calculated and then provides a link to the net price calculator. The College Board website has Expected Family Contribution, College Cost, College Savings, Student Loan, Parent Debt, and Parent Loan Repayments Calculators.

Once financial aid is awarded, students may need additional information to understand their package. The Pennsylvania State University Office of Student Aid provides an explanation of the package, a "to-do" list, a student aid glossary, and a calendar of financial aid deadlines for the coming year. The Penn State website also provides specialized financial aid information for prospective students, undergraduates, graduate students, law and medical school students, and adult students, along with parents of students. Each page is linked to sites that provide more in-depth information. The A-Z site map for financial aid topics makes information easy to find on the Penn State website.

Financial aid is complex, but it is one of the most crucial services for many prospective and currently enrolled postsecondary students. While institutions strive to present this information clearly and accurately online, they also recognize that many students still need the assistance of a financial aid professional. Institutions may want to consider how best to serve their remotely located students, who want to know the best way to communicate with those professionals. For most institutions, the best way is a financial aid home page that presents options for live interaction via chat, phone, or videoconferencing technology. The home page should provide details, such as hours of operations that include the institution's time zone, as well as instructions about how to use chat and videoconferencing.

FINANCIAL PLANNING

Financial planning for college students has never been more important. Because of the gap between the typical student's ability to pay and the cost of attending college, many students leave college with a substantial amount of debt. This occurs even though approximately 75% of students are now working while attending college (Chaloux, 2010). If institutions can find ways to improve their students' financial literacy that results in better financial planning, the payoff might be that students graduate without the burden of unmanageable debt.

Institutions that offer financial planning services provide information about core issues: balancing work and school, contacting a financial planning professional, saving money, budgeting and record keeping, and tracking credit cards and credit scores. The National Endowment for Financial Education has developed a Financial Literacy CashCourse that is being used by 553 institutions. Institutions can use their own logo to brand the course and then customize it by adding modules, such as financial basics, paying for college, college life, world of work, and economic survival tips.

Institutions use this application in various ways. St. Norbert College, which launches its version from its Career Center website, has added a section with calculators and worksheets and an email form that allows students to ask financial literacy questions. Ohio State University Office of Student Life and Undergraduate Student Government has a Financial Life webpage from which the Cash-Course modules are integrated with other information about financial literacy. Stanford University launches the CashCourse from their Financial Aid and Parent Associations pages. University of California, San Diego, links its version from the Student Wellness page.

The National Endowment for Financial Education (NEFE) runs a contest and provides cash awards for innovative ideas that encourage students to use the system. Because these ideas are shared on NEFE's website, they are a universally available knowledge base of innovative ways to improve students' financial literacy. This collaborative effort illustrates one approach to utilizing online student services developed outside a single institution, yet customized to reflect the brand and priorities of individual institutions.

If an institution's goal is to make higher education affordable and available to an increasing number of students, the institution may look for ways to simplify the process and expand the reach of financial aid. Achieving that goal is furthered by effectively delivered online information about financial aid and financial planning.

REGISTRATION

Some of the earliest online student services were web-based registration and related services. Institutions from the *Online Registration Services* (2003) AACRAO study reported they offered the following online services:

- 88% Class schedules
- 92% Catalog information
- 76% Instructor information
- 67% Registration
- 49% Payment processing
- 74% Registrar's office home page
- 52% Schedule planning services
- 75% Community information

When AACRAO conducted a similar study in 1999, only 20–35% of institutions surveyed offered these services online. AACRAO has not surveyed institutions about web-based registration and related services since 2003, presumably because almost all institutions have put these services online.

Students who register for one or more online courses need access to many online services. In addition to a completed application, students may need other services such as the following:

- Placement testing or directions about how to demonstrate completion of course prerequisites
- Understanding of program and degree requirements
- Access to an academic advisor to develop an educational plan
- Application and approval for financial assistance

- Understanding the demands and requirements of online learning
- Understanding how to obtain accommodations from disability support services

Students may also need access to the catalog, a college calendar that includes registration deadlines, final exam schedule, schedule of classes, course planner, course availability listing, waiting lists for closed courses, and instructor information. They need information about how to complete online registration and how to add or drop courses. They may need to know how to contact a person to assist with registration.

Students may also need technical assistance if they have not previously used online registration. They should also have a way to be alerted if any IT systems used to support online registration are not fully operational. Online students are particularly dependent on the institution's network. Institutions might include links to this information on the registration home page. As soon as students register, they need to know how to pay tuition, print their schedule, and buy textbooks and other course materials. Institutions may want to provide a link to orientation to online learning options for those students registering for their first online course.

INNOVATIVE PRACTICE

The Madison Area Technical College registration website contains information about all of the above, and it also provides a series of multimedia tutorials explaining to prospective and current students various processes needed to complete registration and get started at the college. The tutorials include Academic Requirements, Account Activation, Account Creation, Completing the Online Application, Add a Class, Browse Course Catalog, Check Your Enrollment Date, Class Search, Drop a Class, FAFSA Completion, Financial Aid Award Acceptance and E-Refunding, How to Use askMadisonCollege, Message Center, Order a Parking Permit, Planner, Print My Schedule, Student Center Overview, Student Center Training Guide, Updating Personal Information, and View Grades. Each tutorial has a text version. The institution's decision to locate these tutorials on the external website make them readily available to assist students new to the college.

STUDENT RECORDS AND ACCOUNTS

Student records and accounts include a history of most transactions a student has with an institution. Capella University, a regionally accredited, fully online institution, provides its students the opportunity to complete all transactions at a distance through its student records and account portal (the MyAccount area of Capella Universities iGuide). iGuide is the name given to the student portal, which also includes a robust set of tools organized with these tabs: Schools and Programs, Library, Resources, Support and Services, and Community.

From the MyAccount home page, Capella provides links to the Support Team: Learner Technical support is for course room and technical help, Ask Your Tech is for First Course technical support, Learner Support is for general questions, Financial Aid is for questions about finances and billing, Academic Advising is for program planning, Capella University Library is for research and reference materials, Career Center is for career management, and MyAccount is for managing student accounts.

MyAccount has the following organizing categories for its information: Finances, Course Registration, University Enrollment Status, Personal Information, and Grades and Transcripts. Finance topics are listed under either Financial Aid or Account Information. Financial Aid allows students to view financial aid status, accept or decline the award, check the status of any submitted financial aid document, and cancel an award. Other links lead to the steps for applying for aid, financial literacy seminars, loan management and repayment, and additional information about financing an education.

The Course Registration tab provides access to course and colloquia registration, current course schedule, drop a course, and change enrollment status. There are also two sets of frequently asked questions (FAQs): one about course registration and the other about course and program guidelines.

The Grades and Transcripts tab allows students to view final grades from the past quarter, an unofficial history of all grades, and military transcripts. Each area has a convenient print button. From this tab students can also request official transcripts and an enrollment verification letter. The FAQs available from this area are about grades, transcripts, and transfer credits.

The My Academic Plan tab provides access to academic plans plus the policies related to determining appropriate plans. This tab includes course history; program information with a link students can use to change current program, specialization, or concentration; a link to leave a message for help changing current program; and a list of relevant FAQs. There is also a link to how to contact an academic advisor. This page includes a video that explains the purpose of and how to develop an academic plan.

The Enrollment Status tab provides links to information about discontinuing from the university, requesting a medical or military leave of absence, returning from a military leave of absence, requesting a quarter of inactivity, and changing program, specialization, and concentration. All are interactive forms that can be submitted online. Applying for graduation, changing a password, and going to the Student Center are all links that are included in the Enrollment Status area. The Student Center is a summary page with links to a student's enrollment, academic history, account, financial aid, admission, and personal information.

From the Personal Information tab, students can make changes to their name, address, phone numbers, email addresses, and demographic information. Students can also find the Family Education and Privacy Act (FERPA) and Personal Information FAQs.

This is a truly comprehensive set of resources and information that allows students to gather information, make changes, and matriculate easily through the university.

CONCLUSION

Institutions recognize that well-developed services from the Administrative Suite are essential to the success of students and worthy of their thoughtful planning and implementation. Online learners who do not come to campus are dependent on effectively delivered services from the Administrative Suite. When these services are clearly and succinctly described with step-by-step instructions about how to complete each transaction, many students are able to successfully use a self-service approach. Self-service has the potential to decrease staff time and ultimately provide opportunities for institutions to redistribute staffing budgets.

While many Administrative Suite services require detailed explanations, frequently presented via text, institutions may also meet student needs with multimedia presentations that are friendly and engaging. Some institutions use a chat popup window with a picture of a person and a friendly voice to ask if the visitor to the page needs help. Other institutions use a video explanation of services to personalize the presentation of information and engage the student. No matter what approach is used, it is essential that the information be current and accessible to all.

CHAPTER SIX

ACADEMIC SERVICES SUITE

Chapters Six and Seven provide sufficient background information about specific services to give readers without direct experience a basic understanding of the services when delivered on campus. The chapters describe any relevant standards for online delivery, discuss concerns when students and service professionals are separated by time and place, and provide innovative examples of online delivery and how each service meets the needs of online students. Chapter Six discusses the following services from the Academic Services Suite: Academic Advising and Counseling, Assessment and Testing, Bookstore, Library, Technical Support, and Tutoring.

ACADEMIC ADVISING AND COUNSELING

Academic advising is a process by which counselors assist students in developing and implementing course selection and sequencing so that the students may achieve their educational goals. This process, which continues throughout a student's academic career, can include many activities that result in course and program selection, life and career goals, and personal development in the areas of critical thinking, leadership, and social responsibility, to name a few. Institutions understand that the separation of time and place may create challenges for academic advisors and students.

STANDARDS FROM THE NATIONAL ACADEMIC ADVISING ASSOCIATION

Recognizing these challenges, the National Academic Advising Association (NACADA) developed the following standards for advising distance learners:

- Adhere to all applicable federal, state, and accrediting agency regulations and policies.
- Offer a minimum set of core services which assist distance learners in identifying and achieving their education goals.
- Employ a myriad of technologies in the delivery of distance education and related services.
- Provide leadership and an organizational structure that supports students, faculty, and advisors.
- Offer appropriate professional development activities and support for staff and faculty advisors.
- Engage in continuous evaluation of program quality by reviewing factors such as educational effectiveness, student learning outcomes, student retention, and student/faculty satisfaction.
- Commit sufficient technical and financial resources on a continuing basis in the delivery of services to distance learners.
- Present the programs and services available accurately in marketing materials.
- Assess applicants to ensure that they have the knowledge and technical skills needed to undertake the program.
- Provide an orientation to introduce new students to the distance education environment.
- Provide appropriate student support services for distance learners as they would for students on campus.
- Provide a single point of contact for the services commonly accessed by distance learners.
- Create opportunities for connection and community among the institution, faculty, staff, and other students.
- Respond to the unique needs of distance learning students, rather than expecting them to fit within the established organizational structure (*Standards for Advising Distance Learners*, 2010).

These standards emphasize the point that distance learners require advising services equivalent to those that on-campus students receive. While advising goals remain the same, institutions serving online learners may consider developing new methods of delivery for those students who do not come to campus. To do so requires leadership, planning, additional resources, and commitment.

IMPORTANCE AND SATISFACTION

Students consider academic advising an essential service. In a 2009 Noel-Levitz study, *Academic Advising Highly Important to Students,* at four-year public colleges and universities students reported advising as the most important aspect of their educational experience. It was the second most important for students at four-year private institutions, third most important for students at two-year colleges, and fourth most important for students at career/private/for-profit schools.

Students at public and private four-year institutions reported the following strengths of the advising programs: (1) My academic advisor is knowledgeable about requirements in my program; (2) My academic advisor is approachable; and (3) Major requirements are clear and reasonable. Students at career/private/for-profit schools agreed that (1) and (2) were strengths of their advising programs. However, students at two-year colleges found none of the seven academic advising items were strengths (My academic advisor is knowledgeable about my program requirements, approachable, knowledgeable about transfer requirements to other schools, helps me set goals to work toward and is concerned about my success as an individual, the advising staff cares about students as individuals, this school does whatever it can to help me reach my educational goals). To qualify as a strength, students had to rate the item above the midpoint for importance and in the top quartile for satisfaction.

Students at four-year institutions are satisfied with the quality of their academic advising programs. However, students at two-year colleges identified the following items as challenges:

- This school does whatever it can to help me reach my educational goals.

- My academic advisor is concerned about my success as an individual.
- My academic advisor is knowledgeable about requirements in my program.
- My academic advisor is knowledgeable about the transfer requirements of other schools (*Academic Advising Highly Important to Students*, 2009).

This Noel-Levitz academic advising study did not disaggregate responses from online learners; nevertheless, the results illustrate the importance, strengths, and challenges of academic advising programs at various types of schools.

The *National Online Learners Priorities Report* (2010) did include an item directly related to advising online students: "My program advisor helps me work toward career goals." Although this item could not be identified as a strength or a challenge, it was closer to being categorized as a challenge. According to the Priorities Report, academic advisors working with online students at two-year colleges have the most room for improvement. This conclusion is supported by results from the Managing Online Education study, where just over 30% of administrators rated their academic advising services for online students to be good or excellent (Green, 2010a). Institutions that are concerned about the success of their online learners may consider innovative practices for online advising discussed at the end of this section.

ADVISING MODELS

The relationship between advisor and advisee remains important and can take many different forms. Feghali, Zahib, and Hallal (2011) suggest the following four models of academic advising: Prescriptive, Developmental, Integrated, and Engaged Advising.

Prescriptive Advising is when the advisor takes a directive approach and lets students know what courses they need to take and the sequence in which to take them in order to complete a specific degree. Prescriptive Advising might be effective once students confirm their college major. Once college majors are confirmed and students understand the requirements to complete the major, advising becomes a task of sequencing the courses. The order depends on students completing prerequisites and knowing when the institution makes each course available. In this model the advisor is active and the student may be quite passive during the advising process.

Developmental Advising is when advisor and student share responsibility for decisions about course selection and completing degree requirements. The goal is for the advisor to facilitate the student's independence, decision making, and problem-solving skills.

Integrated Advising combines strategies from both the Prescriptive and Developmental models. Some aspects of the advising activities use a prescriptive approach, and others involve the advisor teaching the students how to assume responsibility for making decisions.

Engaged Advising focuses on building a relationship between advisor and student for the purpose of facilitating the student's independence, decision making, and problem-solving skills. The relationship is established before work begins on advising activities such as developing an educational plan.

ADAPTING MODELS TO ONLINE ADVISING

Since Prescriptive Advising is the most concrete, it is quite easily adapted to the online environment. Students and advisors can obtain detailed program and degree information and specific steps for completing degree requirements not only in online catalogs but also from departmental websites or online tools developed by advising departments.

Students should be alerted to some drawbacks of using online advising tools. For example, many degree audit reports can be difficult for students to decipher without the assistance of an advisor. Students may be confused when similar information is available in multiple areas of the institution's website. To overcome these problems, Capella University created an academic planning system that is integrated with its student information system. The academic planning system creates a single view for advisor and student, a standardized format across programs, and a centralized location to store degree plans. It has a degree planner, substitutions and equivalencies, course articulations, and course sequencing modules that track student progress toward a degree. Advisors can easily see when students are off track. Under this system, an advisee can email or call an advisor by phone to clarify any points of confusion from the Academic Plan.

Many students may need more complex interaction with the advisor to help select a major and create an educational plan. For these students, the Developmental, Engaged, or Integrated Models may be more appropriate choices. Through the use of email, phone, Web 2.0 technologies, and desktop videoconferencing software, advisors and students who are in separate locations can develop meaningful relationships. San Diego City College uses WebEx to conduct live online e-counseling and advising appointments and workshops. This technology facilitates the Developmental, Engaged, and Integrated Models of online advising. A student must sign an informed consent statement before registering for any e-counseling services.

Ideally, prior to meeting with advisors, students would begin investigating possible programs using online advising resources: sites with comprehensive information about majors and minors, graduation requirements, degree audits, grade and assignment calculators, transfer in and out information, course schedules, and online tutorials. Information from online student services sites enables students to become more knowledgeable before they interact with their advisor.

When students use online resources to assume responsibility for understanding the requirements for their degree, they are more active participates in the advising process, an essential component of the Developmental, Engaged, and Integrated Advising Models. Kittelson (2009) found that students who completed a pre-advisement online module came to the advising appointment with more understanding of their programs and could participate more fully in making decisions about planning for a degree, setting academic goals, and developing a relationship with the academic advisor. These sessions included more developmental than prescriptive advising interventions as compared to students who did not complete the pre-advisement module.

Innovative Practices

Online advising is an area where innovation is taking place. The Open University of Hong Kong has developed an intelligent online system with iCounseling and iAdvising modules that respond to questions about career development, learning formats, program and course choices, student plans, and graduation checks through the use of avatars, and search technologies. The system, available 24/7, is designed to handle the simple questions while complex issues continue to be handled by the advising staff (Leung, Tsang, Lam, & Pang, 2010).

Valencia Community College's Lifemap is an online advising tool. The content is organized in five main areas: College Transition, Introduction to College, Progression to Degree, Graduation Transition, and Lifelong Learning. Each section links to online information, campus resources, planning tools, and success indicators that students can use to check their progress in each area. Valencia's student information system, Atlas, allows students to personalize and save Lifemap information.

Students at Valencia also have an ePortfolio application to collect artifacts such as results of career inventories, résumés, and course assignments that demonstrate knowledge learned and skills attained to assess personal development and academic learning. The ePortfolio is an especially important resource for career development as it provides a visual portrayal of evidence the student has collected that may help them make a satisfying career choice. The Lifemap handbook provides details about what is included and how to best use Lifemap to develop and accomplish personal and academic goals at Valencia. This comprehensive tool has transformed student success at Valencia.

While the innovative online academic advising tools improve a student's access to academic advising information, online advising also involves the development of advisor and advisee relationships. Chapter Eight describes effective online communication and emphasizes the importance of conveying a caring tone especially as a part of text-based online interaction. The innovative practices described in this section are providing new ways of creating advising relationships. The experience of students who can come to campus for advising is enhanced by these electronic tools. The advising process of students who cannot come to campus is facilitated by a combination of robust online advising practices and Web 2.0 tools, which are more fully described in Chapter Eight.

ASSESSMENT AND TESTING

Assessment and testing are services that some believe are the least ready for online delivery. Those skeptics want to ensure that the person taking the test is the same person who registered for the course and want to minimize the chances that the student taking an online test is cheating. Institutions may consider sophisticated tools like biometrics fingerprints, iris scans, or voice prints to authenticate the person taking the test and to watch that person's actions during the process. However, these tools are expensive and they present privacy concerns. As of 2008, biometric software was used by only 1 out of 55 colleges surveyed (*Academic Integrity and Student Verification Survey*, 2008). Most institutions are looking at approaches other than biometrics to support placement and academic testing for online students.

PLACEMENT TESTING

Placement testing for students new to college is becoming increasingly important. The National Association for Developmental Education (NADE) in a resolution calls for mandatory cognitive and affective assessment and appropriate course placement for all incoming college students. Mandatory testing for course placement improves both the rates of course and college retention. Correct placement enhances self-esteem and academic progress. It is a time and cost savings for the institution and the student (*Mandatory Cognitive and Affective Testing and Placement of Students into College Courses*, 2010). Correct course placement is equally important for online learners.

Institutions may want to offer placement tests for online students who cannot come to campus and who do not transfer in college English composition and math courses. The Illinois Virtual Campus set up a statewide cooperative agreement that enables all students taking online courses anywhere in Illinois to take exams at their local community college. Some colleges charge a fee per test; others do not. Institutions might also consider referring students who do not live close to the college to The Consortium of College Testing Centers, a free proctoring service provided by the National College Testing Association (NCTA) to support online learners. The approved centers must comply with test environment standards set forth by NCTA as an assurance of quality control.

Institutions may decide to set policies and procedures that enable the student to arrange for a private proctor. For example, Virginia Tech University (VT) defines acceptable guidelines for proctors. VT students fill out a request form for a proctored test and send it to the instructor for approval. If approved, proctors fill out a Proctor Agreement Form in which they agree to comply with procedures for administering and returning tests. The VT website provides step-by-step procedures including time lines to be followed by student and proctor. This information is located on the external college website and could be linked inside the learning management system to provide easy access for online students. Proctoring policies and procedures are equally relevant for placement and academic course testing.

Institutions' websites are an always available platform for communicating assessment and testing information to students. Websites might contain information such as options for waiving placement tests, study guides, tutorials, and supplemental materials to help students prepare for placement tests. The institution might communicate to remotely located students how they can obtain an interpretation of their placement test results. Not all students understand the detrimental impact that placing into developmental courses has on their progress toward achieving their educational goals. Students who place in developmental courses may have to delay taking college-level courses, thereby extending the time it takes them to earn a degree. Institutions may want to use websites to emphasize to students the importance of preparing for and putting forth their best efforts when taking placement tests.

ACADEMIC COURSE TESTING

Since the early days of web-based learning—and even back in the days of correspondence courses—institutions have debated the prevalence of cheating in online courses. Many course design and online pedagogy issues contribute to the concern, the details of which are beyond the scope of this book. However, institutions may want to consider a few suggestions from the *Best Practice Strategies to Promote Academic Integrity* (2009) report.

This report suggests that to discourage cheating faculty can use a variety of methods of assessments and emphasize assignments that require written work and problem solving. However, if an online course requires objective assessments, the report has numerous recommendations:

- Use a test bank.
- Pull a small number of questions from a test bank.
- Randomize the order of correct answers.
- Allow students to enter the test only one time.
- Set a short time frame for completion.
- Use password-protected exams.
- Show one question at a time to discourage copying and pasting for others.

The report also recommends the use of a lock-down browser to discourage students from looking answers up on the Internet. A lock-down browser is software that is installed on a computer to prohibit students from leaving the testing page and going to other locations such as the Internet. This software is also bundled with some learning management systems. However, institutions may want to consider the WCET *Academic Integrity and Student Verification Survey* (2008) that found lock-down browsers to be the least effective way to discourage cheating.

For subjective assessments, the report recommends that faculty

- Check the creation date and author for essays or term papers if they suspect it was created by someone other than the student.
- Clarify requirements for accommodations for extended time.
- Change assignment topics each semester.
- Require reference articles with cited text highlighted or annotated bibliographies.
- Require a thesis statement prior to topic approval, drafts of work, concept papers, project plans, or cumulative parts of a project turned in throughout the semester.

- Have students reflect upon and discuss written assignments on the discussion board (*Academic Integrity and Student Verification Survey*, 2008).

CREATING A CULTURE OF HONESTY

Academic honesty is everyone's responsibility. The institution, faculty, and students each have responsibilities for establishing a culture of honesty, creating awareness of how the institution defines academic integrity, and understanding the consequences for violations. Institutions that consistently stress academic honesty are better able to maintain a culture of honesty and integrity. In particular, those who support online students may be well positioned to influence their students if they stress the importance of academic honesty.

The *Best Practice Strategies to Promote Academic Integrity* (2009) report suggested that the institution, faculty, and students have certain responsibilities for academic honesty:

It is the institution's responsibility to

- Establish, publicize, and enforce an academic honesty policy that articulates faculty, student, and institutional expectations and responsibilities for enforcement.
- Include ethics instruction within the curriculum.
- Address academic honesty policies and enforcement at student orientations.
- Encourage faculty to report every suspected violation.
- Publicize policy on the college website.

It is the faculty's responsibility to

- State on the syllabus the institutional academic policy and clarify enforcement in each online course and provide a link to the full academic honesty policy.
- Define, clearly explain, and provide examples of academic integrity and cheating.
- Require students to engage with the policy. Some examples: ask students for suggestions about how to create a community of integrity within the course, ask for a commitment to honesty by signing an agreement, and/or make the policy part of a discussion board or reflection assignment.

- Differentiate between collaboration and cheating and state how much collaboration is permissible on each project.
- Define consequences of violations and enforce the consequences.

It is the student's responsibility to

- Understand the requirements.
- Ask questions when confused.
- Comply with the expectations.

Institutions can use web resources and faculty can use the syllabus and other course materials to express the core value of academic honesty. Some faculty may have concerns about remotely located students who take online courses. To allay these concerns, institutions may provide these students with the option of taking proctored tests. It is important for institutions to clearly communicate academic honesty policies and the consequences for violations.

BOOKSTORE

The traditional concept of a print textbook is being significantly altered through the use of eReaders, digital textbooks, and freely available resources from the Internet. As the traditional textbook is transformed, so will be the services delivered by college bookstores. Although the headline of the article in the November 14, 2010 *Chronicle of Higher Education,* "As Textbooks Go Digital, Campus Bookstores May Go Bookless," may be a hyperbole, the message is clear that change is on the horizon.

Online bookstores provide a convenient way for online and on-campus students to order textbooks. Bookstores' websites display and provide access for purchasing textbooks, other course materials, hardware, software, and college-branded merchandise. Students can find information about the books and supplemental materials required for specific courses, payment and delivery, refund policy, store hours, and how to use financial aid to purchase books. To best serve online students, the bookstore might provide a chat function to answer questions at various times, even beyond typical business hours. This service is particularly important not only for students who work during the day but also for those who live in different time zones. Online students greatly benefit when the bookstore identifies a staff person who understands the needs of online learners.

College bookstores may be thinking about how to reinvent themselves as they compete with low-cost online bookstores that provide equal service and lower purchase prices for academic books. Bookstores may support faculty members who choose new options: textbook rental and return services; open source books; other options for book buy-back; quality online materials that faculty may consider equivalent to textbooks; and self-publication by faculty. As with many innovations, not all will be successful but some may become mainstream in the not too distant future.

PREDICTING THE FUTURE

The 2010 *Horizon Report* identified three emerging technologies that may transform the traditional college bookstore. According to the *Horizon Report,* mobile computing and open content will become mainstream in institutions by the end of 2011, and electronic books will become well established by 2012–2013 (Johnson, Levine, Smith, & Stone, 2010). Institutions should note the skyrocketing sales of mobile devices, especially eReaders, starting with the Kindle and continuing with the iPad and its competitors.

Three additional reports support the predictions from the *Horizon Report.* Forrester Research expects 1 billion dollars to be spent on e-books in 2011 and 3 billion dollars by the middle of the decade. The National Association of College Stores (NACS) reports that digital books account for about 3% of textbook sales, but NACS expects that percentage to reach 10%–15% by 2012 (Waters, 2011). Even though digital textbooks are not as popular as electronic books read for pleasure, this dynamic may change in the near future with improved eReader technology for notation, navigation, and inclusion of multimedia. *The Campus Computing Survey* results found almost 80% of the respondents agree or strongly agree that e-books will be an important platform for instructional content in the next five years (Green, 2010c).

OPEN SOURCE

Open source initiatives make Internet-based course materials free to all. The open content movement in higher education was originally associated with the Massachusetts Institute of Technology (MIT) open courseware project, which celebrated its 10th anniversary on April 4, 2011. Initially, MIT announced it would openly share videos of class lectures, lecture notes, and exams from all courses. In the first decade, MIT made available materials from 2,000 courses to an estimated 100 million individuals worldwide.

Another initiative, created at Foothill-De Anza Community College District, is the Community College Open Textbook Collaborative. Recognizing the sometimes prohibitive cost of textbooks, Foothill-De Anza joined with other colleges, governmental agencies, and educational organizations to create this project that has peer-reviewed over 500 open online textbooks and is considering the development of 250 others. These textbooks are licensed so that users can read, download, and print the materials at no cost to faculty and students.

The state of Washington has an Open Course Library that does not loan textbooks. Instead, faculty and instructional designers stock this library with low-cost online materials to be used in specific courses. The materials are available to students for $30 or less. Institutions choosing this approach will provide students significant cost savings and the convenience of online access to course materials (Overland, 2011).

ADVANTAGES AND DISADVANTAGES OF ELECTRONIC BOOKS

Whether electronic textbooks (eTextbooks) are free, low cost, or just cost slightly less than traditional textbooks, they have some distinct advantages. One significant advantage is the cost of publishing and the purchase price of textbooks compared to costs associated with eTextbooks. eTextbooks can be updated continuously, whereas some print textbooks are out of date soon after publication. Another advantage is better quality control as errors can easily be corrected as soon as they are found, rather than continuing uncorrected until the next edition. Moreover, eTextbooks are accessible from anywhere and students do not have to carry heavy book bags. Print presentation cannot compare with dynamic multimedia delivery of content, not printing textbooks is environmentally friendly, and searchable content might make learning more effective and efficient. For online students either deployed overseas or taking courses abroad, delivery of print textbooks is cumbersome and often not timely. This problem is solved with electronic books.

eTextbooks may have some disadvantages. According to the *Campus Computing Survey*, eTextbook development and pricing strategies are still evolving. Authors of eTextbooks worry about loss of copyright protections and royalties, and not all students have eReaders. Multimedia can be cumbersome on slow computers or computers with slow Internet connections, and effective navigation strategies for electronic books are still evolving.

While electronic textbooks and open source course materials have not yet been widely adopted, several reports predict this will happen in the near future. Currently eTextbooks are widely used at for-profit colleges and universities (Green, 2010c). For example, since 2003, University of Phoenix has mandated that instructors assign digital materials whenever possible. In 2010, about 90% of University of Phoenix course content was delivered electronically, a great savings for students (Kolowich, 2010). The textbook landscape may change significantly in the next few years, thus altering the services delivered by online bookstores.

LIBRARY

Library services are among the best developed of all online student services. In 2008, the Association of College and Research Libraries (ACRL) approved the Standards for Distance Learning Library Services (referred hereafter as Standards). The Standards are based on the Access Entitlement Principle: All students, faculty, administrators, and staff members connected to the institution will have equitable access to all library services, including communication with library personnel, wherever they are located (*Standards for Distance Learning Library Services*, 2008).

The following Standards recognize that a library is an essential resource for online learners' successful academic performance. Libraries must

- Provide access to appropriate library services and resources that are essential for all postsecondary students, regardless of where students, faculty, staff, and programs are located. Access must be extended to all members of the distance learning community, including those with disabilities.
- Provide direct human access with a member of the library staff. This contact must be made available to the distance learning community through instruction, interaction, and interventions from library personnel to facilitate successful use of library resources, particularly electronic resources that require computer and information literacy skills.
- Provide to the distance learning community library resources and services that may require an additional investment, funded separately from the regular library budget.
- Provide for the information needs of distance learning programs by developing and delivering equivalent library services and learning resources to all students, faculty, and other personnel regardless of location.
- Provide technical linkages between the library and complementary resources such as computing facilities, instructional media, support services for people with disabilities, and telecommunication centers.
- Provide evidence that remotely delivered library services meet or exceed national and regional accreditation standards, professional association standards and guidelines, as well as laws such as the Americans with Disabilities Act and Title 504 of the Rehabilitation Act.
- Be informed of detailed analysis of planning, development, evaluations, and changes to the distance learning program.
- Maintain a current strategic plan, vision, evaluation, revision, and updating for services designed to meet the needs of distance learners.
- Make outcomes assessment a major component of distance learning library services.

- Provide information literacy instruction programs to the distance learning community no matter where they are located.
- Assure that libraries are adequately staffed to deliver the mandated services and meet the needs of distance students (*Standards for Distance Learning Library Services*, 2008).

ACRL member institutions are committed to providing equivalent services to remotely located online learners.

LIBRARY WEBSITES

Institutions typically deliver library resources and services through the institution's websites. After analyzing 111 college and university websites, Liu (2008) found that the most common elements on the library home pages were these:

- Contact us
- Suggestions
- Description of library services
- Ask a librarian
- News and announcements of events
- A tool to search the site
- Resources by subject
- Research assistance
- Live chat

Website elements that were less common, but frequently included, were

- Sign-in for library accounts
- Digital collections
- Portals organized by students, faculty, staff, alumni, friends, and visitors

Rare but innovative features included

- RSS (Really Simply Syndication) feeds for library news and events

- My Library (a personalized library space where students can aggregate course reserve materials, library alerts, databases, citation tools, and search preferences)
- Links to the university portal
- Link to Google Scholar
- Link to Windows Live Academic

All of these are important elements for an academic library, along with well-organized and clearly described instruction about how to access and use all library electronic resources and materials. Lui suggests that through the use of emerging technologies library websites can enable students to collaborate, share ideas, and engage in a variety of interactive activities, all of which facilitate learning and provide remote connection to library personnel, other students, faculty, and the institution.

Lui describes a model that provides a single point of entry to many resources launched from a library portal. On the library home page, individuals identify themselves as graduate students, faculty and staff, or friends and visitors. By selecting one of these categories, individuals narrow the available information based on anticipated need. If they choose a path that does not provide sufficient information, they can then access the other areas. Once inside the appropriate website, individuals can continue to personalize their library experience by selecting the needed resources from a list of options. These options are sent to the individuals' personal library space where links to these options are located: My Favorite Library Tools/Resources, My Saved Searches, My Library Collections, My Multimedia, My Online Classes (links to LMS), My Work Space (file storage space), My School Calendar, My School Email, My Portfolio, My Events, My Bulletin Board.

This page also links to My Published Spaces (websites), My Blogs, My Wiki Spaces, My RSS List, My Podcasts, My Tags, My Friends, and Spaces shared by other users (Liu, 2008). When students return to their personalized library portal, they can immediately access the information they have saved. This type of portal could be expanded to other services such as My Academic Plan, My Career Plan, My Tutoring, and My Financial Aid.

Students can benefit greatly by using a library portal. They save time because they can find everything in one location.

They can identify those resources they will use, and remove distracting clutter by eliminating the areas they do not use. They are actively engaged with, and in control of, their learning environment. Using this approach, the institution no longer decides all that a student needs; instead, students are empowered to decide how they can improve the efficiency and effectiveness of their own learning. In sum, this type of library portal enables students to develop communities of inquiry, connect to the institution, and organize the library resources they need to complete their academic goals.

INNOVATIVE PRACTICES

Liu (2008) identified four library websites that provide students some capabilities to customize their library experience: Brown University, North Carolina State University, University of North Carolina, Chapel Hill, and University of Iowa. Here are a few innovative practices from each library website. MyJosiah at Brown University allows students to renew books without having to go to the campus library. North Carolina State University provides a tool to help students find other students studying in the libraries. The University of North Carolina allows students to view and renew items checked out, track recalls, cancel holds, manage email notification, opt-in to reading history, and set or review search preferences. These tools help students customize their online library experience.

The University of Iowa library describes these customizable services on the external library website. Students can check the status of items they have checked out, including due dates and a list of items requested along with the status. They can renew books and request a book, an article, or book chapter through the Interlibrary Loan/Article Delivery Request System. They can use all the functionality of RefWorks, a web-based citation management and bibliography tool. And they can recommend that a library purchase an item. Other colleges may have these functions, but students may not be aware of them until they access the library from within the secure portal.

Institutions understand that remotely located online students are dependent on web-based, comprehensive library services and that their access to library services should be of equal quality to students who visit the library in person. When online students have to use local, physical libraries to research and find resources to complete assignments, the additional time spent compromises the convenience factor, the very reason many students take online courses. Continuing to improve online library services will benefit all students as an increasing number of students are using online libraries.

TECHNICAL SUPPORT

An institution that provides to its online students convenient and effective technical support contributes significantly to their online learning experience. Online students require technical information that on-campus students may not need. Frequently, online courses are delivered through learning management systems that require particular settings on a student's computer. Online courses may require students to download applications and plug-ins to be able to navigate and use the functionality within the learning management system. Students may need timely technical support in order to successfully begin their online courses. How an institution delivers technical services is a quality indicator of online programs.

Although institutions typically include explanations and access to the above information on the distance learning website, students may need additional assistance. Institutions might include these elements on their website to support online learners:

- Hardware and software requirements for specific courses (online and blended) and the ability to test their computer to make sure it meets these requirements.
- Easy access to, and automated updates of, free applications such as anti-virus software, Adobe reader, or a multimedia player.
- Guidelines that explain the scope of technical services, times of operations, delivery options, and typical response time for each option.
- Easy access to, and activation of, student email accounts.

- Multimedia instructional tutorials to explain how to use hardware and software, including the learning management system.
- Schedules for live tech training delivered either on-campus or web-based (using virtual classroom technology).
- Technology alerts when any system is down, either posted on the website or provided to students through email, instant message, call system, text message, blog, wiki, or social network site.
- Frequently Asked Questions (FAQs) that students can search or that are categorized by topic.
- Troubleshooting that allows a support person, with permission, to control a student's computer.

INNOVATIVE PRACTICES

The State University of New York (SUNY), Delhi Online Education website provides a comprehensive one-stop technical support portal where students can select from a broad array of self-service and help desk support services. The services include FAQs, notification when systems are down, and a searchable knowledge base of tutorials. Students can directly contact help desk personnel via live chat, walk-in support, instant messaging, phone, or by submitting a help desk ticket. Delhi uses a variety of Web 2.0 tools, including RSS, Twitter, a wiki, DimDim for screen sharing, and GoogleVoice and GoogleCalendar to facilitate technical support. The technical support portal is linked in every course that uses the learning management system. Live technical help is available 70 hours per week.

Institutions realize that providing live help desk support is labor intensive. What they may not realize is that clear online technical tutorials decrease the time students spend with help desk support. The University of Washington developed a wide array of online technical tutorials as part of the Catalyst Web Tool project. According to the Catalyst website, unique students using the website increased by 11% in 2010 to a total of 109,773 users. These users logged an average of 31,304 sessions each day, a 50% increase over 2009 numbers. From the Catalyst login, students have access to a drop box, project workspace, web-based file management system, discussion boards, a grade book, polls/surveys/ quizzes, college email, and a group space. The University of Washington, which developed these materials over many years, is improving them continuously and is also adding new resources. As the use of Catalyst increased, the number of live help desk calls decreased.

If an institution supports its online students with a combination of an easy-to-understand technical support website or portal, live help desk services (24 hours/7 days a week is best), and effective self-help tutorials, then it is doing its best to ensure that technical barriers do not interfere with the success and retention of online students. All staff who have contact with online students should be aware of the scope of technical resources and services and work collaboratively to encourage students to take advantage of technical support.

TUTORING

Institutions offer tutoring services to bridge the gap between student performance and faculty expectations. Those services are provided to campus-based students in a variety of formats. Students may be tutored by other students, faculty, or learning center support staff. Tutoring most commonly occurs in an individual meeting between student and tutor, but it also may occur in small or large groups. The goals of tutoring can be remediation, supplemental learning, or drill and practice. Tutoring is frequently offered to improve basic skills (writing and math) but also can be discipline or course-specific. Tutoring can cover personal development in such areas as study skills, meta-cognitive skills, self-regulation, organizational skills, and time management. Tutors can serve in an instructional role but can also serve as coaches, supporters, guides, counselors, and mentors. The challenge for many institutions is how to provide these tutoring services for online students.

TUTORING PLATFORMS

An institution can deliver online tutoring through the external or internal institutional website or from within the learning management system. If delivered from within the institution's learning management system, tutoring can be associated with a single course, with a group of courses within a discipline, or be made available to everyone with access to the learning management system.

An institution's tutoring website may contain the general information common to all Generations 2 and 3 services. The website might also include contact information and hours for interacting with a tutor by phone, text, chat, and/or through a virtual classroom. Online students will want to know what tutoring services are available and how to access those services.

Some institutions develop self-paced resources with a variety of formats. Tutorials and study guides can be text only, audio, audio and video, or game simulations. Self-assessment tools can be text-based slides that allow for basic interactivity or be highly sophisticated adaptive self-assessments that generate more challenging problems as students correctly answer previously presented items. Institutions might be interested in a growing body of free online, open source academic tutorials designed to help students anywhere in the world, such as that offered by the Khan Academy. All of these may be linked on an institution's tutoring website.

Calculators are available that help students plan their study time and decide how to achieve their program goals. The University of Minnesota has an assignment calculator that asks students to identify the date they will begin the assignment, when it is due, and the subject area. Grade point average (GPA) calculators have been available for quite some time. Interactive GPA calculators allow students to create "what-if" scenarios that help them identify the grades they need in individual courses to graduate with a particular GPA.

INSTITUTION-BASED ONLINE TUTORING

Some institutions provide students with a variety of self-paced tutoring resources. All of these tools can supplement course-based learning and are available 24 hours, 7 days a week. These are tools developed with an insider's view of the needs of students at a particular institution. In addition to the self-paced online tutoring tools, institutions can build and deliver interactive synchronous and asynchronous online tutoring services using their own hardware and software and their own staff. Students at North Dakota State University submit an online form requesting synchronous tutoring for multiple 100–200 level courses using Wimba, virtual classroom software now owned by Blackboard. Using this software, students and tutors are able to interact in real time, using video, voice, and an interactive whiteboard. The software is webbased, and students have access from any computer connected to the Internet. When the student and tutor use a webcam and a headset, they engage in a dynamic tutoring session that closely approximates in-person tutoring.

Central Piedmont Community College uses the Blackboard learning management system to offer math and writing tutoring. Blackboard provides file-sharing capabilities and online chat. Students can also find tutorials and other learning support materials inside Blackboard. The resources and staff are located in one virtual location. Live Chat is available Monday through Thursday during typical daytime business hours.

Institutions that have internally developed synchronous and asynchronous online tutoring services have an advantage in that their technical and tutoring staff are familiar with the needs of faculty, students, and the policies and procedures. Faculty and staff may be more supportive when online tutoring is consistent with the academic support priorities of the institution. Without faculty support, online tutoring may not be used to full advantage.

In considering the option to develop an in-house online tutoring service, an institution may face several issues: the technology needed to develop, deliver, and support the service; the demands on staff time to train online tutors and deliver tutoring services; and the planning involved in developing and implementing an effective online tutoring program. Because this option is labor intensive, institutions may only be able to provide tutoring for a small number of courses.

VENDOR-PURCHASED ONLINE TUTORING

Institution-based tutoring services are developed from an insider's perspective and are clearly a product of the institution. The same cannot be said when online tutoring services are contracted.

However, there are certain advantages to purchasing services from a vendor.

An institution may find that a substantial benefit of this approach is ease of implementation. The service is activated as soon as the institution signs a contract. The institution is not responsible for software and hardware setup, and the service is typically hosted outside of the institution's network. This option offers the broadest selection of courses and 24/7 tutoring service. The possible downsides are that the institution does not have any control over rising costs of the services; some faculty may be concerned about hiring tutors not directly connected to the institution; and the service does not carry the institution's brand, other than perhaps a logo placed in certain areas of the website.

The oldest online tutoring vendor is Smarthinking. It offers tutoring in basic skills math through calculus II, writing, general and organic chemistry, physics, biology, anatomy and physiology, accounting, economics, finance, Spanish, statistics, nursing and allied health. Ninety percent of its tutors have a Master's or Ph.D. in their discipline and an average of nine years teaching experience. Smarthinking offers live, online tutoring, and asynchronous tutoring. Its site includes a full array of answers to technical support questions along with technical phone support during daytime business hours. Email support turnaround time is one to two business days.

COLLABORATIVE TUTORING

An institution may consider a collaborative option, such as eTutoring sponsored by the Connecticut Distance Learning Consortium (CTDLC). eTutoring provides synchronous and asynchronous online tutoring, creates a master schedule of tutoring, and trains the tutors. The CTDLC owns the platform, hosts the service, and provides technical support. It also provides an experienced consulting service to assist members (in 2011, 12 states) to set up online tutoring for their students. Each institution contributes tutors to eTutoring, and each institution has a coordinator who supervises their tutors. Each institution provides one representative/coordinator to the Advisory Council, which makes policy and chooses subjects for which tutoring is available.

The collaborative option offers some benefits over the other options. Institutions have some input into program development and delivery, but not to the extent of those programs developed by a single institution. It is easier to implement than institution-based programs, but takes more staff time than purchasing the service from a vendor. The subjects and hours of operation may be more extensive than institution-based programs, but not as wide reaching as a vendor can offer. It is the least expensive option.

CHOOSING AMONG ONLINE TUTORING OPTIONS

Some possible benefits of online tutoring are improved learning outcomes, course retention, and academic success. Students may become more confident that they can succeed in subsequent courses, develop improved time management and organizational skills, and feel that the institution cares about their success.

Institutions may want to consider some possible negatives. For example, of the 26 items on the Noel-Levitz 2010 *National Online Learners Priorities Report,* students ranked tutoring services next to last as a service they perceive to be important for their success. The average importance score for online tutoring was 5.87; all other items received an average score of 6.02 or better. Given the low ratings for tutoring services, institutions may consider conducting a faculty and student needs assessment prior to beginning an online tutoring service. The results from a needs assessment might provide institutions with information about student and faculty usage of tutoring services to guide development of this service and determine which delivery option best fits with the institution's goals for online tutoring. Institutions will want to decide whether the services should be developed internally, con-tracted with a vendor, or implemented collaboratively with a con-sortium of other colleges and universities. As previously noted, there are benefits and concerns with each option.

CONCLUSION

The Academic Services Suite contains core services to support the success of online learners. Institutions may best support the success of online learning by informing their students of these services before they register for their first online course. For example, with effective academic advising, students will select appropriate courses based on their placement scores and educational goals. They will understand how to obtain their textbooks as soon as they complete course registration. They will understand the hardware and software requirements, and they will receive technical support for their first online course. Students should be informed about how to use the online library and tutoring services. When students are well prepared before they begin their first online course, they have a better chance of success.

CHAPTER SEVEN

PERSONAL SERVICES SUITE

The Personal Services Suite includes services that historically have been characterized by a high level of human interaction. The Personal Services Suite includes Orientation, Career Services, Personal Counseling Services, Health and Wellness Services, and Ethical and Legal Services. Professionals from these areas work with students on issues that can be of a sensitive nature. Some institutions may be concerned about whether it is appropriate to provide these interactive services at a distance. Reflecting on the discussion about the generational evolution of online student services, institutions may decide that Generation 3 is as far as they want to develop some services, while others are so essential for the success of online students that institutions will decide to develop fully interactive, personalized online services in those areas.

One approach is to look at how fully online colleges might view the inclusion of, for example, personal counseling in their suite of online services. These institutions generally decide not to offer personal counseling services; however, professionals at these institutions will encounter individuals with emotional difficulties that are impeding academic progress. These institutions may refer students to counseling services in their locale or they may want to be able to refer them to web-based resources offered by external vendors, or both.

The other services in this suite are not as controversial. However, for institutions offering services to online students from this suite, it is particularly important to select appropriate technology, ensure confidentiality, and make sure that staff is committed to delivering online personal services.

Orientation to Online Learning

Institutions have long offered orientation activities to facilitate the success of students new to college. Some institutions are realizing that orientation to online learning is just as essential prior to a student's first online course. One goal of orientation to online learning is to improve online course retention. Institutions have looked at online retention research to determine what content to include in orientation activities. Although results from retention research that attempts to determine causes for withdrawal from online courses are preliminary, inconclusive, and often contradictory, one variable that seems important for online course retention is that students must understand the expectations and demands of online learning and know how to use the technology required for their online course. These factors are sometimes referred to as readiness for online learning. One overarching goal of orientation is to improve readiness for online learning.

Importance

The importance of orientation in facilitating online student success is suggested in the following studies. One study recommended stronger orientation programs to help students transition to and understand the demands of the online learning environment (Brescia, Miller, Ibrahima, & Murry, 2004). In another study, Ludwig-Hardman and Dunlap (2003) found that an orientation to online learning is one of the support services that can help online students overcome isolation, lack of self-direction, and decreased motivation. From a faculty and staff perspective, students who participated in orientation activities were reported to be more proficient in accessing online student services and course resources (*Academic Advising Highly Important to Students*, 2009). From the perspective of students who withdrew from online courses, 46% stated they would benefit by orientations (Nash, 2005). Also from a student perspective, orientation to the course media/delivery format was ranked as the most important support service at the beginning of the course (Ozoglu, 2010). In comparing retention rates of students in an online undergraduate business course based on whether they attended a face-to-face orientation, 91% who attended and 18% who did not attend were retained in the course (Ali & Leeds, 2009). Providing orientations seems to make a difference. However, there is no consensus about which formats are most beneficial to students.

FORMATS

Orientations to online learning are delivered in many formats. Wilson (2008) compared three types of orientation events: a general face-to-face session, a prerecorded video developed by the instructor and imbedded in the course, and a live online webinar. Both types of live session had high registrations but poor attendance. Students reported scheduling conflicts. Even though their intentions were to attend, other responsibilities seemed more important than what they thought they would learn at the orientation. Of the three formats, the orientation that was specific to the course and readily available from the course management system received the most positive evaluations. The convenience, availability, and usefulness of the information were reasons cited for the positive comments. The study also found that students appreciated the opportunity to get to know the instructor from the video presentation.

Orientations are commonly launched from the institution's website using text only, or audio podcasts, or audio and video. These are all self-help tools. With this approach, it is essential for institutions to organize content in a way that makes information easy to find. Long Beach Community College, Success in Distance Education website orientation does a particularly good job of presenting information for students when they are considering an online course, getting started in their first online course, and throughout the semester. The Considering tab leads to interactive tutorials that help students understand the types of online courses, personal characteristics that will lead to success, and computer requirements for most courses. The Getting Started tab leads to activities that prepare students for online success. The Succeeding tab provides testimonials from successful online students and an interactive simulation about the peril of procrastination in online learning. A well-organized resource directory on the website provides students easy access to additional information including a variety of online student services. It is noteworthy that each of these multimedia tutorials is accompanied by an alternative text version.

Some institutions have orientations that provide opportunities for students to interact with professional staff and/or the faculty member who is teaching the course. One option is to include a Week 0, which is an orientation conducted within each course site a week prior to the first day of the term. Students can spend time reading the syllabus and exploring the course before starting assignments. The course instructor facilitates activities that allow students to understand the expectations of that course, including how the course is organized. Students may engage with the instructor and other students in various orientation activities such as introductions, a course scavenger hunt, or a syllabus quiz that provide opportunities to practice using the course tools. Week 0 also provides a convenient way of setting the tone and pace of the course and enforcing course expectations before the course begins.

There are other formats for orientation to online learning. Some institutions provide a short course either prior to the start of the semester or during the term to prepare students who want to register for their first online course at the beginning of the following term. Still others create a full-term credit course that combines the contents of a First Year Experience course and orientation to online learning. A few institutions require some form of orientation before students take their first online course. And occasionally institutions make orientation courses available to students free of charge. When students have the option to enroll or are required to enroll in an orientation to online learning course, all information included in the web-based asynchronous delivery method can be delivered from within the learning management system. One advantage of orientation to online learning courses is the measure of accountability that provides evidence that students are actually engaging with the materials and demonstrating an understanding of the tools and resources they need to become successful online learners.

Credit or noncredit courses are the most engaging and the most labor intensive forms of orientations to online learning. These approaches provide the most comprehensive understand-

ing of the demands of online learning. Because students participate in a low-stakes online experience, they begin to learn how
to succeed in an online course without the performance anxiety
that comes with doing assignments for an academic course.

Yet another format is to create a self-paced orientation inside
a demo learning management system (LMS) site. Students are
free to use the demo site to understand the demands of online
learning before they decide to register for their first online course
or to prepare prior to the start of the term once they have decided
to take an online course. These orientations to online learning
courses are sometimes used by instructional faculty as a student's
first assignment. Faculty include a quiz or a written assignment
based on content from the orientation demo course to ensure
that students have learned what they deem necessary to be ready
for online learning. Some institutions make staff available to
answer questions on the discussion board or through email from
inside the demo course site.

Video conferencing software can also be used to facilitate live,
remotely delivered orientation workshops that cover the expectation of online learning, success strategies, and navigation of the
learning management system. Video conferencing orientations
allow students to ask questions and actively engage with the
instructor. Using this type of software to deliver an orientation
to online learning is the approach that is most similar to an experience students might have if they were able to come to an
on-campus session, but students can attend from the convenience
of their home computer.

Measurement of Readiness

Institutions can choose from a variety of approaches to assess
readiness for online learning. Perhaps the most common approach
is for institutions to post a readiness for online learning quiz on
a distance learning website. These self-report quizzes typically
include specific cautions or encouragement to enroll based on
how students respond to each question. Some have questioned
this approach and found that students tend to overestimate their
technical skills and other readiness indicators for online learning
(Bozarth, Chapman, & LaMonica, 2004).

SmarterMeasure (formerly READI) is a vendor-produced online learning readiness tool that assesses a student's likelihood of succeeding in online courses. SmarterMeasure contains some self-report assessments of individual attributes, learning styles, and life factors. The strength of this product is that it also includes tests of technical skills and knowledge, and screen reading and typing speed and accuracy. Results of all assessments indicate whether a skill deficiency might make online learning more challenging for individual students. Institutions can decided to develop remediation materials based on the number of students who are deficient in particular areas. The instrument allows institutions to link to already established support tools for each subtest.

Each year SmarterMeasure analyzes usage and results. In 2009, the most common usage was through an orientation course (33%); second, the institution's website (28%); and third, as an assignment in an online course (27%). Thirty percent of the schools require students new to online learning to take the inventory (Mercer & Simmons, 2010).

CONTENT OF ORIENTATIONS TO ONLINE LEARNING

Institutions prioritize the content they believe to be most important for online student success and retention based on the format used to deliver the orientation. It is easy to overwhelm students with too much content. Institutions may want to consider the literature to see what content research suggests is most important. One study found that including technical skill development in a new student orientation course has the most impact for improving student success (Miller & Pope, 2003). Research on what knowledge, skills, and attitudes should be taught as part of an orientation to online learning course found that students should understand the time commitment and possess good time management skills (Bozarth, Chapman, & LaMonica, 2004). In order to be prepared for success in online courses, students needed the most help with learner control and self-directed learning. Learner control includes the students' ability to direct their own learning and to control distractions. Self-directed learning involves creating study plans, obtaining assistance with content, setting goals, and developing time management skills (Hung, Chou, Chen, & Own, 2010).

Different orientation formats, to some extent, determine what content can be included. When orientations are limited to one-hour to two-hour sessions, delivered on-campus or online through a virtual classroom, institutions may overwhelm students if they include too much information. Live sessions tend to be restricted to information about how to navigate the course management system, expectations about online learning, and information about how to access student support resources. The amount of material presented is also driven by whether the session is interactive or delivered through a lecture. Face-to-face orientations conducted in a computer lab provide opportunities for students to practice navigating the learning management system. One advantage of live orientations is they provide students with the opportunity to connect to professionals from the institution.

Web-based, asynchronous delivery formats have no limit to the scope of information that can be made available to an online student. With these methods, orientation materials can be accessed when students are ready to learn the information. However, institutions should ensure that their web-based orientation materials are well organized so that students can easily find the information they need. Institutions may want to organize information based on enrollment periods when specific information is important for student success.

For example:

Prior to enrollment, students may need to know how to apply to the college and for financial aid; to comply with course placement requirements; to assess whether or not they are a good fit for online learning; and to select and register for an online course.

After enrollment, students may need to understand the demands of online learning and remediate any weaknesses identified from a readiness self-assessment. They can learn how to navigate the course management system, access technical support; find, order, and pay for books and other course materials; and make sure the technical requirements of the course match the hardware and software on the computer they will use. They can learn how to access and use the online library; interact effectively using the course communication tools; contact their instructor; and find their course.

Shortly after the course begins and throughout the semester, students may need to learn about plagiarism and the consequences of violations to academic honesty; how to study effectively online; how to improve concentration, time management, and organizational skills; how to use tutoring services; and how to access test proctoring forms.

Throughout the remainder of their enrollment, students may need to know how to access academic advising and career services, along with the other online services described in this book.

INNOVATIVE PRACTICES

Rowan University has developed self-service orientation modules that students can use either when they need the information or when an instructor uses them for a course assignment. In addition to learning the skills previously mentioned in this section, Rowan University has found that using orientation modules has relieved faculty of orienting online students to the learning environment. The modules contain videos from YouTube.com, which are integrated with instructional materials that students access from inside their LMS.

When a student selects Bucks County Community College (BCCC) online learning website, a popup window provides an audio-video welcome message and encourages students to participate in the live online information sessions. Students may elect to chat with a professional during typical business hours or leave a message after hours. When the prospective online student's link is selected, another recorded message describes essential information about what to expect from online learning. The page contains FAQs and a link to a Getting Started with Online Learning Tour. Flash movies that include a text alternative help prospective students decide whether or not online learning is right for them. Other movies describe policies and procedures for Getting Started. The BCCC online learning website makes it easy for prospective online students to find essential information.

Drexel University has a First Year Experience program for the online Master of Science in Higher Education Program (MSHE). The goals are to engage the students, foster and support community development, and connect students to the institution. The first event of the year is a synchronous online orientation where students meet faculty and support specialists. Support specialists from the writing center noted an increase in the use of writing center services after MSHE started offering these events. As a result they developed a series of online writing workshops. The First Year Experience also includes the following online events: a tea in the fall, a wine and cheese event in winter, a graduation event in the spring, and panel speaker series in the summer. All of these events serve to create a feeling of community outside the online classroom. Drexel University has expanded its invitations to these events to online doctoral students from the Higher Education program and other programs from the Goodwin College of Professional Studies and undergraduate and commuter students. The events are conducted in Wimba, videoconferencing software, or in Second Life, a 3D virtual world. During the summer there is an online Luau with a beach and music in Second Life (Betts, 2011).

This section highlights the importance of providing an orientation to students new to online learning. When students feel comfortable with the learning environment prior to the beginning of their first online course, they are ready to learn the content of the course rather than struggle with the technology or where to find instructional materials. Orientation activities that continue beyond the start of the semester facilitate the use of all student support services and the connection of the students to the institution. As with all online student services, the approach institutions take will depend on a number of factors that include the number of online students served, the mission of the college, and the financial resources available for orienting students new to online learning.

Career Services

Institutions take various approaches to delivering career services. One approach is helping students develop a career profile that includes self-assessment of their career interests, skills, values, experiences, and personality type. Students use this self-knowledge to identify and explore the types of occupation that fit their career profile. Students may select a few occupations for in-depth investigation and then weigh the pros and cons of each, sometimes in the context of selecting a college major. This process can be facilitated as part of a career development course, during individual or group sessions with a career professional, or self-paced online career tools.

Career counseling involves various aspects of career planning, but an important component is the development of a relationship between the student and a career professional. The professional is a guide who encourages the student to examine any barriers that prevent the student from making a career choice. Placement services, which prepare a student to find a job, involve writing résumés, developing interview skills, searching job databases, learning how to network, job shadowing, participating in internships, and volunteering to learn more about potential careers.

STANDARDS

With the increase in the use of the Internet to deliver career services, the National Career Development Association (NCDA), the National Association of Colleges and Employers (NACE), and the Association of Computer-based Systems for Career Information (ACSCI) developed standards to ensure that career services delivered electronically are of equal quality to those delivered in person. While not intended to be a comprehensive review, what follows are highlights of standards from each of these associations.

NCDA developed the Guidelines for the Use of the Internet for Delivery of Career Counseling and Career Planning Services, which require the following:

- Career websites must be developed by professional career counselors.
- Counselors must make clients aware of free online content.
- Online career content must be appropriate for online delivery.
- Clients must be assessed for the appropriateness of online services.
- Online counselors are to abide by the ethical standards of the profession.

- Clients must be made aware of the counselor's credentials.
- Clients must agree to the goals and cost of online services.
- Clients must be made aware of security issues and methods used to keep records confidential.
- The use of career assessments must have been tested for online delivery.
- Online counselors must abide by the same ethical guidelines of in-person counselors.

NCDA standards also provide ethical guidelines for posting and searching job databases and unacceptable counselor behaviors on the Internet.

NACE Professional Standards for College and University Career Services, under the Technology section, require that career service staff be well informed about current career-based technological applications and that these application be used appropriately to deliver career services.

ACSCI created standards for integrated career exploration software. The following are examples of software that comply with these standards: Discover by ACT, Bridges Choices, TypeFocus Careers, and comprehensive career sites such as Oregon, Virginia, Idaho, Minnesota, Wisconsin, New Jersey, and Iowa Career Information Systems.

CAREER WEBSITES

College and university career centers use websites to provide a multitude of resources that support the delivery of career services. However, because students can be overwhelmed by the amount of career information and resources, institutions might stay focused on career resources that are most beneficial for their audiences. When planning career websites, institutions may place particular importance on defining the purpose and goals. Without the focus provided by clear goals, institutions may be tempted to upload all information generally found in a career resource center. Chapter Nine describes detailed information about website planning.

Institutions can choose from several approaches for organizing online career information. Some institutions organize online career information according to functional areas, enrollment periods, or the steps in a career decision-making model. Examples of career service functional areas are choosing a major and finding a job, as well as career information, career events, and networking opportunities. An enrollment period approach would recognize that first-year students have different career needs than do graduating seniors. Organizing career information according to the steps for making a career decision might include understanding the process of career decision making, developing a personal career profile through self-assessment, exploring majors and careers, weighing the options, making a preliminary decision, creating an educational plan that leads to a particular career, and preparing for employment. Well-designed career service websites facilitate ease of use by students, employers, and alumni.

Career websites also contain information unique to the institution: contact information for career and placement personnel, workshops and other career-related events, interviewing opportunities, and job fairs. The websites may have links to college majors and the relationship of various careers to those majors. Institutional career websites may provide links to formal career assessments purchased by the college or informal assessments freely available on the Internet. The fee-based services, such as formal career interest inventories, are typically located behind a secure portal where students may also be able to save their assessment results for later review.

In addition to information unique to a particular institution, institutions' websites provide additional resources through links to a variety of for-profit, nonprofit, and governmental career websites (Jencius & Rainey, 2009). The for-profit websites might be job search sites such as Monster.com or Quintessential Careers. Nonprofit sites may include professional associations that represent a variety of occupations. Government agencies such as the Department of Labor provide career information from two frequently visited sites: the Occupational Outlook Handbook and O*NET Online. Institutions are aware that online career related information is abundant. It is important for institutions to make judicious decisions about what information is of most use to their target audiences.

ONLINE CAREER CENTERS

The NACE 2010–2011 *Career Services Benchmark Survey for Four-Year Colleges and Universities* surveyed 750 four-year college and university career center and provides a perspective about how institutions are delivering online career services.

Respondents reported

- 68% offer online counseling.
- 70% have established a career center Facebook page (59% the previous year).
- 36% have established a Twitter presence.
- Career services websites and online job posting are the most commonly used technologies.
- Online job postings and online interview scheduling systems were rated as being the most effective online services.

Institutions are increasingly delivering online career information, as well as online interactive services such as career counseling. While some students may want more interactive online services that are available around the clock, others will want to come on campus to meet with career service professionals. A blend of on-campus and online—synchronous and asynchronous—services may be the best combination.

ASYNCHRONOUS AND SYNCHRONOUS INTERACTIVITY

Comprehensive online career information is important, but it may not be sufficient for students to make college major or career decisions. Historically, many students make career decisions while meeting face-to-face with a career professional. The personal relationship between student and career professional can be replicated in the online environment. Online interaction might take one of two forms. The first is asynchronous when students and professionals are connected through the Internet but located in different places and signing into a site at different times. The second is synchronous interaction when participants sign in from different locations but are online at the same time. Synchronous sessions provide opportunities for live interaction. Institutions may consider various technologies that facilitate both types of online interaction.

Asynchronous interaction is common in online courses through discussion boards in learning management systems (LMS) and in many social networking service (SNS) applications such as Facebook and Twitter. Interestingly, software that was designed for asynchronous interaction is adding synchronous functions. Both learning management systems and social networking applications are adding a function that allows users to see who is signed into the application at the same time. This encourages live, usually text-based interaction. There is a growing recognition of the value of immediacy provided when users can spontaneously interact with one another. Even though asynchronous applications are adding synchronous functionality, the preponderance of online communication occurs with users separated by time and place.

On the other hand, videoconferencing software applications were developed to leverage the benefits of online synchronous interactivity. This type of software allows participants to replicate much of what is done in a traditional classroom setting by using text, audio, video, a whiteboard, file sharing, and much more for teaching and learning. These virtual classrooms allow a career professional to deliver a PowerPoint presentation, assemble students into small groups to discuss a topic, and then reassemble them back to the main classroom to deliver a summary of their deliberations. The session can be recorded and archived for those who are unable to attend the live session and for review purposes for those who were present. Virtual classroom applications create an online experience that comes closest to the type of interactivity that occurs when career professionals meet with students in person.

These applications have many uses in the delivery of career services. Career development courses have been taught online since the beginning of the twenty-first century. While the primary delivery platform for online career courses has been from learning management systems using primarily asynchronous communication tools, videoconferencing software can be used for one-to-one and for group interactivity. For example, individual sessions between student and career professional can take place within the desktop conferencing software for career assessment interpretation and to practice job interviewing skills. Group sessions might include a faculty lecture, student presentations, and small group discussions. Students can use the text or audio functions to get answers to their questions during the live lectures. Students find great value in being able to replay the session recordings.

Asynchronous tools such as social networking sites and discussion boards inside learning management systems can be used for interactions among groups of students (organized according to major, by internship interests, or into a number of other groupings) to share resources and communicate about topics of mutual interest. Guest lecturers from the community or alumni might visit these sites to provide expert perspectives on the careers being considered by groups of students.

For several years, career professionals have been working with students at a distance using a number of communication devices, some synchronous and other asynchronous: first by phone, then by email, and most recently by learning management systems, videoconferencing applications, and a variety of Web 2.0 technologies. As students ponder their choice of college major and future occupations, they can collaborate with professionals using tools such as Google Docs, social networking sites such as Facebook, video sharing sites such as YouTube, photo sharing sites such as Flickr, and virtual worlds such as Second Life (Jencius & Rainey, 2009).

INNOVATIVE PRACTICES

Some institutions are using emerging technologies to present more dynamic information. The San Jose State University Career Center Exploring Majors and Career website is an example of an online multimedia approach to help students understand the relationship between majors and careers. Students are encouraged to download materials and actively participate in a self-paced tutorial. This approach may work for students who are motivated to make a decision about their college major and career; however, many students need a more structured approach, such as a career development course facilitated by a career professional.

Institutions have embraced a number of ways to organize and share occupational information. Purdue University uses a wiki to organize occupational information because a wiki is easy to keep current and allows many people to contribute to content development. The University of Pennsylvania Career Center uses Facebook to create a community of students interested in sharing career information. The Facebook site is notable because it has created Regional Network Groups whose members share housing information and provide networking opportunities for University of Pennsylvania students and alumni in nine metropolitan U.S. cities, one general International Network, and one group specifically for India. The University of Pennsylvania Facebook page provides podcasts for using Web 2.0 tools, staying safe online, and finding a job.

Rutgers University, recognizing that their graduates are located all over the United States and perhaps the world, offers online career counseling for alums. The institution contracts with ReadyMinds, an organization that trains online counselors and provides online counseling services. The training and services are approved by the National Board of Certified Counselors.

College and university career center websites are among the most comprehensive services available online. Whether they primarily deliver static career information or have dynamic career services delivered using synchronous and asynchronous technologies, well-designed career websites can be very helpful for students who need to determine college major and future career. Online career services are important to the success of all students.

PERSONAL COUNSELING

The focus of personal counseling at colleges and universities is to help students with stressors that interfere with their capacity to achieve their academic goals. Campus counseling centers offer individual and group counseling. These campus-based services typically follow a short-term counseling model. With limited institutional budgets and resources, students cannot always receive counseling support. If a student has needs that exceed the capacity of the college or university counseling center, the student may be referred to a resource in the community.

Ninety-four percent of four-year college and university counseling center directors report that the number of students arriving on campus with significant psychological problems is a growing concern, and 71% report that the number of students with severe psychological problems increased in the 2008–2009 academic year (Barr, Rando, Krylowicz, & Winfield, 2010). There is no question that some students served by institutions of higher learning are coming to college with mental health issues, some of which create barriers to their academic success. Many institutions are making information about mental health issues available from college websites.

COLLEGE AND UNIVERSITY COUNSELING CENTERS

Most counseling center websites would be considered Generation 2 or 3 in their presentation of personal counseling information. Of the 323 college and university counseling center websites listed on the Counseling Center Village Directory hosted by the University of Buffalo, most provide a description of on-campus personal counseling services, biographies of staff, relevant campus events such as workshops and other prevention and educational activities, emergency and referral resources, self-help information, training and internship information, links to Internet resources, and peer education programs. California State University, Long Beach and San Diego State University have online faculty assistance materials with referral resources and guidelines about how faculty can assist students who come to them with a variety of psychosocial issues.

Some centers provide other resources, such as the article "Coping with College" on the Illinois State University website, the Seton Hall University online mental health screenings, or information on St. Mary's College of Maryland's website that associates counseling services to the developmental tasks of college students. College and university counseling centers are closely associated with and provide a link to a number of other campus departments, such as the multicultural affairs, disabled student services, and career planning and placement. Twelve percent of college and university personal counseling centers are fully integrated with health services, as is reflected in how they present both services on the web (Barr et al., 2010).

A few colleges have interactive, Generation 4 personal counseling resources. Randolph-Macon College has an online registration form for counseling services. Go Ask Alice from Columbia

University archives previous questions and responses and has a special section on topics related to Emotional Well-Being. Cornell University uses Dear Uncle Ezra, an online counselor, who provides advice to students anonymously. Duke University uses the Healthy Devil to provide answers to students' health concerns. Self-help assessments can be found at Fairfield and Santa Clara Universities.

College and university counseling centers are using Web 2.0 technologies. Hsiung (2009) found the following uses of Web 2.0 technologies: college and university counseling centers that have a page or group on Facebook (35), Twitter account (3), Blogs (2), and one, the University of Cincinnati, that had an island in Second Life. Certainly these numbers would be larger if the survey was done today.

EXTERNAL RESOURCES

Many college and university counseling centers link to self-help mental health resources that are developed and maintained by outside organizations such as the Unabridged Student Counseling Virtual Pamphlet Collection (developed and maintained by Robert Hsiung). This site links to college and university resources in the following categories: alcohol and substance use, anger, anxiety, assertiveness, attention-deficit disorder, counseling, cults, cultural issues, depression, disabilities, eating disorders, family and childhood issues, grief, impulse control, medication, relationships, sexual assault, sexual harassment, sexual orientation, sleep, stress, study skills, test-taking, time management, traumatic events, wellness, and writing. There is a section for concerned others that links to resources from over 80 institutions for audiences such as friends, parents, faculty, and staff with concerns about the behavior of a particular student.

A total of 1200 colleges and universities participate in the ULifeline network, which is an anonymous, confidential, online resource center targeted at college students looking for mental health and suicide prevention information and services. It provides students with information about helping themselves or a friend and the resources for finding help in their community or on their campus, if it is part of the network. This organization awards innovation grants. All of the six grantees listed on the website were awarded to institutions developing innovative on-campus-based services: Hartwick College for a Peer-Helping Service, Long Island University Brooklyn Campus for an Academic Anxiety Screening Service, Pennsylvania State University Altoona for a Program to Assess and Transform Health, Philadelphia University for a Twelve Month Calendar to educate parents about developmental issues of college students, Stony Brook University for a Meditation Program for Academic Success, and University of Minnesota Twin Cities for a program to help parents distinguish between the blues and depression. Although it does not appear that colleges and universities are making personal counseling services available online, those services have been available from private practitioners since the beginning of the twenty-first century.

Private Online Counselors

Relevant literature provided by the Center for the Study of Technology in Counseling and Career Development at Florida State University reveals that clients with the following concerns are seeking online counseling: relationship development, stress-related disorders, suicide prevention and support, eating disorders, depression, fear of public speaking, panic disorder and agoraphobia, social phobia, epilepsy, substance abuse, and post-traumatic stress disorder. The Center also has conducted many studies about the process and efficacy of online counseling. Private practitioners are using a variety of technologies to deliver online counseling. Some online counselors use audio only, while others combine audio and video. Voice Over Internet Protocol free services such as Skype facilitate interactivity between counselor and client from anywhere in the world. These practitioners are guided in their work by standards and principles set forth by the National Board for Certified Counselors (NBCC) in *The Practice of Internet Counseling*, 2005. In addition to abiding by the ethical standards of all NBCC counselors, online counselors must

- Authenticate the identity of the client.
- Obtain parental/guardian consent if the client is a minor.

- Explain the procedures for contacting the counselor when she is offline and specify expected response time.
- Explain the possibility of technical problems and identify alternative methods of communication.
- Explain the possibilities of misunderstanding when visual cues do not exist.
- Identify counseling professionals in the clients' locale.
- Create barrier-free websites in compliance with ADA and the Rehabilitation Act.
- Be sensitive to different cultures and time zones and local events that may impact clients.
- Communicate issues of confidentiality.
- Communicate how long archives of sessions or email records will be preserved.
- Follow customary procedures for releasing client information.
- Make credentials, legal and ethical codes of practice available to clients with links to all certification bodies and licensure boards (*The Practice of Internet Counseling*, 2005).

As of the writing of this book, college and university counseling centers are offering many personal counseling-related information resources to assist students with mental health issues, but typically not online personal counseling.

HEALTH AND WELLNESS

There is a wide range of health services available on college campuses. Some colleges do not have health services, while other colleges and universities have fully staffed health clinics. Many institutions are members of the American College Health Association (ACHA). The ACHA does not have specific policies or guidelines that address the needs of distance learners. Rather, the ACHA General Standards of Ethical Principles and Guidelines apply to all students. Of particular interest to all institutions is the principle of maintaining standards of confidentiality when using electronic means for health and wellness communication. Institutions must keep in mind issues of confidentiality as they strive to engage and educate students through interactive online health and wellness services. One example is Virginia Tech (VT), which provides students a secure Online Student Health Portal where they can make appointments, receive secure messages from the health center, and view immunization records.

HEALTH AND WELLNESS WEBSITES

Institutions' health services websites may contain the following information:

- Scope of health services
- Policies and procedures about how to obtain health services
- How to make appointments
- How the college community will be notified in case of emergency
- Insurance
- Billing
- Pharmacy
- Medical leave of absence policies, procedures, and forms
- Health and wellness information

Institutions typically organize health and wellness information according to individual topics or by categories. One approach is to organize information in six broad categories: general health and wellness, addiction and substance abuse, sexual health, diet and nutrition, mental health, and safety and violence. Another approach is used by Virginia Tech as a result of a health and wellness information needs assessment of online learners (Scheer & Lockee, 2003). The researchers asked online learners what wellness services they would use if the resources were linked inside their online course. Their survey questions covered the categories of Intellectual, Social, Occupational, Emotional, Spiritual, and Physical Wellness. They used those categories to organize resources as they developed the Online Wellness Resource Center (Scheer & Lockee, 2003). In the decade after this study was conducted, Virginia Tech created a comprehensive health services website, with internally developed resources and links to external wellness websites. Whatever approach an institution employs, the addition of an A-Z subject index helps users find information.

INNOVATIVE PRACTICES

Health alerts may be posted on an institution's health services website or delivered to students through email, instant message, a call system, blogs, wikis, or social network sites. Institutions are providing social networking sites, such as Facebook, as places for students to ask questions of professionals and engage with other students. For example, Ohio State University uses its Student Health Services Facebook page to provide information and encourage discussion about current topics, events, and services. Students can access YouTube health videos or go to other external resources related to health issues. The Really Simple Syndication (RSS) feed allows students to subscribe to the health blog, a good way for students to keep current on health issues. Ohio State University tags its blog articles to indicate the main topics included in each article. Because tagging results in an organizational structure of content that is automated and easy to understand, students can readily find the health topics of most interest to them. Ohio State University Student Health Services provides an example of how students can be kept informed electronically about health-related issues.

Until recently, college and university personal counseling and health and wellness services were typically separate departments with individual reporting lines and functional responsibilities. At some institutions those separations are beginning to blur. When institutions develop online services that are driven by the needs of the student, institutions seamlessly present content from both personal counseling and health and wellness services, regardless of whether they are joined organizationally. When an institution adopts this approach to developing online student services, the action is known colloquially as "breaking down the silos." For further details about health and wellness resources and innovative practices, revisit the Personal Counseling section of this chapter.

ETHICAL AND LEGAL SERVICES

Online ethical and legal services are designed to ensure that online students have access to legal services provided by an attorney and/or ombudsperson. The focus is on communicating students' rights and providing services to remotely located learners if those rights are violated. The core component of this service is to provide an avenue for students to seek redress if institutional ethical policies and procedures are violated. As with other services to remotely located students, it is important that this service be equal to that which is available for on-campus students.

If students are accused of cheating in an online course, the institution should have procedures that accommodate remotely located students. At a minimum, a student accused of dishonesty should know whom to contact and the steps to follow to address the accusation. Some schools have ombudsperson services to support students through this process. It is important to make contact information available along with academic honesty policies and procedures.

This book discusses various ethical issues related to online learning and student services. Chapter Six (under Assessment and Testing) discusses issues of cheating and academic honesty. Chapter Ten discusses an institution's responsibility to authenticate the identity of online learners, a requirement of the 2008 Higher Education Opportunity Act. Chapter Six (under Academic Advising and Counseling, and Library) and Chapter Seven (under Personal Counseling, and Health and Wellness) discuss ethical standards of professional conduct for delivering online services.

INNOVATIVE PRACTICE

Kansas State University (KSU) created a one-credit Development and Integrity course in 2000. Prior to this course, if a student violated the institution's honor code, a commonly used sanction was to fail the students and post an "XF" on the student's transcript, indicating the student had failed due to academic dishonesty. KSU created the Development and Integrity course to respond to an interest in helping the student learn from the experience and be able to remove the designator from the transcript that the failure was due to dishonesty. An online version of this course was developed and delivered in the spring term 2008. This version is fully accessible to on-campus and online students who have violated the honor code (Roberts & Hai-Jew, 2009).

CONCLUSION

As institutions establish more interactive online services, they may look for ways to blend the high-tech and high-touch services described in the Personal Services Suite. Orientation services, career services, personal counseling, and academic advising from the Academic Services Suite are perhaps the services that have the most potential to impact student success and retention and are the most challenging to deliver effectively online. These services, when offered on campus, are frequently based on the relationship that develops between student and professional. Institutions are challenged to find ways to deliver these services when students do not come to campus. Development of interactive services in these areas are in their infancy. Institutions are faced with how to creatively develop and deliver these services to support the success of online learners. Institutions will benefit by working collaboratively with consortia and peer institutions and through associations such as NACADA (Distance Learning Advising Commission) and WCET to share innovative practices that help students overcome barriers to success.

CHAPTER EIGHT

COMMUNICATIONS SUITE

Institutions are striving to determine the best way to communicate at a distance with their students, faculty, and other audiences. They are challenged in their efforts to determine which electronic tools are most effective for specific goals and purposes.

EFFECTIVE ONLINE COMMUNICATION

Effective communication occurs when the receiver understands a message just as the sender intends. In face-to-face communications, the parties benefit from using the five senses, nonverbal cues, body language, facial expression, and/or voice intonation in assessing and understanding the intended meaning of the message. These benefits are not available in most online communications. However, even face-to-face communication does not guarantee complete accuracy. Given the complexity added by the separation of time and place and by using text-only means of conveying messages, institutions acknowledge the challenges of accurate online communication. This chapter reviews strategies for selecting technology that maximizes the effectiveness of electronic communication that supports the needs of online learners.

TEXT-ONLY COMMUNICATION

Institutions may want to examine ways to improve the effectiveness of their text-based online communication: for example, communication of information from an institution's website, from within an online course, and from Web 2.0 applications.

Institutions might want to consider when to use formal communication and when to use informal and personal communication. However, institutions may find that a few basic ideas apply to most text-based electronically delivered communications: develop a clear writing style, be concise while providing sufficient detail for understanding, and deliver information in small chunks.

Betts (2009b) recommends that institutions carefully note the tone of online communication; that is, the choice of words and how those words are put together to convey the sender's attitude. For example, many student service professionals as part of their in-person interactions with students show concern and empathy, two core feelings that professionals can also express in online communication. When determining the best tone, institutions may want to ensure that the media type they use is the best vehicle for engaging the intended audience. For example, using Facebook to deliver a message sets a tone different from that when using email.

Institutions may also want to answer various questions before deciding which form of communication best accomplishes the intended goal. Should the communication be private or is there value in publically communicating the message? Does the content necessitate a secure environment because of privacy and confidentiality concerns? Is the purpose of the message to inform, engage, instruct, or promote? And, perhaps most important, how does the form of presentation and tone respond to the needs of the target audience? The institutions' thoughtful consideration of and answers to these questions can improve the effectiveness of online text-based communication.

MULTIMEDIA COMMUNICATION

Multimedia communication is the expression of thoughts using two or more of the following: text, graphics, audio files, video, music, photos, and/or animation. Face-to-face interaction typically involves audio and visual elements, and it is virtually always a form of multimedia communication. This is not the case with online communication. A large body of research supports the importance of using multimedia in online communication (Mandernach, 2009).

When examining the seven principles of multimedia learning, institutions may want to focus on the *personalization principle:* in-depth learning is more likely when words in a multimedia presentation are conversational rather than formal. Subsumed within this principle is the finding that learning is facilitated when messages are spoken by a human rather than a mechanical voice and that people do not necessarily learn more from multimedia presentations when the speaker's image is included on the screen. This principle is supported by a body of empirical research (Mayer, 2005).

Mandernach (2009) conducted a mixed-method study comparing two identical courses taught by the same instructor; the only difference was that one course included multimedia supplements and the other did not. The study measured the impact of instructor-personalized multimedia supplements on student engagement in an online course. While the quantitative results showed no significant difference in engagement or learning, the qualitative feedback clearly indicated that the multimedia supplements provided a positive learning experience.

If institutions move from text only to incorporating audio and video in their online student services, they may bring back high-touch elements that have historically characterized the delivery of student services. Students feel more connected to the institution when they have a perception that the electronic communications are personalized. Institutions might strive to make the students' experiences with the virtual campus as hospitable, inviting, and worthwhile as those available at the physical campus.

ISOLATION

Institutions may find it important to keep in mind how some students experience the online learning environment. Various studies have reported that online students may have a feeling of isolation, a risk factor that may contribute to their lack of success (Bambara, Harbour, Davies, & Athey, 2009; Lee & Chan, 2007; Ludwig-Hardman & Dunlap, 2003; McInnerney & Roberts, 2004; McPherson & Nunes, 2004; Walker, 2007; Willging & Johnson, 2004). Bambara et al. studied community college online courses defined as high risk (a course with withdrawal rates of 30% or higher). The studies revealed the common theme of students' feeling isolated. Contributing to the sense of isolation were a static environment that lacked interactivity between student and instructor and among students, and a sense that the learning environment was not real, but merely a space where instructional materials had been made available to students for self-paced learning. Students described instructors as either not responsive or providing monosyllabic responses or feedback. One commented that the grades seemed to be automatically generated. When Lee and Chan (2007) studied the use of supplementary audio podcasts to reduce anxiety caused by isolation, they found that hearing an instructor's voice may promote a sense of inclusivity. With these positive results, they suggest that podcasting has potential to aid online students with their integration into the social and academic life of the institution, despite the physical separation.

Unquestionably, online instructors can play a significant role in helping students overcome a sense of isolation. However, Ludwig-Hardman and Dunlap (2003) also found that support services helped students overcome a sense of isolation, lack of direction, and low motivation. The McInnerney and Roberts (2004) study suggested the use of supplementary synchronous communication tools to assist with the development of online community. They found that the online environment is made more personal and less mechanical by the power of voice, the ability of interacting live with the instructor and other students, and the spontaneity that generates feelings of trust. See sections about multimedia tutorials and virtual classroom applications later in this chapter. The studies examining student isolation both inside and outside the online classroom confirm that isolation is a real concern. Institutions may conclude that interventions can make a difference in issues of isolation, especially for students who do not come to campus.

COMMUNITY OF INQUIRY

The Community of Inquiry (CoI) framework, developed about ten years ago, is designed to define, describe, and measure elements of collaboration and meaningful educational experiences.

Institutions may use the CoI framework, in particular the concept of social presence, to better understand how to effectively communicate with online students and to select media that facilitate meaningful interaction. Although most studies of these concepts are based on online course instruction, the research findings include suggestions that may help student service professionals understand how to respond to the needs of online students. These concepts contribute to an institution's understanding of how to develop a welcoming virtual campus that facilitates online students' connection to the institution, faculty, student service providers, and other students. These connections seem to help students overcome feelings of isolation. However, further research is needed to validate a connection, but the idea is compelling enough to consider for a discussion about how to create a welcoming virtual campus.

The Community of Inquiry framework is based on three elements and how they interact with one another: *social presence, cognitive presence,* and *teaching presence.* Social presence, viewed as an emotional sense of belonging, is most relevant for the discussion of online student services. Social presence has three dimensions: participants identifying with the community, communicating purposefully in a trusting environment, and developing interpersonal relationships (Garrison, 2009 as cited in Garrison, Anderson, & Archer, 2010). Social presence is further defined as the ability of learners to project themselves socially and emotionally in an online environment, as well as to perceive others with whom they interact as real people (Gunawardena & Zittle, as cited in Garrison & Arbaugh, 2007).

Research has identified three main factors that allow for effective projection and establishment of social presence: *affective expression, open communication,* and *group cohesion* (Boston, Diaz, Gibson, Ice, Richardson, & Swan, 2009). Affective expression, which includes emotional content when appropriate, contributes to making the interaction feel real. Open communication contributes to the development of a trusting environment. Both affective expression and open communication contribute to the development of interpersonal relationships and group cohesion in online courses. These factors facilitate the ability of participants to identify with and feel like a member of an online community.

Briefly, cognitive presence is the extent to which students learn through reflection and discourse. It is a four-stage process: triggering event, exploration, integration, and resolution. Teaching presence has a three-part structure: instructional design and organization, facilitation of discourse, and direct instruction (Boston et al., 2009). Though both are important for effective online instruction, cognitive and teaching presence are less relevant for the delivery of services for online students.

Boston et al. (2009) used an instrument, the Community of Inquiry Survey, which was developed based on this framework, to explore whether the CoI Survey could predict students' likelihood of remaining in an online program of study. The CoI Survey was administered to 28,877 students attending American Public University, an online, for-profit institution. The CoI survey contains 34 items, 21 of which were found to be statistically significant predictors of reenrollment. All but one of the social presence indicators (five out of six) were a significant predictor of reenrollment, suggesting that social presence in general and affective expression in particular are important determinants of persistence. The authors of this study suggest that these findings have profound implications for academic and student affairs. Student affairs may be especially interested in the study's suggestion that programming designed to enhance student engagement may need to include opportunities for online interaction (Boston et al., 2009).

Effective online communication is not easily defined, nor is there a formula for communicating with online students that is appropriate for all circumstances. Institutions may look at the culture of their physical campus and attempt to communicate that culture online. Institutions without a physical presence may create a unique online culture. Whether it is text only or various combinations of social and multimedia, students will derive a sense of the institution by the way online information is presented. Engaging and personalized presentations assist online students in overcoming a feeling of isolation.

STUDENT ENGAGEMENT

"Student engagement represents the time and effort students devote to activities that are empirically linked to desired outcomes

of college and what institutions do to induce student to participate in these activities" (Kuh, 2009). When institutions measure
student engagement, they consider the quality of the learning
experience both inside and outside the classroom, focusing on
interventions that they can provide to improve a student's educational experience that facilitates progress toward completing
educational objectives. There is an abundance of literature that
describes activities, programs, and services that engage students
who come to campus and research that demonstrates impact on
student success. This section explores ways that the delivery of
online support services can facilitate student engagement.

For many years institutions have used the National Survey of
Student Engagement (NSSE) and the Community College Survey
of Student Engagement (CCSSE) to measure educationally
purposeful activities that lead to student engagement in five benchmark areas: *academic challenge*, defined as institutions set high
expectations and student put forth time and effort to meet
faculty expectations; *active and collaborative learning*, defined as
students collaborate with other students inside and outside the
classroom; *student-faculty interaction*, defined as faculty interact
with students and become role models, mentors, and guides, and
students seek faculty feedback and advice on careers, discipline-
based ideas, and research; *enriching educational experiences*, such as
internships, community service, senior capstone projects, independent study, and other forms of applied learning; and *supportive
campus environment*, where students build relationships and develop
skills through participation in campus activities (Kuh, 2009).

NSSE results show that measures of engagement make positive contributions to student learning and personal development
which contribute to academic success. CCSSE results show that
measures of student engagement are positively associated with
persistence and academic achievement (Kuh, 2009). While these
instruments were designed and are used primarily with on-campus
students, their theoretical basis, the *Seven Principles of Good Practice
in Undergraduate Education*, is also relevant for online students
(Chen, Lambert, & Guidry, 2010; Chen, Gonyea, & Kuh, 2008;
Robinson & Hullinger, 2008).

There have only been a few studies that examine the engagement of online learners. A review of literature describing three
studies using NSSE results and one study using CCSSE results

provides insight that can be used to develop online student services that facilitate student engagement. As part of the 2006 administration of NSSE, a question was asked to identify survey participants who, during the term in which the study was conducted, were taking all of their courses online. In addition to the 3,894 students identified by this question, 35 institutions agreed to ask 14 more questions on the 2006 NSSE that further explored online learning issues. Analysis of these responses found that online students are as engaged or more engaged than campus-based students (Chen, Gonyea, & Kuh, 2008).

Online learners scored higher than their on-campus counter-parts on the following measures of student engagement:

- Academic challenge, which measures amount of reading, writing, and higher-order thinking activities and amount of time spent studying
- Reflective thinking, which measures deep thinking in the areas of critically examining their view, considering the views of others, and adapting their thinking on the topic
- Practical competence, which measures career skills, interpersonal skills, and technological proficiency
- Personal and social development, which measures developing values and ethics, understanding people from diverse backgrounds, and self-understanding
- Satisfaction with educational experience

First year online students reported interacting more with faculty in the context of discussing grades, ideas from classes, and career plans. These students reported receiving prompt feedback. Fourth year online students reported that the online learning environment was more supportive and that they experienced gains in skills such as writing, speaking, and analyzing quantitative problems. Online learners reported significantly less engagement than the on-campus students in only one area: active and collaborative learning. They were less engaged in working with other students on class projects and outside of class to prepare for class assignments (Chen, Gonyea, & Kuh, 2008).

Chen, Guidry, and Lambert (2009) examined data from the 2008 administration of the NSSE to analyze the impact on student engagement of web-based technologies used to deliver course content. In their analysis, they disaggregated the findings based on the course delivery method (web only, hybrid only, some web, face-to-face and hybrid, and face-to-face only). Their overall analysis supports the positive relationship between using learning technologies and student engagement found in Chen et al. (2008). Of particular interest is the suggestion that students who participate in courses using technology would also use technology to engage in other ways with students and the institution. Institutions may reasonably conclude that as technology is increasingly infused into the curriculum, it can also be increasingly used to deliver student support services.

Another study used a modified version of the NSSE to explore the engagement of 201 students from three universities who were taking at least one online course. Only four of the five student engagement benchmarks were included in this study. The fifth benchmark, on-campus engagement, was thought not to be relevant. The NSSE results from these 201 students were compared to the total student 2006 NSSE results. Online students reported a higher level of engagement than students responding to most of the individual questions in each of the four benchmarks. The one exception was a lower level of engagement in the areas of speaking skills and some areas of student-faculty interaction (Robinson & Hullinger, 2008). These studies were conducted before institutions began using social media to engage online learners. Perhaps the use of social media may facilitate the connection of online students with the institution.

SOCIAL AND MULTIMEDIA

Selecting social and multimedia applications suitable for online student services is a complex process. This section discusses communication platforms that use text, audio, video, and graphics to present information and encourage students to become actively involved in the use and creation of educationally meaningful materials. Institutions not only can communicate content but also can engage learners through interactive, personalized, and customizable tools such as social networking services (SNS), multimedia tutorials, and virtual classroom software.

Social Networking Services (SNS)

The most popular SNS are Facebook and Twitter, where users share experiences, communicate personal information, and build community (Lester & Perini, 2010). Institutions use social networking sites in a variety of ways: as vehicles for marketing, announcing events, learning, interacting, and building community.

Institutions may recognize the great potential for using SNS for engaging online students. SNS can facilitate active learning and collaboration, core components of student engagement. Collaborative efforts can begin in the context of class assignments and continue after the end of the term because some SNS exist outside the boundaries of a learning management system. SNS make it easy to invite experts to join the site and participate in the discussion. Sometimes a true community of learners is begun: students who participate in online class discussions continue the interaction after class, thereby establishing an ongoing community of support beyond the classroom.

Examples of Social Media

Some social media websites have been around for a relatively long period, are stable, and will probably continue to be available. Others come and go on a daily, if not hourly, basis. Brian Solis and Jesse Thomas developed *The Conversation Prism,* which describes categories of social media, organized by how people use each type of network, and examples of each type of social media. Table 8.1 lists the categories and provides one example from each category. To view more examples for each category, visit the *Conversation Prism* at its website, which is found at www.theconversationprism.com.

Several SNS tools provide more than one function. For example, Facebook, while most commonly used for asynchronous communication, allows text messaging, posting links to video and audio files, signing up for events, playing games, and video conferencing via Skype. Facebook is continuously developing new functionality. Students select the media that are most relevant to them and individualize the way they use the platforms.

Table 8.1 Categories and Examples of Social Network Sites

Pictures	Flickr
Social bookmarks	Diigo
Comment and reputation	Disqus
Wisdom of the crowds	Digg
Questions and answers	Quora
Collaboration	Google Docs
Social commerce	Groupon
Blog platforms	Blogger
Blogs/conversations	Technorati
Social curation	Flipboard
Streams	Twitter
Nicheworking	Yammer
Custom social networks	Ning
Discussion boards and forums	Google Groups or Sites
Social networks	Facebook
Listening or targeting	Collecta
Attention/communication dashboards	TweetDeck
Business networking	LinkedIn
Reviews and ratings	Yelp
Location	Foursquare
Video	YouTube
Social customer relations management	Crowd Sound
Documents and contents	Slideshare
Events	Event Brite
Music	Pandora
Wiki	PB Wiki
Virtual worlds	Second Life

Source: Adapted from The Conversation Prism, www.theconversationprism.com.

Many students come to college with the knowledge and willingness to use these tools as demonstrated by the usage statistics discussed in Chapter One. Research is beginning to show evidence of an impact on student engagement and learning outcomes. Junco, Heiberger, & Loken (2010) found that students using Twitter in a pre–health professional first year seminar course were more highly engaged in the learning process and had higher grade point averages than students who did not use Twitter (Junco, Heiberger, & Loken, 2010).

However, faculty, staff, and administrators tend to be less knowledgeable than are the students and hence are less inclined to use the tools (Junco & Cole-Avent, 2008). To meet the needs of potential users, institutions may want to provide professional development for employees, and training or online tutorials for students. Two websites describe many of these tools. The Educause, *7 Things You Should Know About,* series defines individual tools, how they work, where social media are going, and why it matters to teaching and learning. A commercial site, Commoncraft.com, uses videos (*In Plain English)* to explain many aspects of technology. Both sites clearly present basic information that might be useful to those planning to develop educational applications for social media.

PLANNING FOR SOCIAL MEDIA ADOPTION AND IMPLEMENTATION

To determine the best use of social media that support the needs of online learners, institutions might carefully consider the goals of the project, the needs of the student, and the functionality of the tool. On the micro level, tactical planning is important. However, institutions may consider integrating social media planning into existing strategic planning processes, or create a new mechanism to plan for college-supported social media. The social media goals and assessments should align with the vision, mission, and strategic plans of the department that is sponsoring the application. They should also be realistic in the context of staff resources.

When institutions establish a plan to implement a variety of social media tools, it is important to ensure that staff are available to implement and support use of the tools to create meaningful student experiences. Implementation and support may include regularly posting engaging information, queries, and activities. By promoting SNS, engaging students, and creating reasons for students to return to the application, an institution improves the possibility that the SNS will contribute to the development of a welcoming virtual campus that improves student success and retention.

Social Media Policy

Junco (2011), who acknowledges the positive and negative effects of social media, suggests the following process for developing a social media policy:

- Create a social media policy committee that includes students, departmental staff, student affairs professionals, faculty members, administrators, trustees, and other members of the community.
- Make the work of the committee transparent and easily accessible by posting minutes to a website, blog, a Facebook group, or Twitter.
- The committee process should reflect how the benefits of social media can contribute to the academic and personal development of students.
- The finished product should be readable, accessible, brief, and clearly written.

He further suggests a policy that

- Has a positive tone and is designed to help the students have a positive social media experience.
- Clearly describes standards, such as how the student code of conduct applies to social media.
- Acknowledges the important contributions that connecting, collaborating, and communicating via technology make toward the development of the whole student.
- Recognizes the value of open sharing and sharing diverse opinions for civil debate.

- Includes an explanation of the limits of privacy in online social spaces.
- Emphasizes the importance of tone in online communication.
- Clearly states the expectation that students be respectful, careful, responsible, and accountable.
- Describes negative and potentially dangerous online behaviors.
- Describes consequences of online violations of social media policy.
- Provides guidance for handling negative behaviors.
- Recognizes the role of faculty and staff in modeling appropriate online behavior (Junco, 2011).

The University of Texas, Austin posts Social Media Guidelines on its website for faculty, staff, and social media community managers. The site links to related institutional policies, including the Acceptable Use Policy, Copyright and Fair Use, FERPA and Student Privacy, and Guiding Principles for Engaging with Social Media. The links also include a variety of institutional standards for developing web resources.

Multimedia Tutorials

Along with social media, multimedia tutorials can be used to teach and engage students. Institutions can develop multimedia tutorials using a variety of software applications, such as Camtasia, Captivate, Adobe Presenter, or PowerPoint. Tutorials can be developed for numerous services: library instruction, technology skill development, orientation, academic advising and planning, career services, and financial aid instruction, to name just a few. Some tutorials use audio, video, and animation and can include interactive functionality that requires students to actively participate in the tutorial. With the increased use of YouTube, professionals from the institution and resourceful students are creating multimedia products both inside and outside the classroom. These resources can be posted or linked on the institutions' websites or as part of social media tools that might further engage students into the fabric of the institution.

VIRTUAL CLASSROOM

A meta-analysis of distance learning studies found that the best learning outcomes resulted from blended learning, a combination of online and traditional classroom instruction (Means, Toyama, Murphy, Bakia, & Jones, 2009). Blended learning can also be delivered fully online. This model combines asynchronous online course formats with synchronous online sessions, using desktop videoconferencing applications, such as WebEx or Blackboard Collaborate. These virtual classroom applications most closely resemble in-person communication: while participants may be located all over the world, they meet and interact at the same time, using audio, video, file sharing, text messaging, and a whiteboard that provides opportunities to make presentations and collaborate. Virtual classrooms allow for breaking students into small groups and then bringing them back to the main classroom to continue discussions with the entire class.

In addition to course instruction, institutions have used these tools for counseling and advising, seminar and workshop presentations, orientation sessions, group meetings, career assessment interpretations, and job interview practice sessions. Virtual classroom applications are valued because they allow a session to be recorded and reviewed repeatedly, or viewed for the first time by students who could not participate in the live session. Virtual classrooms are particularly effective for developing relationships and conducting sessions that rely on spontaneous responses from participants.

Institutions that use social media, multimedia tutorials, and virtual classrooms provide numerous options for engaging and supporting online students. Innovative practices using these tools are discussed in Chapters Six and Seven. The next three sections describe innovative practices that facilitate communication between faculty and students, the institution and students, and among students.

FACULTY-TO-STUDENT

Online faculty and students communicate both inside and outside the course site, just as do on-campus faculty and students. However, in an online course, faculty members may be the only contact a student has with the institution. A common scenario may be the following: after a student registers for an online course, that student may email the instructor about how to get started or to receive clarification about course expectations. Instructors may post on the institution's website biographies, photos, research interests, publications, and other scholarly information. In an ideal world, the student visits the institution's website to find the instructor's course syllabus prior to the beginning of the course. This is the beginning of faculty-to-student communication.

QUALITY MATTERS

Once students enter the online course site, faculty members provide a variety of student support resources and functions in addition to their instructional and course management responsibilities. Quality Matters (QM) identifies standards of student support that faculty should integrate into online course design. QM, a widely recognized program for evaluating online course design, provides a rubric that defines eight categories of online course design standards (QM standards). The eight categories or *General Standards* are Course Overview and Introduction, Learning Objectives, Assessment and Measurement, Resources and Materials, Learner Engagement, Course Technology, Learner Support, and Accessibility.

Learner Support is the category most relevant for this discussion. The Learner Support *Specific Review Standards* encourage faculty members to include information about the scope, purpose, and how to access technical support, academic support, student support, and services to develop writing, research, and technical skills ("Quality Matters Rubric Standards 2008–2010 Edition with Assigned Point Values"). However, even if faculty members provide links and referral to online these services, that alone may not be sufficient to support the success of online learners. Faculty encouragement along with integration of these services into the course materials may improve the chances that students will participate in these support services. Course integration of student support services was recommended by the Community College Survey of Student Engagement (CCSSE). Results from the 2010 CCSSE survey found that many students are unaware of, or do not take advantage of, the support services that are available to them. It recommends that, to overcome these problems, faculty integrate student support into the coursework (*The Heart of Student Success: Teaching, Learning, and College Completion*, 2010).

STUDENT SUPPORT SERVICES INSIDE AN ONLINE COURSE

Many benefits accrue when an institution integrates student support services within online course content. Including support services as part of an online academic course eliminates the obstacles of students not knowing that the service exists or how to access those services. Having services as part of an online course provides the development of community as students assist other students. When faculty create assignments that require students to use writing, math, or other skill labs, as well as library services, academic advising, or online tutoring, students will learn how to access and use the service if a future need arises. When support staff are invited to become guest lecturers or answer questions on the discussion board about a service, students are provided a more comprehensive understanding of the service. When student support service tutorials are linked inside the learning management system, not only do students have easy access to the information when they need it, but also faculty can create assignments based on the tutorials to ensure that students have viewed and understood the material.

If an institution establishes a supportive virtual community both inside and outside the online classroom, it can reduce the sense of isolation felt by some online learners. Student support personnel, faculty, and other students all play significant roles in the development of a welcoming community in which students can be academically successful, develop personally, and feel connected to the institution.

FACULTY-TO-STUDENT INNOVATIVE PRACTICES

Betts (2009a) provides an example of how Drexel University's Master's of Science in Higher Education (MSHE) Program has accomplished tight integration between online course instruction and student support. The MSHE program developed *A Faculty Student Resource Portal* that includes weekly announcements, an academic calendar, learning resources, job postings, alumni interviews, photos, student biographies, a discussion board, and a newsletter.

By using this space, both students and faculty have multiple opportunities to interact, including attending a Virtual Tea and other events that are conducted throughout the year synchronously in a Virtual Classroom and in Second Life. Faculty and students discuss current issues in higher education. During these events, student support specialists are introduced to faculty and students. Two or more classes are invited to each event, giving students the opportunity to meet students from other courses and other faculty in the program.

These informal online events encourage faculty and students to engage with one another and to better understand student support resources. Students become comfortable and develop relationships with support personnel, even before they need the services. These developed relationships increase the likelihood that students will utilize online student support services (Betts, 2009a). This program, aptly named the Online Human Touch, shows how an institution can develop a welcoming virtual environment for students who may come to campus only for graduation. Additional information about this program can be found in Chapter Seven (under Orientation).

INSTITUTION-TO-STUDENT

In the not-so-distant past, institutions used their home page as their primary source to communicate emergency alerts, technical outages, events, news, announcements, and deadlines. Now, however, institutions are using various social media platforms to inform and engage audiences.

Research done by Slover-Linett and Stoner (2011), in collaboration with the Council for Advancement and Support of Education (CASE), provides a detailed view of how educational institutions (of which 76% were colleges and universities) are using social media. Facebook, Twitter, and LinkedIn are the three most frequently used platforms to communicate with alumni (92%), friends and supporters (77%), current students (66%), current faculty and staff (62%), donors (61%), prospective students (56%), parents of current students (47%), media (43%), parents of prospective students (41%), employers (37%), high school guidance counselors (26%), and government organizations (21%).

The top goals for social media are to engage alumni, create an improved brand image, engage current students, and increase awareness, advocacy, and rankings. Most institutions acknowledge they have a long way to go before they evaluate their social media efforts as successful, as demonstrated by the following survey results: 62% of the institutions responding to the survey rated their program as somewhat successful, 10% not very successful, 3% not at all successful, thus leaving only 25% very successful or a model for successful use of social media. The top barriers to success are staffing for day-to-day content management, staffing for site development, and lack of staff with expertise in how to implement social media applications (Slover-Linett & Stoner, 2010).

Management of social media is located in the following departments: 44% Communications, 40% Alumni Relations, 36% Development, 30% Marketing, 19% Advancement Services, 8% Enrollment Management/Admissions, and 9% other (Slover-Linett & Stoner, 2011). It is the responsibility of professionals within these departments to decide which platform works best for which type of institutional message. Institutions are increasingly delegating this authority to individuals with job titles such as the director of web marketing and communication or social media manager. The staff they supervise may be a combination of full-time employees and student workers, who bring to the job experience, knowledge of the platform, and credibility because of their role as a peer, along with an enthusiasm and conversational tone that resonates with the audience (Roscorla, 2011).

INSTITUTION-TO-STUDENT INNOVATIVE PRACTICES

Many institutions are at the beginning stages of planning and implementing broad-based use of social media. However, some institutions have already embraced innovative practices. The whitepaper from the 2010 Stoner and CASE survey found Oregon State University (OSU) to be the best example of a coordinated social media deployment. OSU uses Facebook, Twitter, LinkedIn, Flickr, YouTube, blogs, and a Google map Mashup to communicate with many constituencies. Applications are launched from a well-organized Social Media Directory. The activity on these platforms is substantial. For example: 70,418 people have "liked" the OSU Facebook page, the OSU YouTube page has 145,185 channel views and 1,576,648 total views, the OSU Twitter account has 2,020 tweets and 4,223 followers. Many departments have individual pages on each of these platforms. It did not appear that any applications were specifically targeted to the needs of online learners.

Although services that an institution puts online are available to all students (including online learners), Pennsylvania State University (PSU) World Campus provides an assortment of multimedia tutorials and social media applications specifically targeted to the needs of online learners. These tutorials include an orientation to online learning and to college; information about financial aid, a military student welcome video, how to use the learning management system, how to use the academic and financial systems; and individual tutorials about how the institution is using YouTube, LinkedIn, Flickr, Twitter, and Facebook. Visitors can access the student blog from World Campus home page. Users can access direct links to the most recent entries and a topical organization of past entries from the social media launch page, called "Bleed Blue & White." Students can also find links from the Academic Advising entry page. PSU has infused social media throughout their comprehensive portal for online students.

STUDENT-TO-STUDENT

Student-to-student interactions are a core component of the college experience. Institutions can facilitate relationship building between students through a variety of electronic means. For example, online students who do not come to campus may have difficulty making connections with other online students, especially those who are not in their courses. To assist students in overcoming these difficulties, institutions may make available student contact information, including biographies, photos, email addresses, personal websites, and Facebook, Twitter, or LinkedIn account names through a student directory. Students may search the directory by last name, department, major, research interests, or nonacademic interests. Institutions can facilitate relationship building between students through a variety of electronic means.

STUDENT ACTIVITIES

Institutions cannot overemphasize how important it is for their online students to feel and to be connected to the institution. It is one factor that leads to academic success and improved rates of retention. Online student activities may be one approach colleges can use to engage online learners. The college experience of online learners can be enhanced when they have access to and are interested in participating in online student activities such as an online newspaper, student government, and special interest clubs and organizations.

Some schools develop virtual student unions, web-based portals that link all student activities. If an institution plans a virtual student union, the institution may adopt a strategic planning approach just as it would if it were developing an on-campus program. As part of the planning process, it may adopt a mission, vision, and goals; do an assessment of audience interests and needs; identify resources, including an advisor; market the program; and measure outcomes.

STUDENT ACTIVITIES INNOVATIVE PRACTICES

The website of the Associated Students of Washington State University Online Degree Programs (ASWSU-Online) describes the organization as a supportive leadership organization that serves as an advocate for online students and that meets their nonacademic needs and interests. The goals and objectives are to increase online students' awareness of resources, strengthen their relationships with the larger college community, raise their awareness of online learning, foster online student achievements, and build a sense of community within the online student body. The website provides links to leaders, events, how to get involved, how to communicate, a home town locator, and resources. Committee meetings are held via video conferencing software that is accessible to all students with an Internet-connected computer.

University of Maryland University College (UMUC) takes a different approach. Clubs and organizations at UMUC are structured around college majors and "meet" inside the learning management system. Student leaders and faculty advisors work together to bring additional information, relevant activities, and answers to questions from participants to the club or organization LMS site. The objectives are the following:

- Social integration—to create a global community of students with similar interests.
- Professional exploration—to provide networking opportunities and help students learn about potential careers.
- Student development—to encourage students to participate in scholarly, leadership, and community activities outside the classroom.
- Navigation of the university—to create a central location where students can go to ask questions and receive program updates and announcements (Hintz, 2010).

All club spaces in the learning management system allow students to introduce themselves to one another and include a discussion board for information and experience exchanges. Some clubs sponsor other activities, such as guest speakers who present seminars, book discussions, writer's workshops, and charity drives. Online clubs provide a venue for honors society and professional meetings. Some clubs have Facebook and LinkedIn accounts to encourage communication of a more public nature.

Because most UMUC students are busy adults and reside in many different time zones, they cannot always come to synchronous sessions. Yet they are still accommodated, as most clubs also conduct ongoing, asynchronous activities. A survey of 250 online club members during 2008 found that 80% participated to network with faculty and students, learn about their field of study and relevant careers, and gather additional information; 73% were satisfied with the amount of information received and the level of activity within the club (Hintz, 2010).

Institutions can facilitate student engagement outside the online classroom through the effective use of online student activities. As with social media applications, the easy part is creating clubs and organizations; the challenge is to solicit and maintain meaningful participation. To meet this challenge requires the work, cooperation, and dedicated leadership of students and a faculty advisor. Adult online students are interested in connecting not only with other students but also with faculty, staff, and professionals in the field in which they may seek future employment opportunities.

Student-to-Student Innovative Practices

Many colleges and universities are using Facebook to communicate with students. However, a May 2011 Facebook search for online learning or distance education resulted in very few college or university pages specifically targeted for online learners. For those distance learning departments that have a Facebook presence, the staff was using the space to make announcements. Professionals, not students, were contributing on these spaces and there was little if any activity between students. Because adult online learners tend to be very busy students, perhaps social media applications may not always be the best approach to helping this population develop a sense of community with other online students. Adult students might be more inclined to use social media if institutions offered options that were more closely aligned to online learners' needs and concerns. Washington State University (WSU) uses Virtual Mentors to help build community and overcome feelings of isolation. Virtual Mentors are experienced, motivated students who are available to students inside the online course site. These mentors can answer most questions not directly related to the content of the course.

What does it take to develop a community of online learners outside of the online classroom? Rio Salado Community College answered this question by creating an online student union where 20,268 students have uploaded 3,979 pictures, posted 2,463 notes, and set 695 goals for themselves in the first six months of 2011. In this password-protected space, students can study, meet people, participate in discussions, and set goals for themselves. They have access to articles, videos, and surveys about online study skills, balancing work and school, and help with majors and careers. Students can personalize their profiles, upload photos, find students with similar interests, and start a discussion about something they learned in class or share tips about being a successful online student. Only enrolled students at the college can use this restricted private space ("RioLounge," 2011).

Because student-to-student community building is important to the retention and success of online students, institutions might consider a variety of options that may be meaningful as a way for online students to connect with one another.

CONCLUSION

This chapter discusses issues that institutions are addressing as they plan and implement strategies for communicating with online students via a variety of emerging technology platforms. In line with expectations of students, institutions are starting to use social media and virtual classroom platforms. The innovative practices described in this chapter illustrate the point that institutions are in the early stages of figuring out how to use social media applications to deliver online student services.

Only a few institutions have taken a strategic approach to the deployment of these new tools. At other institutions, someone in a particular department may have made an ad hoc decision to pilot these applications. Some social media in particular have been around for almost as long as has web-based learning, but just recently have these media started to be deployed at colleges and universities to engage students.

When planning for social media deployment, institutions might want to align mission, vision, goals, audience needs, and staffing requirements as they add these platforms to current forms of communication. Institutions are just beginning to benchmark and assess whether social media will have a sufficient return on the investment of resources required to develop, implement, and support these tools. Although website traffic is the easiest and most common measure, it does not tell an institution whether a student's experience using these tools has contributed to the student's academic or personal development. Measuring impact of social media is an important part of implementation planning.

CHAPTER NINE

PLANNING AND IMPLEMENTATION

Institutions may be investigating ways to improve their online student services. To do so, they may establish a plan that, when implemented, meets the needs of an ever-expanding base of students who want easy access to online learning and support services. Institutions may choose from various approaches. One approach is to adopt and follow a planning process already in place at the institution. Or, after considering the needs of its online student population, an institution might conclude that a new planning process is the best choice to improve online student services.

Strategic planning for online student services might become a part of each campus-based department's strategic planning process. Or perhaps the development of online student services might be a component of a strategic plan for the design and delivery of an institution's website. Online student services, as defined in this book, encompass a significant percentage of the content on institution's websites. Whether strategic planning for online student services originates from the department charged with developing the institution's website, the office of distance learning, or student and academic affairs departments, it is important that all stakeholders collaborate in the planning, implementation, maintenance, assessment, and improvement of online student services.

Collaboration is a key component to effective strategic planning for online student services. Institutions may decide to bring together teams of key stakeholders to make decisions about the most effective ways to serve students who are remotely located or local students who prefer using online services. Teams established to develop online student services might be composed of representatives from areas of the institution who have different motivations for putting services online. For example, some may have a substantial interest in placing all services online, while others may be concerned with the potential decreased demand for face-to-face services. One department may be interested in providing increased access for remotely located students for the purpose of increasing enrollment, while another may be concerned with enforcing course placement and prerequisite requirements, which may be seen as a barrier to growth. These and other differences may need to be addressed early in the planning process.

Most stakeholders have many shared values, such as the importance of providing a consistent message from the various departments by improving the accuracy and currency of all online information. The institution may acknowledge that quality online student services are enhanced when strategic planning involves a coordinated effort from stakeholders across the institution.

Because of the complexities of the processes and the ever-present issues of responsibilities, an institution may anticipate friction that might potentially derail the team's planning process. Understanding that some friction might be unavoidable, throughout the planning process the planning group might focus on open and continuous communication, stressing inclusiveness, respect for colleagues, and, most important, keeping the needs of students at the forefront of discussions and decisions.

If an institution's ultimate goal is to develop a full array of online student services, its planning process will be rigorous, comprehensive, and attentive to details. An institution may have already identified objectives for starting or expanding its distance learning program and may recognize that in order for online students to be successful they may need to complete most or all transactional services at a distance.

Institutions are sometimes motivated to develop a strategic plan for developing online student services in response to low online course rates of retention. The discussion of developing an online student service strategic plan may begin with an analysis of what is known about online student rates of retention.

Online Student Retention

To define retention in the context of online learning means over-coming some obstacles. Broad-based studies that provide year-to-year retention rates across multiple institutions for students taking all of their courses online currently do not exist. Many students take a combination of online and on-campus courses, and many online students are enrolling as part-time students. Many institutions that offer online courses do not offer a full range of online programs. For these reasons, this chapter defines retention as whether a student successfully completes an online course.

Retention rates for online students are hard to find. Currently, no national statistics exist. Individual schools do measure online course retention and program retention. Because each institution is unique, findings are difficult to generalize beyond the single institution. Prior to 2000, distance learning was delivered via correspondence and telecourses. Students taking courses using these delivery modes shared some of the challenges of today's online learners. However, web-based or online learning provides opportunities for interactive instruction and engaging online support services that were not previously possible. Therefore, early distance learning retention studies may not be relevant to the current mode of distance education.

Three studies found retention rates for online courses are 10–20% lower in online courses than in on-campus courses (Ali & Leeds, 2009; Angelino, Williams, & Natvig, 2007; Holder, 2007). Individual institutions have reported very high and very low course retention rates; some exceed 90% while others are lower than 50% (Ali & Leeds, 2009; Boston et al., 2009; Boston, Ice, & Gibson, 2011; Dietz-Uhler, Fisher, & Han, 2007; Doherty, 2006; Drouin, 2008; Fike & Fike, 2008; Fisher, 2005; Herbert, 2006; Heyman, 2010; Hossler, Ziskin, & Gross, 2009; Huett, Kalinowski, Moller, & Huett, 2008; Liu, Gomez, & Yen, 2009; Ludwig-Hardman & Dunlap, 2003; Nash, 2005; Nichols, 2010). While this is clearly an area that needs additional empirical research, this chapter assumes that retention rates in online courses could improve, and online student service strategic planning and implementation is one process that may improve online student retention.

Why Do Online Students Withdraw?

Both personal and institutional variables may contribute to the reasons that online students withdraw from their courses.

Personal or Demographic Variables

- Demographics include age, gender, ethnicity, low income, first generation, and military.
- Personal characteristics include lack of independence, motivation, self-efficacy, self-management of learning, meta-cognitive skills, self-confidence, computer self-efficacy (willingness to troubleshoot or recognize when to contact help desk), patience with computer and online course glitches. Other factors may include learning preferences, attitude about online learning, procrastination, need for direction and encouragement from faculty, and unrealistic expectation of online learning demands.
- Academic factors include program of study, previous experience in online courses, previous record of online course withdrawals, prior academic record, early in program (less investment), later in program (more invested in completion), relevance of course content, interest in course content, academically underprepared, study habits, developmental course placement, and course satisfaction.
- Life circumstances include work, family commitments, part-time or full-time enrollment, financial concerns, health, relocation, deployment, access to adequate computer hardware, software, or Internet connection.
- Prerequisite skills for online success include technical skills, online communication skills, typing speed, online screen reading speed, time management skills, and organization skills.

Institutional Variables

Institutional variables can create an environment where online students have an increased likelihood of academic success. Students have an increased chance of succeeding in online courses when they are well prepared for online learning, have excellent technical and personal support, are enrolled in well-designed online courses taught by faculty trained in the pedagogy of online instruction, and are in an environment where online student academic support services are provided throughout their enrollment.

The Studies

While research has not been conducted for online learning on all of the above mentioned personal and institutional variables, institutions might want to consider results from the studies listed in Table 9.1 as they decide which online student services are most important to develop. Table 9.1 provides a summary of the variables shown to influence student success and course retention. This summary includes only studies about web-based learning.

Table 9.1 lists a diverse set of variables that researchers have examined in an effort to determine predictors of online course and program completion. In addition to these variables, institutions may want to consider interventions the literature indicates may interrupt a student's decision to withdraw from an online course. Institutions involved in strategic planning for online student services may consider implementing some of these interventions.

HIGH-IMPACT INTERVENTIONS

A few recent studies have emphasized the importance of providing early, intrusive, frequent, and sometimes mandatory support service interventions for online students. Nistor and Neubauer (2010) found more dropouts occur at the beginning of an online course than at any other time. Based on research by Park and Choi (2009), institutions might consider the importance of supporting online learners when family and organizational support is low. Several studies have highlighted the importance of providing orientations for students new to online learning (Ali & Leeds, 2009; Allen & Seaman, 2006; Bozarth et al., 2004; Hossler et al., 2009; Ludwig-Hardman & Dunlap, 2003; McKimmy & Leong, 2004; Moore, Med, & Edwards, 2004; Nash, 2005; Ozoglu, 2010; Scagnoli, 2001; Tyler-Smith, 2006; Wilson, 2008; Wojciechowski, 2005).

The results of three surveys show what students and administrators are identifying as the highest-impact retention interven-

TABLE 9.1   VARIABLES SHOWN TO INFLUENCE STUDENT SUCCESS
AND COURSE RETENTION

Variable	Source
Student Characteristics (Demographic and Personal)	
Self-efficacy, effort regulation, rehearsal, elaboration, meta-cognitive self-regulation	Doherty, 2006; Holder, 2007; McQuaid, 2010 Puzziferro, 2008
Time management and study environment	Doherty, 2006; Holder, 2007; Puzziferro, 2008;
Number of previous online courses	Aragon & Johnson, 2008
Academic readiness	Aragon & Johnson, 2008
Gender (F)	Aragon & Johnson, 2008
Satisfaction	Levy, 2007; Park & Choi, 2009
Life Circumstances	
Organizational, family, emotional support	Holder 2007; Park & Choi, 2009; Pelowski, Frissell, Cabral, & Yu, 2005
Institutional Variables	
Offering an array of student support services	Heyman, 2010
Attending face-to-face orientation	Ali & Leeds, 2009
Sense of community	Drouin, 2008
Faculty feedback	Doherty, 2006
Collaborative group assignments	Puzziferro, 2008
Learning communities	Fisher, 2005
Relevance of content	Park & Choi, 2009

tions. Table 9.2 summarizes the results of the *National Online Learners Priorities Report* (2010), *What Works in Student Retention* (2010), and *Student Retention Practices and Strategies at Four-Year and Two-Year Institution* (2009). Two of these studies include online students. The third study provides a broad view of high-impact retention interventions.

Table 9.2   Interventions That Facilitate Retention

Intervention	Source
Administrative Suite	
Adequate financial aid is available	Noel-Levitz, 2010
Billing and payment procedures are convenient	Noel-Levitz, 2010
Registration for online courses is convenient	Noel-Levitz, 2010
Tuition paid is a worthwhile investment	Noel-Levitz, 2010
There are sufficient opportunities with my program of study	Noel-Levitz, 2010
Students are aware of whom to contact for questions about programs and services	Noel-Levitz, 2010
Online student services including registration and financial aid are available	Noel-Levitz, 2009
Academic Services Suite	
Online library resources are provided	Noel-Levitz, 2010
Remedial/developmental coursework	ACT, 2010
Mandated placement of students in courses based on test scores	ACT, 2010
Academic advising/training for academic advisors	ACT, 2010
Early warning and intervention systems	ACT, 2010; Noel-Levitz, 2009
Tutoring	ACT, 2010
Technical support to address online connection issues	Noel-Levitz, 2009
Academic support services specifically for online learners	Noel-Levitz, 2009
Faculty advisors are assigned to each online learner	Noel-Levitz, 2009
Supplemental instruction	ACT, 2010
Personal Services Suite	
Freshman seminar/University 101	ACT, 2010
Orientation program for online learners	Noel-Levitz, 2009
Communications Suite	
Feedback mechanisms to identify program improvements for online learners	Noel-Levitz, 2009

TABLE 9.2 (CONTINUED)

Intervention	Source
Assignments clearly defined in syllabus	Noel-Levitz, 2010
Instructional materials appropriate for program	Noel-Levitz, 2010
Faculty are responsive to student needs	Noel-Levitz, 2010
Faculty provide timely feedback about student progress	Noel-Levitz, 2010
Quality of online instruction is excellent	Noel-Levitz, 2010
Faculty develop includes online pedagogy and technology	Noel-Levitz, 2009
Mandatory online interaction between faculty and students	Noel-Levitz, 2009
Student Communities	
Advising interventions with selected student populations	ACT, 2010

The first study, the *National Online Learners Priorities Report*, Noel-Levitz 2010, asked two groups of online students (those primarily taking online courses and those primarily taking on-campus courses plus a few online courses) to rate the importance of, and their satisfaction with, specific components of online courses and support services. The students identified the following items as the most important and with which they were most satisfied: student assignments are clearly defined in the syllabus; registration for online courses is convenient; instructional materials are appropriate for program content; and billing and payment procedures are convenient. The following high-importance items received the lowest satisfaction scores: the quality of instruction is excellent; faculty are responsive to student needs; tuition paid is worth the investment; faculty provide timely feedback about student progress; there are sufficient opportunities within my program of study; and adequate financial aid is available. Many within the institution, especially online faculty and course designers, may collaborate to address these concerns.

In the second study, *What Works in Student Retention*, ACT 2010, 316 representatives of two-year and four-year institutions responded to a survey conducted in April and May 2009. Only representatives from institutions who had online programs responded to the nine questions about the effectiveness of their programs for retaining online learners. According to this study, the key student services for online learners are registration, financial aid, an early warning system, technical and academic support, and an orientation program. The most frequent responses are included on Table 9.2.

In the third study, *Student Retention Practices and Strategies at Four-Year and Two-Year Institution,* Noel-Levitz (2009), asked chief academic affairs officers from 3360 institutions of higher education to answer survey questions about what works in student retention. Participants were asked to rank the three campus retention practices that had the greatest impact on student retention. All respondents identified at least one of the following: freshman seminar/university 101 for credit, tutoring program, advising interventions with selected student populations, mandated course placement testing program, and comprehensive learning assistance center/lab.

The compiled summary of results from the three surveys, organized using the framework of the WCET Spider Web, are found on Table 9.2. The Noel-Levitz and ACT studies make a strong case for providing comprehensive support services for online learners.

INNOVATIVE PRACTICES

Institutions are aware that when students lag behind in online courses, they have more difficulty catching up than do students in a traditional course. A particularly effective retention intervention with online learners is an early alert system. Sinclair Community College has developed electronic early alert notifications that make it easy for faculty to alert the student's advisor or counselor. The system is used in all developmental courses, select math, the first college English composition course, and First Year Experience courses.

Once the instructor identifies a problem, the instructor sends an alert through the Student Success Plan System (see Chapter

Two, under Student Taking Developmental Courses, for more details). The software contains a series of options, including an alert to be sent to the student as well as the advisor. Once the advisor makes contact with the student and develops an Action Plan, the Early Alert is closed. The Early Alert is also closed if several unsuccessful attempts have been made to contact the student. The Action Plan includes another series of screens on the Student Success Plan System that provides a system of tracking and accountability.

The system has yielded very favorable results. From 2005 to 2008, 59% of the participating students who had direct contact with an advisor were retained and had a GPA that was 0.26 points higher than those who had indirect contact (mail, email, or voice mail message). Forty-six percent of the students who had indirect contact with an advisor were retained.

Chapters Five, Six, and Seven describe other examples of innovative retention practices as part of the description of individual online student services. Taken together, these strategies provide an array of ideas that institutions can implement to improve online course retention. However, institutions will continue to face challenges such as prioritizing which services will have the most impact on retention for an institution's online population, to what extent should services be made remotely available, and the degree to which they can afford to develop personalized, customizable online student services.

PREVALENCE OF ONLINE STUDENT SERVICES

Institutions sometimes begin to make online student service implementation decisions based on what peer institutions are making available. Fully online institutions may need to develop interactive online student services that facilitate electronic completion of most transactions students have with the institution. These institutions might encourage students to accomplish most tasks independently, thereby using the least amount of the institution's staff time. For online institutions, especially those without a physical campus, this may be the only option available to them.

Dual-purpose institutions have choices to make about which services will be fully interactive and remotely delivered and which ones may require students to interact with a professional either online or on-campus. Dual-purpose institutions are delivering an increasing number of services online. For example, the 2010 *Trends in eLearning: Tracking the Impact of eLearning at Community Colleges* found the following:

- 94% have online admissions, with 4% intending to implement the service in the next year.
- 60% have online counseling and advising services, with 17% intending to implement the service in the next year.
- 86% have online information and application for financial aid, with 6% intending to implement the service in the next year.
- 94% have online library services and resources, with 4% intending to implement the service in the next year.
- 93% have online payment of tuition and fees, with 5% intending to implement the service in the next year.
- 94% have online registration for classes, with 2% intending to implement the service in the next year.
- 54% have online student organizations, with 21% intending to implement the service in the next year.
- 79% have online orientation for distance learning classes, with 16% intending to implement the service in the next year.
- 75% have online textbook sales, with 8% intending to implement the service in the next year.
- 71% have online tutoring assistance, with 17% intending to implement the service in the next year (*Trends in eLearning: Tracking the Impact of eLearning at Community Colleges,* ITC, 2010).

Once institutions decide which services to put online, institutions can concentrate on how best to present these services on the Web. A basic goal is to present the service in a way that students clearly understand and that empower students to take full advantage of the interactive online services available to them. The range of possibilities includes presenting basic text-only information through progressively more interactive services that allow students to complete transactions and make increasingly complicated decisions using sophisticated web-based technology.

PRIORITIES OF ONLINE SERVICE DEVELOPMENT AND DELIVERY

Institutions have a variety of factors to consider and decisions to make before deciding how to present online student services. Most institutions are faced with ongoing concerns: balancing budgets, student expectations, competition for students, and fulfilling their mission. These concerns weigh heavily as institutions decide whether to present online student services in an text-based information-only format or to create interactive comprehensive tools where students can use technology to assist with completing transactions.

STUDENT EXPECTATIONS AND COMPETITION

Students' first impressions of an institution may be shaped by their initial response to the institution's website. Sixty-five percent of prospective students go directly to the institution's home page where they want to quickly find information about academic programs, tuition and fees, and a tool to estimate their cost of attending the institution.

The Noel-Levitz 2010 *E-Recruiting Practices and Trends* recruitment survey of high school seniors led to the following recommendations:

- Recognize that external websites are the number one marketing tool
- Use unofficial social media to supplement official content
- Set up a private official social networking sites
- Focus on social media that have the greatest impact on enrollment
- Look for ways to engage students by providing opportunities for them to send their email address
- Know the recruiting techniques of the competition

The Noel-Levitz 2009 study, *Making Web Sites an Effective Recruitment Asset,* recommends website content that may be important for prospective students coming directly from high school. However, busy adult students may be looking for different content and presentation. For example, they may be less interested in using social media to interact with the institution and other students. An Eduventures report, *The Adult Learner: An Eduventures Perspective,* found that adults making enrollment decisions are most interested in the ease of use of an institution's website and want access to the online course catalog. They also prioritize cost, scheduling, reputation, and class size. Virtually all student populations want to know the cost of higher education.

Convenience is the most important reason students take online courses. Students enroll in online courses, expecting they will be able to receive support services at convenient times for them, rather than exclusively during typical business hours. Putting student services online responds to these expectations.

Students want personalized services that make them feel part of the institution, and they want to be able to customize the available online services so they can easily find the information that is most relevant to them. Students want to be able to choose formats and views that allow them to place the information most important to them at the top of their MyInstitution portal home page. This technology, which is similar to that used by Yahoo or iGoogle, let users populate their portal page by selecting channels of relevant information and moving the most important information to the top of their page. Institutions may identify some channels of information that everyone receives and that cannot be deleted or moved around the portal page and allow students to select all other information from a menu of channels.

WHAT ONLINE STUDENTS NEED AND WHEN THEY NEED IT

Floyd and Casey-Powell (2004) suggest specific services that online students may need at various periods of enrollment. Institutions that provide these services contribute to the development of a supportive virtual academic environment. Their Inclusive Student Services Process Model suggests five phases of student support services:

1. *Learner Intake Phase* is the stage at which students are setting goals and assessing their readiness for online learning. The

services they need include admissions, placement testing, registration, financial aid, technology training, and orientation.

2. *Learner Intervention Phase* is during a student's introduction to online instruction. The required services focus on developing independent learning skills. Success strategies include providing help desk support and online faculty advising.

3. *Learner Support Phase* is when students need help managing their learning environment. Services that facilitate a student's sense of belonging such as counseling, academic advising, instructional support, tutoring, library and disability services are part of this phase.

4. *Learner Transition Phase* prepares students as they depart from the institution. Most important during this phase are career and transfer advising and job placement services.

5. *Measurement Phase* includes evaluating online programs and delivery systems. Components of this phase are tracking of retention, graduation, and persistence rates, along with course evaluations for the purpose of improving online student support services.

HOW ARE OTHER INSTITUTIONS DOING?

Surprisingly, very little research has been conducted about the effective use of institutions' websites. However, Katrina Meyer (2008a, 2008b) analyzed the home pages of 40 public two-year and four-year colleges and universities, both urban and rural, representing all regions of the United States. Her three research questions asked how institutions are using their home pages, how well they perform, and what home pages say about higher education in the United States. Meyer found that 35 out of 40 institutions segmented information by audience (future students, current students, faculty and staff, alumni, donors, community, business, parents). This form of navigation helps users access information that is most relevant to them.

Thirty-four percent of links from the institution's home pages lead to functional areas such as information and services of interest to students. Users want to be able to quickly access needed information. Institutions can organize website information in a variety of ways, such as by audience or functional area. Rather than using these two paths of finding information, some users would prefer to search the institution's website or browse an A-Z index. In Meyer's study, 33% had site search engines and 7.5% had an A-Z index. Four out of 40 home pages did not have any site-based search or index capabilities (Meyer, 2008a, 2008b). It is generally considered advisable to create more options for finding information that will accommodate users with the broadest array of learning styles.

A common measure of how easy it is to use a website is how many clicks it takes a user to access information from the home page, and whether or not the information can be found at all. Information available within one to three clicks is thought to be easy to find. Meyer and Wilson (2010) examined websites at 40 institutions to determine how many services were within the one to three click range from the institution's home page. They found that 40/40 had online application to the college, 35/40 had online registration, 11/40 had specific information about additional fees for taking online courses, and 40/40 had library resources that were within three clicks from the home page. While online library services are ubiquitous, only 12/40 have a link to Ask a Librarian, a service that students appreciate.

The Meyer and Wilson (2010) study investigated special services available for online learners. Online course schedules were universal, as were registering for online courses and logging into the learning management system. A few of the 40 websites offered a variety of other services: bookstore, employment aids, student organization, an online orientation program, online training for the learning management system, and online academic advising specifically targeted to the needs of online learners.

Another purpose of the Meyer and Wilson study was to help public institutions assess their competitive advantage. Meyer and Wilson concluded that many of the institutions in the sample were not fully prepared to support online learners, but acknowledged the University of South Dakota and University of Alabama for providing comprehensive online student services. Traditional institutions serving remotely located online students or students seeking the convenience of online student service might be concerned about losing students to institutions that have comprehensive online student service programs.

INNOVATIVE PRACTICES

From the Off-Campus and Distance Learning home page, the University of South Dakota provides online learners with easy access to online course schedules that define different delivery modes, a list of fully online programs with links to each department, and links to a variety of online services specifically created with the needs of online learners in mind, including an online orientation guide. The University of Alabama uses *Bama by Distance* to clearly label most web pages pertaining to the needs of online learners. The site identifies three audiences—current students, prospective students, and high school students—and provides paths to the information they need. Both websites include features that support the needs of online learners.

USE OF THE CENTSS AUDIT TOOL FOR PLANNING

The Center for Transforming Student Services (CENTSS) has developed an audit tool (CENTSS Audit Tool) that provides institutions with a systematic process for examining 31 remotely delivered student services. The CENTSS Audit Tool, developed as a part of the *Beyond the Administrative Core* FIPSE grant, a collaboration among WCET, the Minnesota State Colleges and Universities, and Seward, Inc., provides a framework for evaluating both the content and the presentation of online student services.

The CENTSS Audit Tool provides a mechanism for institutions to assess current online student services and to plan for improvements. Generation 1 is when no evidence of the services can be found on the website, Generation 2 is text-only information presented using the organizational structure of the institution, Generation 3 is information presented based on student needs, and Generations 4 and 5 are online student services that are interactive and customizable that allow students to complete transactions, make decisions, and save information for future use. Chapter Four provides additional details about the generational development of online student services.

For each of the 31 services, the Audit Tool identifies between 5 and 14 critical components that describe the content and the mode of presentation, which together constitute a comprehensive online delivery of each service. Users of the audit are asked to examine the institution's website and report whether they can find the critical components and are asked questions to help them identify the generation of each component. A report is generated that combines the results of several reviewers to provide planners an agreed upon baseline for each service. Planning teams can use these data to make decisions about how they want to improve content and presentation of each online service.

In planning for the development and improvement of online support services, institutions may use the CENTSS Audit Tool or another means to establish a baseline of current online student services. When institutions have a clear picture of what services are available online, they can set goals for how they want to improve those services. Ananthanarayanan (2000), as cited in Shelton and Saltsman (2005), suggests that institutions develop a flow chart that traces each action required by students in order to access and complete online transactions. For example, if students want an unofficial copy of their transcript, the planning team may devise a flow chart to determine the path and how many clicks it requires to complete that transaction. After analysis of the flow chart, the planning team may determine a more efficient way to accomplish that task.

Using this sort of analysis, the planning team might identify where gaps exist between current services and what the team deems to be important improvements. The overarching goal is to provide students a smooth online experience that improves their chances for academic success.

PHASED APPROACH TO ONLINE STUDENT SERVICES PLANNING

Beyond the Administrative Core recommends a phased approach to strategic planning for online student services: prelaunch, assessment, planning, design, development, implementation, and evaluation. During prelaunch, the institution considers what it wants to achieve by developing online student services that reflect the mission, campus culture, and resources. The institution selects a director of the project and a leadership team and might identify essential attributes and qualities of an effective project leader. That person might be a creative thinker who understands the big picture but also attends to the details. The person might have the ability to motivate student service staff who are overworked, some of whom may be inclined to focus on the challenges rather than the benefits of putting services online. Other important qualities are good communication skills and the ability to set and meet realistic goals and time lines.

The prelaunch phase is also an opportunity to develop a cross-functional team to provide project oversight. The team might include representatives from each of the service areas, along with marketing, IT, and students. Even though the team may seem large, a larger team allows for inclusion of team members who represent and communicate with each functional area.

Possibly the most important prelaunch activity is for the team to garner support from top leadership, buy-in that may well determine the success of the project. The team might identify key stakeholders, campus leaders, and champions who will facilitate acceptance of the necessary changes. During the prelaunch phase, the leadership group envisions the project, sets realistic goals and time lines for each phase, and defines the tasks to be accomplished during each phase. It also determines how the project will be communicated to the institution and the process the college community will use to provide feedback to the group. Some institutions want external assistance to guide the institution through the process of improving online student services and decide to hire a consultant to facilitate the process.

During the assessment phase, the team may develop a working relationship and a joint understanding of all functional areas. A key element of this phase is that the team members develop a mutual trust and agree to a common understanding of the project. The common understanding might include the scope of student services, the target audiences, and technology available to support the project. This phase also includes visioning and scanning the environment for innovative best practices being used by peer institutions.

Teams may use a variety of technology tools to communicate with team members and resource people between meetings. A key task during the assessment phase is to evaluate current online student services. The team may decide to use an evaluation instrument such as the CENTSS Audit Tool to gather information about current online student services from experts within the institution and from other stakeholders. Through an analysis of current online student services, the leadership team develops a clear picture of which online services are information-only, which are interactive, personalizable, and customizable, and which services are not currently online.

The team can use these data to set improvement goals. During this phase, some institutions use focus groups or surveys to conduct a needs/gap analysis of expected users of online student services (Sener & Baer, 2002). An institution may conduct a needs assessment to determine which online services students are most likely to use.

During all phases, but especially during the assessment phase, the team may strive to maintain ongoing communication among team members and with the college community, stay on task, determine and publish the project scope, and update the time line as decisions are made. The team may anticipate changes to the scope of the project and time lines as the assessment results are analyzed. During the planning phase, the team uses the needs assessment results to redefine the goals of the project, adopt guiding principles, and further define a vision of online student services. When institutions have a clear understanding of the needs of their target audiences, they will be better prepared to identify which online services they want to transform into interactive, personalized, customizable online delivery and which services might remain a static presentation of information.

Once a vision for improvements of online student services has been redefined, the team may want to analyze current institutional policies, practices, and attitudes to identify any inconsistencies. If inconsistencies are identified, the team may involve all stakeholders in deciding what changes are necessary. If putting services online is in conflict with institutional policies that cannot be changed, that conflict will limit how that service can be delivered online. For example, if there are FERPA concerns that cannot be satisfactorily addressed, perhaps that service will never become more interactive than Generation 3.

Based on the information gathered as a result of previous discussions and analysis, the team may decide to alter its vision and time line, and, if necessary, reevaluate and reset priorities. The team may use various criteria to determine the sequence of interactive online student services development. If the team decides that its primary criterion is which services seem to have the greatest influence on student success, studies from student support and retention literature show that academic advising and orientation activities have been identified as two important services (*Academic Advising Highly Important to Students*, 2009; Ali & Leeds, 2009; Bozarth et al., 2004; Bresciani, 2005; Curry & Barham, 2007; Hossler et al., 2009; Ludwig-Hardman & Dunlap, 2003; Nash, 2005; Ozoglu, 2010; Steele & Thurmond, 2009; Tyler-Smith, 2006; Wilson, 2008). If an institution has yet to put services from the Administrative Suite online, those might be the first priority.

In the design phase, the team decides whether to develop online student services internally or use a Request for Proposal (RFP) process to select a vendor. In either case, internal subject matter experts (SMEs) from each functional area might work with IT and a vendor (if one is hired) to transform the service for online delivery. The team facilitates discussions about how to track usage, keep materials updated, and measure learning during this phase. Some institutions are using content management systems to assist with these tasks. During the design phase, the team decides how to phase in the development of online services for each functional area, as institutions rarely can afford to develop all online services at one time.

During the development phase, SMEs work with developers (internal or external) to establish a realistic work plan. If the institution agrees on a consistent look and feel that might be shared across student services, the result might make it easier for audiences to find information. Other institutions might decide that each student service should have an individual brand. Sometimes storyboards are developed to help SMEs articulate how each functional area wants the service to be developed. The developer creates a prototype to ensure the service is being developed the way the SME has envisioned.

Institutions may consider refinements to the budget during this phase. After final approval of the prototype and development of the enhanced online service, institutions might find it helpful to conduct a usability test. One type of usability test is to ask questions, watch, and take notes as novice users navigate the new online service. Even small modifications at this point can help ensure a smooth launch. The next steps might include marketing the new service and piloting it with a subset of users.

During the implementation phase, a primary task is training the staff and students who will use the enhanced online student services. The new online services are deployed after adjustments have been made from the user and pilot tests. Some institutions have a feedback mechanism that allows users the opportunity to assess the effectiveness of the online service.

The last phase is an ongoing process of evaluating online student services by getting input from students and college employees. Information from a formal evaluation process provides institutions a rational basis for making revisions and improvements. Evaluation is discussed in Chapter Ten.

CONCLUSION

Online students need a wide array of services to support their success, and those services must be electronically delivered. Online student service planning covers two broad areas: the content and presentation of each online service. Historically, campus-based student services have been developed within a single department, with perhaps occasional collaboration from closely related services. A collaborative approach to developing online student services often results in a seamless support experience for online students. With careful planning and well-developed methods of presentation, some institutions have established a virtual student service center from which online students may easily access all services. This approach provides a clear path leading online students to the information they need for academic success.

CHAPTER TEN

EVALUATION

This chapter begins with a discussion about the importance of measuring the quality of online student support services, followed by a review of approaches to evaluating those services. It then describes a brief history of how standards of web-based learning in general have evolved, primarily since the beginning of this century. The remainder of the chapter reviews standards and guidelines related to the delivery of online student services, quality indicators, tools used to measure quality, and ways for using results.

IMPORTANCE OF MEASURING QUALITY

Institutions of higher education are hearing the call for increased accountability that is coming from multiple sectors: the general public, accreditation agencies, U.S. Congress, the Department of Education, and students and their families, to name a few. This push for accountability is especially applicable for distance education programs and is one driver for the ongoing cycle of program evaluation and improvement. Institutions are aware of increasing college costs and the challenges of clearly defining and measuring student learning outcomes. Institutions may find themselves justifying the expense and effort required to develop or expand distance learning programs. To do so, they may be assisted by a solid evaluation plan for the development and delivery of online student services (Bresciani, 2011).

Distance learning has experienced rapid growth, but its critics suggest that the learning outcomes from distance learning are not as good as those outcomes from traditionally taught courses. However, studies do not support their position. A meta-analysis of experimental and quasi-experimental studies comparing learning in blended, online, and face-to-face instruction found online instruction to be at least as good as traditionally delivered courses. The same study found that blended instruction was better than instruction taught exclusively in traditional classrooms (Means, Toyama, Murphy, Bakia, & Jones, 2009). Even with the publication of this research, some are still skeptical. Although concerns about quality are not as compelling as before, many institutions want to demonstrate equitable learning outcomes when students take courses at a distance. Accordingly, institutions view the development of a comprehensive evaluation plan as a means of improving quality.

Retention rates in online courses are typically not as high as they are in traditionally taught courses. Chapter Nine reviewed many factors that may contribute to student withdrawal from online courses: demographic and personal factors, life circumstances, and institutional barriers. Chapters Two and Three discussed additional demographic and personal factors that may contribute to a student's decision to withdraw from an online course: having disabilities, being first generation students, placing in developmental coursework, having a low income, being an adult student or a student of color, or being a veteran. When evaluating support mechanisms for online students, institutions might consider how well services are supporting the needs of specific populations of online learners.

Institutions may want to ensure that the same quality support services are available to online students as are available to those students taking courses on campus. Although student services is a single component of a distance learning program, it is the one that perhaps gets the most attention when institutions have concerns about online student retention. Institutions and students benefit when rates of online retention improve after institutions make improvements based on evidence obtained from an effective evaluation plan. An effective evaluation plan is one that provides evidence to justify the investment of resources, ensure quality goals are being achieved, guide improvements in learning outcomes, and provide a basis for decisions to expand distance learning programs (Thompson & Irele, 2007).

An Approach to Measuring Quality

Institutions of higher learning have been evaluating student services for many years. When students participate in remotely delivered services, many things are different, not the least of which are matters involving relationship building. The effectiveness of in-person student services is sometimes influenced by the quality of the relationship between the professional and the student. Relationships change dramatically when mediated by electronic communication tools. Although those relationships are different, they are not necessarily better or worse.

Student service professionals may benefit from the lessons learned by distance learning program administrators who have spent many years comparing online and face-to-face courses. Years of research have produced primarily the same results: "no significant difference" between the learning outcomes in the two modes of delivery (Russell, 1999). Some students choose to participate in online services for a number of reasons, while others must use online services because they live far from campus or because there may not be a campus. The best approach to measuring quality of online student services may be to avoid comparison with the same services delivered in person, and simply concentrate on independently improving the quality of each method of delivery.

Well-established approaches to educational evaluation are applicable to evaluation of online student services. Educational evaluation is a process of examining and reporting on the strengths and weaknesses of programs, policies, personnel, processes, products or outcomes, and organizations for the purpose of improving effectiveness. Evaluation provides answers to quality questions for stakeholders: learners, instructors, staff, administrators, policymakers, boards, vendors, and accrediting associations. Institutions use results of assessments to justify the distribution of resources, examine quality and effectiveness, measure progress toward goals, establish a baseline for improving quality and effectiveness, and provide a basis for strategic planning (Thompson & Irele, 2007).

Obtaining and analyzing comprehensive evaluation results facilitate effective data-driven decision making that can improve the effectiveness of online student services.

Bresciani (2011) suggests the components of an outcomes-based assessment (OBA) plan and report. The components of Bresciani's model are program name, program mission or purpose, program goals, outcomes, planning for delivery of outcomes, evaluation methods and tools, implementation of the assessment process, results, reflection, interpretation, decisions and recommendations, documentation of higher-level feedback, and appendices.

Institutions might find it useful to view this model through the lens of online student services:

- Program name helps clarify what is being evaluated. With respect to online student services, if institutions use the WCET Spider Web as an organizing framework, as many as 31 services could be represented in a comprehensive assessment plan. Institutions might want to decide which services will be included in the assessment plan. Bresciani suggests identifying a contact person for each service to be assessed.
- Program mission or purpose of an online student services program requires alignment with institutional, student affairs and other relevant departmental missions, visions, values, and priorities.
- Program goals (broad statements of what students will be able to do and know, how evaluators will know what students have learned, and what the program will do to facilitate acquisition of this knowledge) should also be aligned with department, division, and institutional goals and initiatives, along with professional accreditation standards. With respect to online student services, this alignment is particularly significant, as frequently the same services are also available to students via an in-person delivery method. The goals are the same, but delivery is different when student and professional are separated by place and time.
- Outcomes are measureable and will clearly define what students are expected to know as a result of participating in each online student service. Each outcome should be aligned with a program goal.

- During the planning for delivery of each service, institutions identify ways in which students will be provided opportunities to achieve each of the desired outcomes. At this point a connection is made between the specific service(s) and the desired outcome(s).
- Evaluation method and tools is the component in which institutions identify the population included in the evaluation, the method of evaluation, and the tools to be used to measure each outcome. Tools are discussed later in the chapter.
- Implementation of the assessment process is the institution's plan for when and how the assessment will take place. A comprehensive assessment plan for evaluating online student services could be a massive undertaking, depending on how many services an institution decides to assess. Assessment cycles for individual services might be tied to when the online service was developed. For example, as interactive online services are developed, assessments are implemented within a specific time after launch and, thereafter, repeated annually.
- Results are summarized and verified for accuracy. Institutions might develop linkages between the outcome results of closely related online student services.
- Reflection, interpretation, decisions, and recommendations start with a summary and provide additional detailed analysis. Institutions identify gaps between desired outcomes and results, discuss evidence, and suggest improvements to the assessment process.
- Documentation of higher-level feedback is the point at which decisions are made about how the results will be used for program improvements. The assessment team might discuss recommendations, the decision-making process, and who has the authority to make decisions.
- Appendices are part of the report that includes additional materials that support the findings and describe the assessment process.

Sources of Standards and Guidelines

Essential elements of an online student assessment program are identifying standards and developing institution-based benchmarks of online services against which to measure student performance. Those standards may be developed internally and/ or extracted from external sources, several of which are described in the next section.

Quality measures of student services come from a variety of resources, including regional accrediting commissions, professional organizations, and the Council for Advancement of Standards in Higher Education (CAS). Some of these organizations are more specific in describing online student service standards and guidelines than others. This section begins with a brief history of the development of online student services standards from these organizations, along with standards established from a study that validated and revised early benchmarks developed by the Institute for Higher Education Policy (IHEP).

REGIONAL ACCREDITING COMMISSIONS

The distance learning standards and guidelines that regional accrediting commissions had in place prior to the beginning of web-based distance learning were revised in 2000 by the *Statement of Commitment by the Regional Accrediting Commissions for the Evaluation of Electronically Offered Degree and Certificate Programs*. It was the first time all commissions jointly issued a set of rules and guidelines (Lezberg, 2007). The preamble delineates several values and principles; the one most relevant to this book is, "institutions accept the obligation to address student needs related to, and to provide the resources necessary for, their academic success" (Lezberg, 2007, p. 411).

The general statement of commitment was supplemented by *Best Practices for Electronically Offered Degree and Certificate Programs*. This document describes concrete standards useful to institutions in the development of distance learning programs. The Best Practices document has five areas: Institutional Context and Commitment, Curriculum and Instruction, Faculty Support, Student Support, and Evaluation and Assessment (Lezberg, 2007). Especially important to note is the early requirement that Student Support standards must meet the needs of remotely located students and be of equal quality to those provided to on-campus students. Until the passage of the 2008 Higher Education Opportunity Act, the regional accrediting commissions used a separate set of standards for evaluating distance learning programs.

HIGHER EDUCATION OPPORTUNITY ACT

The 2008 Higher Education Opportunity Act (HEOA) changed the approach regional accrediting commissions take when evaluating distance learning programs. While HEOA no longer requires separate standards, policies, and procedure for evaluating distance learning programs, it does require the regional accrediting commissions to address issues of quality, particularly student achievement. HEOA requires that regional accrediting commissions have effective standards for evaluating distance education program quality, ensure that members of review teams understand distance education, and monitor significant growth in distance education enrollments.

Under HEOA, evaluators of distance learning programs now look at new indicators of quality. First, HEOA distinguishes correspondence courses from distance education courses. Distance education courses must include significant interactivity between instructor and student, either synchronously or asynchronously.

Second, institution must have in place a process to verify student identity in all distance programs. Typically, students use secure login and passwords to enter learning management systems. Institutions must track the identity of students participating in distance education and correspondence courses. This change has generated a broader discussion about academic honesty. Chapter Six (under the heading Assessment and Testing) contains a detailed discussion of these issues.

Third, regional accrediting commissions more closely monitor the rate of growth in online student enrollments. Institutions are now required to submit to the regional accreditation commission their intent to make substantive increases in distance learning enrollments prior to doing so. Under this change, regional accrediting commissions look more closely at measures of student success.

Fourth, regional accrediting commissions use the same guidelines and standards to evaluate all instructional programs. Previously, separate criteria were used for distance learning programs. As a result of HEOA, each regional accrediting commission more carefully evaluates distance learning programs at institutions within their region.

STUDENT AFFAIRS ASSOCIATIONS

Student affairs, while guided by regional accreditation commission standards, also have standards developed by professional organizations. In 1986, the Council for Advancement of Standards in Higher Education (CAS) established and disseminated the first student services standards to help student affairs professionals self-assess the quality of their work. As of 2007, there were 37 standards, including specific standards for distance learners. The Educational Services for Distancé Learners standards, established in 2004, includes many functional areas covered by the regional accrediting commission's standards. CAS standards emphasize that services to online learners must be equal to and accessible to all students no matter where they are located.

In its 2000 report, *Distance Learning and Student Affairs: Defining the Issues*, the National Association of Student Personnel Administrators (NASPA) identified key issues related to the support of distance learners. NASPA acknowledged that virtually all services provided by student affairs professionals could be remotely delivered; that institutions would be challenged to retain their distance learners; and that student affairs professionals must develop a sense of community among online students and a sense of affiliation between online students and the institution. NASPA outlined next steps to continue the discussion about how to best support distance learners. NASPA suggested that student affairs professionals start a discussion about how student affairs might play a leadership role in the support of online learners; identify student affairs units that were supporting online students; develop a database of resources; address the training of student affairs professionals; identify other organizations with which student affairs professionals might collaborate; and promote research about supporting online learners. NASPA has been slow to provide leadership for these next steps. NASPA does not currently have divisions, communities, or knowledge groups identified to support online learners.

In a 1999 report, the American College Personnel Association (ACPA) identified the growth of distance education as a trend that would shape the future of student affairs. The report acknowledged that institutions were not monitoring the support of online learners (Upcraft & Terenzini, 1999). As of the writing of this book, ACPA has no commissions or standing committees devoted to the support of online learners. ACPA uses the CAS Educational Services for Distance Learner standards as benchmarks for the effective support of distance learners (Wall, 2011).

Student affairs professionals consider that their core work is to develop the whole student, which includes learning in the cognitive and affective domains. To be educated as a whole student, online learners need essentially the same services that student affairs professionals provide to all students. Although student affairs professionals at individual institutions are successfully supporting the needs of online students, student affairs, as a professional organization, might want to more fully commit to support the needs of this population. Many authors have called for greater leadership, proactive programming, and transformative delivery of services for online students (Crawley & LeGore, 2009; Dale & Drake, 2005; Dare, Zapata, & Thomas, 2005; Kleemann, 2005; Kleinglass, 2005; Kretovics, 2003; Lowery, 2004; Taylor & Holley, 2009). Given the growth of online learning and growing concerns about student retention, student affairs professionals might consider how important it is to provide online learners with the services they need for academic success and personal growth.

A QUALITY SCORECARD FOR THE ADMINISTRATION OF ONLINE EDUCATION PROGRAMS

In 2000, the Institute for Higher Education Policy (IHEP) commissioned the National Educators Association (NEA) and Blackboard, Inc., to establish benchmarks of quality for distance education programs. The group generated the report, *Quality on the Line: Benchmarks for Success in Internet-Based Distance Education* (Phipps & Merisotis, 2000). Shelton (2010) used the original benchmarks developed from this report as a starting point and conducted a six-round Delphi study with 43 seasoned administrators of online education programs. The study resulted in the validation of 70 quality indicators that administrators might consider when evaluating online programs (Shelton, 2010). The quality indicators from this study, CAS, and the regional accrediting commissions are combined in Table 10.1 to provide a summary of standards and guidelines for online student services.

TABLE 10.1 SUMMARY OF ONLINE STUDENT SERVICES GUIDELINES AND STANDARDS

WCET Web of Student Services	Sample Standard	Source
Administrative Suite		
Admissions	Students receive (or have access to) information about programs, including admission requirements, tuition and fees, books and supplies, technical and proctoring requirements, and student support services prior to admission and course registration.	Shelton, 2010
Admissions	Applications for admission must be provided in a manner that is practical and can be completed without undue assistance.	CAS, 2004
	Application and admission counseling must be made available to distance learners.	
	The admissions process must be specific and described in a step-by-step fashion.	
	Applications should be made available online and in print along with clear instructions.	
	Deadlines should be specific and explicit.	
Admissions	The institution seeks to admit online students whose interests, goals, and abilities are congruent with its mission and fit the student profile. The institution seeks to retain them through the pursuit of the students' educational goals.	MSCHE, 2009

TABLE 10.1 (CONTINUED)

WCET Web of Student Services	Sample Standard	Source
Admissions	The institution determines that students admitted to its DE programs are able to benefit from these programs.	ACCJC/ WASC, 2010
Admissions	The institution regularly evaluates admissions and placement instruments and practices to validate their effectiveness while minimizing biases.	ACCJC/ WASC, 2010
Registration	Distance students must be provided registration services for each new term or course in a clear, timely, and user-friendly manner. Policies and processes should be clearly described. Alternative methods of registration should be identified.	CAS, 2004
Registration	The online course site includes a syllabus that outlines course objectives, learning outcomes, evaluation methods, textbook information, and other related course information, thus making course requirements transparent at the time of registration.	Shelton, 2010
Registration	Students receive (or have access to) information about programs, including admission requirements, tuition and fees, books and supplies, technical and proctoring requirements, and student support services prior to admission and course registration.	Shelton, 2010
Student Accounts/ Records	The institution maintains student records permanently, securely, and confidentially, with provision for secure backup of all files, regardless of the form in which those files are maintained.	AACJC/ WASC, 2010
	The institution publishes and follows established policies for release of student records.	

(Continued)

TABLE 10.1 (CONTINUED)

WCET Web of Student Services	Sample Standard	Source
Financial Aid	Information about financial aid must be provided to distance students and the application process must be described clearly. Eligibility requirements must be specifically outlined including all institutional financial aid policies. Deadlines for application for financial aid must be clearly stated. General information about financial aid, types of aid, specific cost of attendance, average percentage of financial need met, and all relevant forms should be made available.	CAS, 2004
Schedule of Classes	Scheduling of online learning courses and programs provides students with a dependable pathway to ensure timely completion of degrees.	NEASC/ CIHE, 2009
Course/ Program Catalog	The institution provides a catalog in print and electronic formats for its constituencies with precise, accurate, and current information including major policies affecting students, and provides locations of publications where other policies may be found.	ACCJC/ WASC, 2010
Catalog	When programs are eliminated or program requirements are significantly changed, the institution makes appropriate arrangements so that enrolled students may complete their education in a timely manner with a minimum of disruption.	ACCJC/ WASC, 2010

TABLE 10.1 (CONTINUED)

WCET Web of Student Services	Sample Standard	Source

Academic Services Suite

Academic Advising	Academic advisors must be available at times convenient to both students and advisors.	CAS, 2004
	Academic advising programs should be designed around the needs of distance learners and commensurate with services provided for on-campus students.	
	Academic advising should include access to advisors, information about general education and major requirements, and self-help pointers for educational planning and course selection, articulation information, curriculum guides, and access to personal academic records.	
Academic Advising	The institution makes available to its online students clearly stated transfer-of-credit policies in order to facilitate the mobility of students without penalty.	ACCJC/ WASC, 2010
Technical Support	The institution must provide information concerning hardware, software, and type of Internet connection needed for full participation in online courses and programs, must take steps to ensure students have technical skills necessary to fully participate, and must provide technical support at times convenient to the students enrolled in distance courses.	CAS, 2004
	Technical support information should include who is eligible for technical support, tutorials for common problems, self-help tools, and access to a help desk.	

(Continued)

TABLE 10.1 (CONTINUED)

WCET Web of Student Services	Sample Standard	Source
Technical Support	Throughout the duration of the course or program, students have access to appropriate technical assistance and technical support staff.	Shelton, 2010
Academic Counseling	The institution designs, maintains, and evaluates counseling and academic advising programs to support student development and success and prepares faculty and other personnel responsible for advising online students.	ACCJC/ WASC, 2010
Retention Services	Institutions determine achievement outcomes of distance education programs including the extent that students progress through and complete degrees and certificates, gain employment, or transfer to four-year institutions.	ACCJC/ WASC, 2010
Bookstore	Students are provided relevant information and policies (ISBN numbers, suppliers, etc.) and delivery modes for all required instructional materials (digital format, e-packs, print format, etc.) to ensure easy access.	Shelton, 2010
Tutoring	Information about academic support services must be made available.	CAS, 2004
	Online students should have opportunities for developing learning strategies and getting assistance with content comprehension.	
	Tutoring services, supplemental instruction, and other academic support services should be available to all distance education students.	

TABLE 10.1 (CONTINUED)

WCET Web of Student Services	Sample Standard	Source
Library	The institution must provide an orientation to library services that includes effective online search strategies geared to the programs of study offered at a distance, access to reference materials, periodicals, and books needed to fulfill course requirements, reference support, convenient access to document delivery services, and online tutorials on conducting library research.	CAS, 2004
Library	The institution provides ongoing instruction for users of library, access, and other learning support services so that students are able to develop skills in information competency regardless of their location.	AACJC/ WASC, 2010
Assessment and Testing	The institution regularly evaluates admissions and placement instruments and practices to validate their effectiveness while minimizing biases.	AACJC/ WASC, 2010
Assessment and Testing	Institutions provide policies and procedures to help online students obtain test proctoring services.	AACJC/ WASC, 2010
Assessment and Testing	Documented procedures ensure that security of personal information is protected in the conduct of assessments and evaluations and in the dissemination of results.	SACSCOC, 2010

(Continued)

TABLE 10.1 (CONTINUED)

WCET Web of Student Services	Sample Standard	Source
Disability Services	Accommodations must be made available to online students with disabilities.	CAS, 2004
	The policies for these students must be equal to those of students with disabilities that come to campus.	
	Web pages must conform to W3C accessibility guidelines.	
	Assistive technology must be provided.	
Personal Services Suite		
Orientation	Orientation to the institution and to the processes of online learning must be offered.	CAS, 2004
	Orientation may employ a variety of methods of communication and should be accessible.	
	Orientation should be interactive and must provide opportunities for student-to-student and faculty/staff-to-student exchanges.	
	Orientation must include requirements of distance learning, tips for success, academic integrity and related policy issues, and all applicable student codes of conduct.	
Orientation	Institutions must provide prospective distance education students with self-assessment of their skills, motivation, and self-discipline for distance learning, give students an idea of how they will fare in a distance education course, provide a description of how the courses will be offered, how students will get textbooks and other materials, the kinds of equipment needed, any on-campus requirements, and a way to contact an advisor.	Evidence of Quality, 2006

TABLE 10.1 (CONTINUED)

WCET Web of Student Services	Sample Standard	Source
Orientation	Expectations for any required face-to-face, on-ground work (e.g., internships, specialized laboratory work) are stated clearly.	NEASC/CIHE, 2009
Orientation	Issues of academic integrity must be discussed during the orientation for online students.	NEASC/CIHE, 2009
Orientation	Before starting an online program, students are advised about the program to determine if they possess the self-motivation and commitment to learn at a distance.	Shelton, 2010
Orientation	Before starting an online program, students are advised about the program to determine if they have access to the minimal technology required by the course design.	Shelton, 2010
Personal Counseling	Counseling services essential to assist distance students to achieve their goals must be provided. Reasonable efforts should be made to extend counseling services to distance learners that are comparable to those available for on-campus students. Counseling services must be offered in accordance with applicable ethical standards for the practice of online counseling. Services should include descriptions of available counseling services for those experiencing a mental health crisis, contact with a personal counselor on campus, referrals to local emergency care resources, and phone numbers for crisis hotlines.	CAS, 2004

(Continued)

Table 10.1 (Continued)

WCET Web of Student Services	Sample Standard	Source
Career Counseling	Career services must be provided to distance students that are appropriate for their needs and remotely accessible. These may include, but are not limited to, self-exploration, self-assessment, goal setting, decision making, educational planning, career planning, career information, and co-op education.	CAS, 2004
	Self-help tools for career decision making and online searches for positions should be provided.	
	Opportunities for experiential learning, such as internships, service learning, cooperative education, and part-time jobs, should be effectively marketed and accessible for distance learners.	
Placement Services	Job search services should be made available to online students.	CAS, 2004
Wellness Services	Information about health and wellness programs should be made available to distance education students.	CAS, 2004
	Referrals to local health care providers and prescription by mail may be made available.	
Ethical and Legal Services	The institution has in place effective procedures through which to ensure that the student who registers in a distance education course or program is the same student who participates in the course or program and receives academic credit.	NEASC/CIHE, 2009
	The institution makes clear in writing that these processes protect student privacy and notifies students at the time of registration or enrollment of any projected additional costs associated with the verification procedures.	

TABLE 10.1 (CONTINUED)

WCET Web of Student Services	Sample Standard	Source
Ethical and Legal Services	The institution establishes and publishes clear expectations concerning student academic honesty and the consequences for dishonesty.	ACCJC/ WASC, 2010
Ethical and Legal Services	The institution's policies on academic integrity include explicit references to online learning.	NEASC/ CIHE, 2009
Ethical and Legal Services	Training for faculty members engaged in online learning includes consideration of issues of academic integrity, including ways to reduce cheating.	NEASC/ CIHE, 2009
Ethical and Legal Services	A structured system is in place to respond to student complaints. Specific grievance policies and procedures are clearly described.	NEA/Bb, Evidence of quality, Shelton 2010

Student Communities Suite

Student Activities	Distance learners must be provided a reasonable opportunity to connect with other students and their instructors through such means as newsletters, frequent announcements, creation of virtual communities, and creative use of other means of electronic communication to enhance a sense of community.	CAS, 2004
Student Activities	Leadership development programs should be made available to distance learners in forms equivalent to those on campus.	CAS, 2004

(Continued)

TABLE 10.1 (CONTINUED)

WCET Web of Student Services	Sample Standard	Source
Student Activities	Information about student activities, including organizations, leisure and recreational activities, and cultural and entertainment events, may be provided when possible to promote identity with the institution.	CAS, 2004
Student Population Segments	The institution identifies and seeks to meet the varied educational needs of its students through programs consistent with their educational preparation and the diversity, demographics, and economy of its communities.	AACJC/ WASC, 2010
	The institution relies upon research and analysis to identify student learning needs and to assess progress toward achieving stated learning outcomes.	
Student Population Segments	Delivery of student support services should be flexible in nature and should vary depending on the modes and levels of educational delivery.	MSCHE, 2009
	Consistent with institutional mission, programs should be available to provide this support to diverse student populations such as older students, students with disabilities, international students, distance and distributed learning students, and students at sites other than a main campus.	

Communications Suite

Institution-to-student	Efforts are made to engage students with the program and the institution.	Shelton, 2010
Institution-to-student	Students are instructed in the appropriate ways of enlisting help from the program advisors.	Shelton, 2010

TABLE 10.1 (CONTINUED)

WCET Web of Student Services	Sample Standard	Source
Institution-to-student	Student conduct policies relevant to online learners are communicated through a student handbook or some other source.	
Student-to-student/ faculty	Students are instructed in the appropriate ways of communicating with faculty and students.	Shelton, 2010
Student-to-student/ faculty	Student-to-Student interaction and Faculty-to-Student interaction are essential characteristics and are facilitated through a variety of ways.	Shelton, 2010
Student-to-student/ faculty	Students should be provided a way to interact with other students in an online community.	Shelton, 2010
Faculty-to-student	Course syllabus contains specific information about how long faculty will take to respond to various forms of communication and provide feedback on assignments.	Evidence of Quality, 2006

General Standards

Access	Institutions must provide appropriate student services for all students enrolled in Distance Education Programs. These services must be sufficiently comprehensive to be responsive to the special needs of all distance students.	CAS, 2004
Access	Some services, such as those found in the Administrative Suite, as well as library, bookstore, technical support, orientation, academic advising, and career services, must be accessible to online students who cannot or will not come to campus.	CAS, 2004

(Continued)

TABLE 10.1 (CONTINUED)

WCET Web of Student Services	Sample Standard	Source
Access	The institution must provide support services to students in formats appropriate to the delivery of the online learning program.	WASC, 2009
Equity	Services to online students must be of comparable quality to services provided to on-campus students.	CAS, 2004
Equity	Program demonstrates a student-centered focus rather than trying to fit service distance education students in an on-campus student services model.	Shelton, 2010
Planning	Planning documents are explicit about any goals to increase numbers of programs provided through online learning courses and programs and numbers of students to be enrolled in them.	NEASC/ CIHE, 2009
Evaluation/ Effectiveness	The institution provides student support services reasonably necessary to enable each student to achieve the institution's goals for students.	MSCHE, 2009
Evaluation/ Effectiveness	The institution evaluates student support services to ensure their adequacy in meeting identified student needs. Evaluation of these services provides evidence that they contribute to the achievement of student learning outcomes. The institution uses the results of these evaluations as the basis to improve services.	ACCJC/ WASC, 2010

TABLE 10.1 (CONTINUED)

WCET Web of Student Services	Sample Standard	Source
Evaluation/ Effectiveness	The institution provides an environment that encourages personal and civic responsibility, as well as intellectual, aesthetic, and personal development for all of its students. The institution designs and maintains appropriate programs, practices, and services that support and enhance student understanding and appreciation of diversity.	ACCJC/ WASC, 2010
Evaluation/ Effectiveness	The institution ensures the quality of student support services and demonstrates that these services, regardless of location or means of delivery, support student learning and enhance achievement of the mission of the institution.	ACCJC/ WASC, 2010
Evaluation/ Effectiveness	The institution identifies student learning outcomes for courses, programs, certificates, and degrees; assesses student achievement of those outcomes; and uses assessment results to make improvements.	ACCJC/ WASC, 2010

Note: The regional accrediting commissions and abbreviations are as follows: Middle States Association of Colleges and Schools Middle States Commission on Higher Education (MSCHE), New England Association of Schools and Colleges Commission on Institutions of Higher Education (NEASC), North Central Association of Colleges and Schools/The Higher Learning Commission (NCA/HLC), Northwest Commission on Colleges and Universities (NWCCU), Southern Association of Colleges and Schools Commission on Colleges (SACS), Western Association of Schools and Colleges Accrediting Commission for Community and Junior Colleges (ACCJC), and Western Association of Schools and Colleges Accrediting Commission for Senior Colleges and Universities (WASC). Also referenced: Council for Advancement of Standards in Higher Education (CAS).

SUMMARY OF STANDARDS

Table 10.1 provides examples of online student services guidelines and standards. Many regional accrediting commissions have the same standards as those listed on Table 10.1. A single example was selected to avoid duplicating information. Table 10.1 is presented using WCET Spider Web as the organizing framework for online student services standards. At the bottom of the table are general standards that do not fall within the WCET Spider Web structure but are relevant to the overall development of online student services.

The regional accrediting commissions began the process of establishing quality standards for web-based learning early in the century through the *Statement of Commitment by the Regional Accrediting Commissions for the Evaluation of Electronically Offered Degree and Certificate Programs*. The parties to this agreement expected that the original document would be a work in progress and be revised to meet the changes brought by emerging technologies and the application of technology to online learning. The 2008 Higher Education Opportunity Act mandates oversight of some of those changes. The regional accrediting commissions have responded to HEOA by updating approaches and standards for evaluating distance learning programs. As institutions prepare themselves for their reaccreditation visits, they may want to consider using these standards as quality benchmarks for online student services. The next section discusses tools institutions might use to measure these standards.

MEASUREMENT INSTRUMENTS

Rovai, Ponton, and Baker (2008) offer a distance learning program evaluation model that includes three tracks, each led by the following program components: technology resources, teaching and learning, and student affairs. The model includes key performance indicators and outcomes within each component. Rovai and others suggest student affairs might assume leadership responsibility for the following evaluation elements: student enrollment, support services, engagement, student evaluations, persistence, and student achievement. The performance indicators for each of these elements can be found in Table 10.2.

TABLE 10.2 ELEMENTS OF ONLINE STUDENT SERVICES ASSESSMENT PROGRAM

Effects (Outcomes)	Performance Indicators
Student enrollment	Number of contacts/prospects, number of enrollments, student quality
Support services	Usage, processing turnaround, client satisfaction, meeting client needs, staff satisfaction, effects on personal development, effects on academic performance, cost-effectiveness
Engagement	Student-student, student-instructor, and student-system interactions
Student evaluations	Student ratings/recommendations, program relevance
Persistence	Course/program completion rates
Student achievement	Course grades, alumni/employer feedback, job placement/advancement, certification exam results, parity with on-campus programs, achievement gap by race/ethnicity/disability, student gratification

Note: Adapted from Rovai, Ponton, & Baker and others (2008, p. 115).

Institutions can choose from various instruments to evaluate campus-based student services. Because only a few instruments are designed exclusively to measure the quality of online student services, institutions will have to be creative in developing a comprehensive approach to evaluating online student services. The institution's object may be to combine results from multiple instruments in order to gain a comprehensive view of the quality and impact of online student services.

STUDENT EVALUATIONS

To organize the types of instruments that might be used to evaluate distance learning programs, Bresciani (2009) uses the following categories: pre-assessment surveys, student satisfaction surveys, utilization data, needs assessments, and outcomes-based assessments. This section focuses on those categories that are relevant for student services.

An institution might use pre-assessment surveys to collect information about a student's readiness and expectations of online learning. SmarterMeasure (formerly READI) is an instrument that measures several factors associated with online student success. The Orientation section of Chapter Seven contains more details about this instrument. Institutions can view results of students who are surveyed individually, by predefined subgroup, or by all students at the institution who took the instrument within a certain period. SmarterMeasure provides opportunities for institutions to compare their results to a general population of students who took the instrument. An institution's SmarterMeasure results might help them develop appropriate orientation options as students begin their first online course, tutorials to remediate skills necessary to be a successful online learner, and links to those resources that students need most to be successful in the online learning environment.

Student satisfaction surveys measure the level of satisfaction with particular online services. Institutions might take a satisfaction survey used for in-person student services and add to it questions about students' satisfaction with their experiences in finding and utilizing electronically delivered services, in using technology, and in accessing support personnel. The Noel-Levitz, *National Online Learners Priorities Survey* measures student satisfaction inside and outside the online classroom. The survey asks questions about program requirements and advising, tuition, opportunities to collaborate with other students, financial aid, institutional response time, sufficiency of offerings, response to student complaints, technical assistance, registration, career services, library, knowing whom to contact for difference services, billing and payment procedures, tutoring, and bookstore along with questions about the quality of instruction (*National Online Learners Priorities Report*, 2010). An institution can compare its results on this type of national survey with a broader audience beyond those students attending their institution.

Institutions might develop their own online course evaluations or they might purchase them from vendors. If institutions include questions about technical support, student academic and personal support, and student preparation prior to the start of the course, they will have the opportunity to aggregate the results of these questions as they decide how to improve online student services. Chaney and others developed an instrument to assess student opinions of the quality of distance education courses that includes items of interest to student service professionals (Chaney, Eddy, Dorman, Glessner, Green, & Lara-Alecio, 2007). Student service personnel might use these end-of-course evaluations as another data source to consider as part of a comprehensive assessment plan.

If institutions want data about the use of its websites in the delivery of online student services, they can obtain some data relatively easily. They may use a website tracking tool to count the number and duration of visits to each student service web page. Institutions can assess the quality of information presented on student services web pages by adding a quick feedback survey that provides users an opportunity to express satisfaction or concerns. Capella University has a feedback link on the bottom of each webpage on the student portal with a textbox that allows users to submit suggestions for improvements. Rather than present an opportunity to respond to an open-ended question, institutions can use questions based on the type of information they want to collect.

Student needs assessment are an important part of the strategic planning process. Institutions might use student needs assessments to determine what online student services are the ones most likely to be used by online students. Institutions might use the results of a needs assessment to prioritize the order in which they develop online services. They might gather demographic and geographic information to better understand the population who will be taking online courses. Institutions might use a needs assessment to obtain information about which services are most important to students during different periods of their enrollment. When institutions can compare student needs to currently available online services, institutions are better able to identify gaps and develop services in the areas most likely to be utilized.

Institutions might also consider outcome-based assessment (OBA). Institutions using OBA for campus-based assessment of student services can use a similar instrument and processes to assess online student services. Institutions may develop quality online student services when they use the OBA concept of identifying these items: what goals they want their students to accomplish from participating in an online service, how well students are accomplishing these goals, what means they will use to know this, how they will use this information to improve the service, and whether the improvement in the service also improves student outcomes (Bresciani, 2009). Institutions might use the same approach to outcomes-based assessment for online student services that they use for campus-based delivery of services, with appropriate modifications to account for the time and place shifting of distance learners and professionals.

PROGRAM EVALUATION

The Quality Scorecard for the Administration of Online Education Programs is one of the few tools available to measure quality in online programs. It contains 17 student services items that may help institutions assess the quality of online student services (Shelton, 2010). Institutions can analyze results from the Quality Scorecard for student services to identify the strengths and weaknesses of their services to online students. The weaknesses can be incorporated into the strategic planning process the institution uses for improving student services.

The CENTSS Audit Tool, which has been discussed extensively throughout the book, can be used to measure the level of interactivity the institution uses to present each of 31 online student services. As institutions recognize specific services whereby students would benefit from being able to interact and become more actively engaged through enhancements, these services could be identified for improvement.

Taken together, the results from the instruments described in this section might provide a comprehensive view of the quality of online student services. Institutions might take the approach of using some of the suggested tools to establish baselines, create a cycle to repeat administration of the instruments to evaluate change, use the data to determine where improvements are most needed, and continue the cycle of evaluation and improvement. A comprehensive student service evaluation plan benefits students and the institution by providing a structure for ongoing quality improvements.

CONCLUSION

This chapter provides ideas about how institutions can measure the current quality of their online student support services to establish baseline criteria and then create a cycle of evaluation for ongoing improvement. For most institutions, providing quality, comprehensive online student services is a work-in-progress. Institutions understand that providing quality online services enhances the educational experience and the success of their students. In times of limited budgets, some institutions might be inclined to use their websites only to describe campus-based student services and to provide opportunities for students to complete online those transactions included in the Administrative Suite. These institutions might decide not to fully develop opportunities for online access to services for the other service areas.

Such an approach may have some significant shortcomings. For online students who cannot or will not come to campus, limiting online services to the areas of admissions, registration, financial aid, course catalog, and course schedule would severely restrict their access to other services that lead to academic success. Students need personal and academic support in many additional areas, such as orientation, academic advising, career services, tutoring, and library, to name a few. With so many educational options available to them, some students may consider attending other institutions that do provide comprehensive online student services available around the clock.

FINAL THOUGHTS

As students enroll in more online courses and programs, institutions may want to focus on effective and efficient methods of supporting student success from their initial decisions to enroll, to their preparations for their first online course, and throughout their college years and beyond. In deciding ways to better support student success, institutions can consult standards and guidelines available from many higher education associations. Throughout this book are innovative examples of the services needed to support the success of online students.

This book has described various approaches to planning for and evaluating the implementation of online student services. Chapter Three describes a process for planning that would result in improved website, course materials, and hardware/software accessibility. Chapters Five, Six, and Seven provide planning ideas particular to the implementation of those services described in those chapters. Chapter Eight describes the essential components needed to plan for the launch of a comprehensive social media program. Institutions understand that planning for all services shares common elements: for example, consideration of institutional mission, vision, and current strategic planning processes. As with all other strategic planning processes, institutions recognize the importance of identifying and including key stakeholders in the development and delivery of online services and communicating progress throughout the institution.

This book has not fully discussed an issue that is ripe for exploration, discussion, and, ultimately, an institutional commitment: Which departments are responsible for the development, delivery, and maintenance of both content and presentation of online student services? The results of the 2010 Managing Online Education Survey show that reporting structures for distance education programs are still in transition: 44% of the respondents indicated that they had reorganized the management of online education in the past two years, 59% expected to reorganize in the next two years, and 31% reported they had reorganized in the past two years and expected to reorganize again in the next two years. The same survey found that the senior operating officer for online programs had various titles: chief information officer (42%), provost (19%), VP/dean continuing education (18), associate/assistant VP (15%), and other (5%) (Green, 2010a). While the organizational locations of offices of distance learning are in transition, even less clear is the department responsible for the support of online learners.

Neither the Managing Online Education report nor the other annual distance learning reports discussed in this book identify which department is ultimately responsible for the support of online learners. Certainly individual institutions are providing effective support of online students, but innovative practices have not been widely shared. With the growing concern about poor online student rates of course and program retention, institutions might want to identify and share those practices that have improved rates of online student success.

REFERENCES

"About WebAIM." (2011). *WebAIM Web Accessibility in Mind.* Utah State University, Center for Persons with Disabilities. Retrieved July 31, 2011 from http://webaim.org/about

Academic Advising Highly Important to Students. (2009). Coralville, IA: Noel-Levitz.

Academic Integrity and Student Verification Survey. (2008). Boulder, CO: WCET/Wiche Cooperative for Educational Technologies.

The Adult Learner: An Eduventures Perspective. (2008). Boston: Eduventures.

Ali, R., & Leeds, E. (2009). The impact of face-to-face orientation on online retention: A pilot study. *Online Journal of Distance Learning Administration, 12*(4).

Allen, I. E., & Seaman, J. (2010). *Class Differences: Online Education in the United States, 2010.* Newburyport, MA: Babson Survey Research Group and The Sloan Consortium.

Angelino, L. M., Williams, F. K., & Natvig, D. (2007). Strategies to engage online students and reduce attrition rates. *The Journal of Educators Online, 4*(2), 1–14.

Aragon, S. R., & Johnson, E. S. (2008). Factors influencing completion and non-completion of community college online courses. *American Journal of Distance Education, 22*(3), 146–158.

Bailey, T. (2009). Challenge and opportunity: Rethinking the role and function of developmental education in community college. *New Directions for Community Colleges* (Vol. 2009, pp. 11–30). San Francisco: Jossey-Bass.

Bambara, C. S., Harbour, C. P., Davies, T. G., & Athey, S. (2009). Delicate engagement. *Community College Review, 36*(3), 219.

Barr, V., Rando, R., Krylowicz, B., & Winfield, E. (2010). *The Association for University and College Counseling Center Directors Annual Survey.* Association for University and College Counseling Center Directors.

Best Practice Strategies to Promote Academic Integrity in Online Education. Version 2.0. (2009). WCET/Wiche Cooperative for Educational

Technologies, University of Texas TeleCampus, & the Instructional Technology Council.

Betts, K. (2009a). Lost in translation: Importance of effective communication in online education. *Online Journal of Distance Learning Administration, 12*(2).

Betts, K. (2009b). Online human touch (OHT) training and support: A conceptual framework to increase faculty engagement, connectivity, and retention in online education, Part 2. *Journal of Online Learning and Teaching, 5*(1).

Betts, K. (2011, April 15). Pro-active proretention program pays dividends. *Distance Education Report,* Magna Publications.

Boston, W., Díaz, S. R., Gibson, A. M., Ice, P., Richardson, J., & Swan, K. (2009). An exploration of the relationship between indicators of the community of inquiry framework and retention in online programs. *Journal of Asynchronous Learning Networks, 13*(3), 17.

Boston, W., Ice, P., & Gibson, A. M. (2011). Comprehensive assessment of student retention in online learning environments. *Online Journal of Distance Learning Administration, 4*(1).

Bozarth, J., Chapman, D. D., & LaMonica, L. (2004). Preparing for distance learning: Designing an online student orientation course. *Educational Technology & Society, 7*(1), 87–106.

Brescia, W., Miller, M., Ibrahima, P., & Murry, J. (2004). Orientation practices for effective distributed learning coursework: Students speak their minds. *Online Journal of Distance Learning Administration, 7*(3). Retrieved from http://www.westga.edu/~distance/ojdla/fall73/brescia73.html

Bresciani, M. J. (2005). Electronic co-curricular student portfolios–Putting them into practice. *New Directions for Student Services, 112,* 69.

Bresciani, M. J. (2009). Implementing assessment to improve student learning and development. *The Handbook of Student Affairs Administration* (3rd ed., pp. 526–544). San Francisco: Jossey-Bass.

Bresciani, M. J. (2011). Assessment and evaluation. *Student Services: A Handbook for the Profession* (5th ed., pp. 321–333). San Francisco: Jossey-Bass.

Burgstahler, S. (2006). The development of accessibility indicators for distance learning programs. *Association for Learning Technology Journal, 14*(1), 79–102.

Career Services Benchmark Survey for Four-Year College and Universities. (2011). Bethlehem, PA: National Association of Colleges and Employers.

"The Center for Universal Design." (2008). *Universal Design Principles.* North Carolina State University. Retrieved February 5, 2011, from http://www.ncsu.edu/www/ncsu/design/sod5/cud/about_ud/udprinciples.htm

Chaloux, B. (2010). Overcoming the financial barrier for e-learners. *Journal of Asynchronous Learning Networks, 12*(2).

Chaney, B. H., Eddy, J. M., Dorman, S. M., Glessner, L., Green, B. L., & Lara-Alecio, R. (2007). Development of an instrument to assess student opinions of the quality of distance education courses. *American Journal of Distance Education, 21*(3), 145–164.

Chen, P., Gonyea, R., & Kuh, G. (2008). Learning at a distance: Engaged or not. *Innovate: Journal of Online Education, 4*(3).

Chen, P.S.D., Guidry, K. R., & Lambert, A. D. (2009). Engaging online learners: A quantitative study of postsecondary student engagement in the online learning environment. *Annual Meeting of the American Educational Research Association*, San Diego, CA.

Chen, P.S.D., Lambert, A. D., & Guidry, K. R. (2010). Engaging online learners: The impact of web-based learning technology on college student engagement. *Computers & Education, 54*(4), 1222–1232.

Chen, X. (2005). *First Generation Students in Postsecondary Education: A Look at Their College Transcripts* (Postsecondary Education Descriptive Analysis Report). Washington, DC: National Center for Educational Statistics.

Compton, J. I., Cox, E., & Laanan, F. S. (2006). Adult learners in transition. *New Directions for Student Services* (Vol. 2006, pp. 73–80).

"Constructing a Perceivable, Operable, Understandable, Robust Website." (2011). *WebAIM Web Accessibility in Mind*. Utah State University, Center for Persons with Disabilities. Retrieved February 4, 2011, from http://webaim.org/articles/pour/

Cook, B. J., & Kim, Y. (2009). *From Soldier to Student: Easing the Transition of Service Members on Campus*. Washington, DC: American Council on Education.

Coombs, N. (2010). *Making Online Teaching Accessible: Inclusive Course Design for Students with Disabilities*. San Francisco: Jossey-Bass.

Crawley, A., & LeGore, C. (2009). Supporting online students. *The Handbook of Student Affairs Administration* (3rd ed., pp. 288–309). San Francisco: Jossey-Bass.

Curry, R. F., & Barham, P. D. (2007). Academic advising in degree programs. *Handbook of Distance Education* (2nd ed., pp. 123–136). Mahwah, NJ: Lawrence Erlbaum Associates, Publishers.

Dale, P. A., & Drake, T. M. (2005). Connecting academic and student affairs to enhance student learning and success. *New Directions for Community Colleges, 131*, 51.

Dare, L. A. (2011, May 4). Student Affairs Information Technology. Google Docs. Retrieved from https://spreadsheets.google.com/ccc?key=0AqjFSA5XV3GFdEdfRlRkWGNDaVJJVFV0b2xYcGFQUnc&hl=en&authkey=CO-c8cQI#gid=0

Dare, Leslie A., Zapata, L. P., & Thomas, A. G. (2005). Assessing the needs of distance learners: A student affairs perspective. *New Directions for Student Services*, (*112*), 39–54.

Dietz-Uhler, B., Fisher, A., & Han, A. (2007). Designing online courses to promote student retention. *Journal of Educational Technology Systems, 36*(1), 105–112.

Diploma to Nowhere. (2008). Washington, DC: Strong American Schools.

Distance learning and student affairs: Defining the issues. (2000). *NASPA—Student Affairs Administrators in Higher Education.* Retrieved from   http://www.ed.gov/about/bdscomm/list/acsfa/distnaspa.pdf

Doherty, W. (2006). An analysis of multiple factors affecting retention in web-based community college courses. *The Internet and Higher Education, 9*(4), 245–255.

Drouin, M. A. (2008). The relationship between students' perceived sense of community and satisfaction, achievement, and retention in an online course. *Quarterly Review of Distance Education, 9*(3), 267.

Edgecombe, N. (2011). *Accelerating the Academic Achievement of Students Referred to Developmental Education (30).* Community College Research Center: Teachers College, Columbia University.

"Eight-step Implementation Model." (2011). *WebAIM Web Accessibility in Mind.* Utah State University, Center for Persons with Disabilities, Retrieved February 4, 2011, from http://webaim.org/articles/implementation/#themodel

E-Recruiting Practices and Trends Report (2010). Coralville, IA: Noel-Levitz.

Erickson, W., Trerise, S., Lee, C., VanLooy, S., & Bruyère, S. (2007). *Research Brief: Web-Based Student Processes At Community Colleges—Removing Barriers to Access* (p. 126). ILR School of Employment and Disability: Cornell University.

Erickson, W., Trerise, S., VanLooy, S, Lee, C., & Bruyere, S. (2009). Web accessibility policies and practices at American community colleges. *Community College Journal of Research and Practice, 33*(5), 403–414.

"Essential Components of Web Accessibility." (2005, August). *W3C Web Accessibility Initiative (WAI).* Retrieved February 4, 2011, from http://www.w3.org/WAI/intro/components.php

Evidence of Quality in Distance Education Programs Drawn from Interviews with the Accreditation Community. (2006). Washington, DC: U.S. Department of Education. Retrieved from http://www.itcnetwork.org/Accreditation-EvidenceofQualityinDEPrograms.pdf

Falk, C. F., & Blaylock, B. K. (2010). Strategically planning for the "newer students" in higher education. *Academy of Educational Leadership Journal, 14*(3).

Feghali, T., Zahib, I., & Hallal, S. (2011). A web-based decision support tool for academic advising. *Educational Technology & Society, 14*(1).

Fike, D. S., & Fike, R. (2008). Predictors of first-year student retention in the community college. *Community College Review, 36*(2), 68.

Final Regulations Implementing Accreditation Provisions in the Higher Education Opportunity Act of 2008. (2009). Federal Update. Council for Higher Education Accreditation.

Fisher, M. (2005). Online learning design that fosters student support, self-regulation, and retention. *Campus-Wide Information Systems, 22*(2), 88–107.

Floyd, D. L., & Casey-Powell, D. (2004). New roles for student support services in distance learning. *New Directions for Community Colleges* (Vol. 2004, pp. 55–64). San Francisco: Jossey-Bass.

Focusing Your E-Recruitment Efforts to Meet the Expectations of College-Bound Students. (2009). Coralville, IA: Noel-Levitz.

Focusing Your E-Recruitment Efforts to Meet the Expectations of College-Bound Students. (2010). Coralville, IA: Noel-Levitz.

"Foundation Giving $110 Million to Transform Remedial Education." (2010, April 20). Bill & Melinda Gates Foundation. Retrieved July 31, 2011 from http://www.gatesfoundation.org/press-releases/Pages/new-ideas-for-remedial-education-in-community-college-100420.aspx

Fox, S. (2011). *Americans Living with Disability and Their Technology Profile.* Internet and American Life Project. Washington, DC: Pew Research Center.

"Gaining Online Accessible Learning Through Self-Study." (2005). *National Center on Disability and Access to Education.* Utah State University, Center for Persons with Disabilities. Retrieved February 4, 2011, from http://ncdae.org/goals/

Garrison, D. R., & Arbaugh, J. B. (2007). Researching the community of inquiry framework: Review, issues, and future directions. *The Internet and Higher Education, 10*(3), 157–172.

Garrison, D. R., Anderson, T., & Archer, W. (2010). The first decade of the community of inquiry framework: A retrospective. *The Internet*

and Higher Education, 13(1–2), 5–9. DOI: 10.1016/j.iheduc
.2009.10.003

Garrison, D. R., Cleveland-Innes, M., & Fung, T. S. (2009). Exploring causal relationships among teaching cognitive and social presence: Student perceptions of the community of inquiry frame work. *The Internet and Higher Education.*

Goldstein, D. F. (2010, November 12). ADA Title II and Section 504 of the Rehabilitation Act: The Pennsylvania State University.

Green, K. C. (2010a). *Managing Online Education.* Encino, CA: The Campus Computing Project. Retrieved from http://www.campus-computing.net/2010-managing-online-education

Green, K. C. (2010b). *Survey of Community College Presidents.* Encino, CA: The Campus Computing Project. Retrieved from http://www.campuscomputing.net/survey/community-colleges

Green, K. C. (2010c). *The Campus Computing Survey.* Encino, CA: The Campus Computing Project. Retrieved from http://www.campus-computing.net/2010-campus-computing-survey

Gunderson, J. (2010). Best and worst college web sites for blind students. *Chronicle of Higher Education.* Washington, DC.

The Heart of Student Success: Teaching, Learning, and College Completion (No. CSD5970). (2010). Center for Community College Student Engagement.

"Help and FAQ." (2009). *World Wide Web Consortium (W3C).* Retrieved February 4, 2011, from http://www.w3.org/Help/#activity

Herbert, M. (2006). Staying the course: A study in online student satisfaction and retention. *Online Journal of Distance Learning Administration, 9*(4).

Heyman, E. (2010). Overcoming student retention issues in higher education online programs. *Online Journal of Distance Learning Administration, 13*(4).

The Higher Education Act Reform Amendments of 2005 (Section-by-section analysis). (2006). Washington, DC: Department of Education. Retrieved from http://www2.ed.gov/policy/highered/leg/hea-analysis.pdf

Higher Education and Disability: Education Needs a Coordinated Approach to Improve Its Assistance to Schools in Supporting Students (No. GAO-10–33). (2009). Washington, DC: U.S. Government Accounting Office.

Higher Education Opportunity Act—2008. U.S. Department of Education. Washington, DC.

Hintz, S. (2010). Presented at the 16th Annual Sloan Consortium International Conference on Online Learning, Florida.

Holder, B. (2007). An investigation of hope, academics, environment, and motivation as predictors of persistence in higher education online programs. *The Internet and Higher Education, 10*(4), 245–260.

Holder, E. (2010, November 15). Revised ADA regulations implementing Title II and Title III. *ADA Regs 2010.* Department of Justice. Retrieved February 4, 2010, from http://www.ada.gov/regs2010/ADAregs2010.htm

Hossler, D., Ziskin, M., & Gross, J.P.K. (2009). Getting serious about institutional performance in student retention: Research-based lessons on effective policies and practices. *About Campus, 13*(6), 2–11.

Hsiung, R. (2009). *Student Counseling Centers Using Social Media.* Counseling Center Village: University of Buffalo.

Huett, J. B., Kalinowski, K. E., Moller, L., & Huett, K. C. (2008). Improving the motivation and retention of online students through the use of ARCS-based e-mails. *American Journal of Distance Education, 22*(3), 159–176.

Hung, M. L., Chou, C., Chen, C. H., & Own, Z. Y. (2010). Learner readiness for online learning: Scale development and student perceptions. *Computers & Education, 55*(3), 1080–1090.

Jaggars, S. S. (2011). *Online Learning: Does It Help Low-Income and Underprepared Students* (No. 52). Community College Research Center: Columbia University, Teachers College.

Jaggars, S. S., & Xu, D. (2010). *Online Learning in the Virginia Community College System.* Community College Research Center: Teachers College, Columbia University.

Jencius, M., & Rainey, S. (2009). Current online career counseling practices and future trends. *Career Planning and Adult Development Journal, 25*(3).

Johnson, L., Levine, A., Smith, R., & Stone, S. (2010). *The Horizon Report.* Boulder, CO: Educause.

Junco, R. (2011). The need for student social media policies. *EDUCAUSE Review, 46*(1).

Junco, R., & Cole-Avent, G. A. (2008). An introduction to technologies commonly used by college students. *New Directions for Student Services* (Vol. 124, pp. 3–17). San Francisco: Jossey-Bass.

Junco, R., Heiberger, G., & Loken, E. (2010). The effect of Twitter on college student engagement and grades. *Journal of Computer Assisted Learning.* San Francisco: Jossey-Bass.

Kendall, J. R. (2005). Implementing the web of student services. *New Directions for Student Services* (Vol. 112, p. 55). San Francisco: Jossey-Bass.

Kittelson, L. (2009). *Millennials, Modules, and Meaningful Advising*. Duluth University of Minnesota.

Kleemann, G. L. (2005). Weaving silos—a leadership challenge: A cross-functional team approach to supporting web-based student services. *New Directions for Student Services* (Vol. 112, pp. 89–101). San Francisco: Jossey-Bass.

Kleinglass, N. (2005). Who is driving the changing landscape in student affairs? *New Directions for Student Services* (Vol. 112, pp. 25–38). San Francisco: Jossey-Bass.

Knowles, M. S., Holton, E. F., & Swanson, R. A. (2005). *The Adult Learner: The Definitive Classic in Adult Education And Human Resource Development* (6th ed.). Amsterdam: Elsevier.

Kolowich, S. (2010, June 8). The e-book sector. *Inside Higher Ed.*

Kretovics, M. (2003). The role of student affairs in distance education: Cyber-services or virtual communities. *Online Journal of Distance Learning Administration, 6*(3).

Kuh, G. D. (2009). What student affairs professionals need to know about student engagement. *Journal of College Student Development, 50*(6), 683–706.

Lee, M.J.W., & Chan, A. (2007). Reducing the effects of isolation and promoting inclusivity for distance learners through podcasting. *Turkish Online Journal of Distance Education-TOJDE, 8*(1).

Lester, J., & Perini, M. (2010). Potential of social networking sites for distance education student engagement. *New Directions for Community Colleges* (Vol. 150, pp. 67–77). San Francisco: Jossey-Bass.

Leung, C. M., Tsang, E.Y.M., Lam, S. S., & Pang, D.C.W. (2010). Intelligent counseling system: A 24x7 academic advisor. *EDUCAUSE Quarterly, 33*(4).

Levy, Y. (2007). Comparing dropouts and persistence in e-learning courses. *Computers & Education, 48*(2), 185–204.

Lezberg, A. K. (2007). Accreditation: Quality control in higher distance education. *Handbook of Distance Education* (2nd ed.). Mahwah, NJ: Lawrence Erlbaum Associates.

Liu, S. (2008). Engaging users: The future of academic library web sites. *College & Research Libraries, 69*(1), 6.

Liu, S. Y., Gomez, J., & Yen, C. J. (2009). Community college online course retention and final grade: Predictability of social presence. *Journal of Online Interactive Learning, 8*(2). Retrieved from http://www.ncolr.org/jiol/issues/PDF/8.2.5.pdf

Lowery, J. W. (2004). Student affairs for a new generation. *New Directions for Student Services* (Vol. *106*, pp. 87–99).

Ludwig-Hardman, S., & Dunlap, J. C. (2003). Learner support services for online students: scaffolding for success. *International Review of Research in Open and Distance Learning, 4*(1).

Making Web Sites an Effective Recruitment Asset. (2009). Coralville, IA: Noel-Levitz.

Mandatory Cognitive and Affective Testing and Placement of Students into College Courses. (2010, December 2). National Association for Developmental Education.

Mandernach, B. J. (2009). Effect of instructor-personalized multimedia in the online classroom. *International Review of Research in Open and Distance Learning, 10*(3).

Manning, K., & Munoz, F. M. (2011). Framing student affairs practice. *Student Affairs: A Handbook for the Profession* (5th ed., pp. 281–285). San Francisco: Jossey-Bass.

Mariger, H. (2005). Cognitive disabilities and the web: Where accessibility and usability meet. *National Center on Disability and Access to Education.* Retrieved February 5, 2011, from http://ncdae.org/tools/cognitive/more_cognitive.cfm

Mayer, R. E. (2005). Principles of multimedia learning based on social cues: Personalization, voice, and image principles. *Cambridge Handbook of Multimedia Learning* (pp. 201–212). Cambridge: Cambridge University Press.

McInnerney, J. M., & Roberts, T. S. (2004). Online learning: Social interaction and the creation of a sense of community. *Educational Technology & Society, 7*(3), 73–81.

McKimmy, P. & Leong, P. (2004). Online in a hurry: Intensive technology orientation for distance education students in Hawai'i teacher preparation programs. In L. Cantoni & C. McLoughlin (Eds.), *Proceedings of World Conference on Educational Multimedia, Hypermedia and Telecommunications* 2004 (pp. 2936–2942). Chesapeake, VA: AACE.

McPherson, M., & Nunes, M. B. (2004). The failure of a virtual social space (VSS) designed to create a learning community: lessons learned. *British Journal of Educational Technology, 35*(3), 305–321.

McQuaid, J. W. (2010). Using cognitive load to evaluate participation and design of an asynchronous course. *American Journal of Distance Education, 24*(4), 177–194.

Means, B., Toyama, Y., Murphy, R., Bakia, M., & Jones, K. (2009). *Evaluation of Evidence-Based Practices in Online Learning: A Meta-Analysis and Review of Online Learning Studies.* Washington, DC: U.S. Department of Education.

REFERENCES 239

Mercer, R., & Simmons, M. (2010). *Using Learner Readiness to Improve Online Student Retention*. Deatsville, AL: SmarterServices, LLC.
Meyer, K. A. (2008a). The "virtual face" of institutions: Why legislators and other outsiders view higher education as aloof. *The Internet and Higher Education,* *11*(3–4), 178–185.
Meyer, K. A. (2008b). The "virtual face" of institutions: What do home pages reveal about higher education? *Innovative Higher Education,* *33*(3), 141–157.
Meyer, K. A., & Wilson, J. L. (2010). The "virtual face" of planning: How to use higher education web sites to assess competitive advantage. *Planning for Higher Education,* *38*(2), 11.
Miller, M. T., & Pope, M. L. (2003). Integrating technology into new student orientation programs at community colleges. *Community College Journal of Research & Practice,* *27*(1), 15–23.
Milliron, M. D. (2010, November). *An optimist's education agenda: Moving to increase access and success in higher education.* Presented at the WCET Annual Conference, La Jolla, CA. Retrieved from http://delta.cpcc.edu/resources/iti/video-support/linked-videos/Keynote_Presentation_by_Mark_Milliron.flv/view
Moltz, D. (2011, April 27). Completion agenda for baby boomers. *Inside Higher Ed.*
Moore, S. L., Med, P. D., & Edwards, M. (2004). Strategies for Success: Developing a Web-Based Orientation for Online Learning. *15th International Nursing Research Congress.*
Nagel, D. (2011, January 26). Online learning set for explosive growth as traditional classrooms decline. *Campus Technology.* Retrieved from http://campustechnology.com/articles/2011/01/26/online-learning-set-for-explosive-growth-as-traditional-classrooms-decline.aspx
Nash, R. D. (2005). Course completion rates among distance learners: Identifying possible methods to improve retention. *Online Journal of Distance Learning Administration,* *8*(4).
National Online Learners Priorities Report. (2010). Coralville, IA: Noel-Levitz.
Nichols, M. (2010). Student perceptions of support services and the influence of targeted interventions on retention in distance education. *Distance Education,* *31*(1), 93–113.
Nistor, N., & Neubauer, K. (2010). From participation to dropout: Quantitative participation patterns in online university courses. *Computers & Education,* *55*(2).
Nondiscrimination on the Basis of Disability; Accessibility of Web Information and Services of State and Local Government Entities and Public

Accommodations (CRT Docket No. 110; AG Order No. RIN 1190-AA61). (2010). Department of Justice, Civil Rights Division.

Oblinger, D. (2005). *Educating the Net Generation: An Educause ebook.* Retrieved from http://www.educause.edu/educatingthenetgen/5989

Online Registration Services. (2003).Washington, DC: American Association of Collegiate Registrars and Admissions Officers.

Overland, M. A. (2011, January 9). State of Washington to offer online materials as texts. *Chronicle of Higher Education.*

"Overview of the CENTSS Online Student Services Audit." Center for Transforming Student Services. Retrieved July 31, 2011 from http://www.centss.org/services/audit_services.html ("Overview of the CENTSS Online Student Services Audit," 2010).

Ozoglu, M. (2010). Assessment of learner support services in the Turkish open education system. *International Journal of Instructional Technology and Distance Learning, 7*(11).

Park, J., & Choi, H. J. (2009). Factors influencing adult learners' decision to drop out or persist in online learning. *Educational Technology & Society, 12*(4), 207–217.

Parsad, B., Lewis, L., & Tice, P. (2006). *Distance Education At Degree-Granting Postsecondary Institutions: 2006–07* (No. NCES 2009044). Washington DC: National Center for Educational Statistics.

Pelowski, S., Frissell, L., Cabral, K., & Yu, T. (2005). So far but yet so close: Student chat room immediacy, learning, and performance in an online course. *Journal of Interactive Learning Research, 16*(4), 395–407.

Pennington, H., & Milliron, M. D. (2010, September). Completion by design concept paper. Gates Foundation. Retrieved from http://www.completionbydesign.org/sites/default/files/CBD_Concept_paper_.pdf

Perez, T. E., & Ali, R. (2010, June 29). Electronic book reader joint "Dear Colleague" letter: Electronic book readers. Retrieved from http://www2.ed.gov/about/offices/list/ocr/letters/colleague-20100629.html

Phipps, R., & Merisotis, J. (2000). *Quality on the Line: Benchmarks For Success in Internet-Based Distance Education* (Bb & NEA). The Institute for Higher Education Policy.

The Practice of Internet Counseling. (2005). National Board for Certified Counselors, Inc. and Center for Credentialing and Education, Inc.

Principles of Effectiveness for Serving Adult Learners. (2005). Adult Learning Focused Institution Initiative. Chicago: The Council for Adult & Experiential Learning.

Puzziferro, M. (2008). Online technologies self-efficacy and self-regulated learning as predictors of final grade and satisfaction in college-level online courses. *American Journal of Distance Education*, 22(2), 72–89.

"Quality Matters Rubric Standards 2008–2010 Edition with Assigned Point Values." Maryland Online, Inc. Retrieved July 31, 2011 from http://www.qmprogram.org/files/RubricStandards2008–2010.pdf

Radford, A. W., & Associates, M.P.R. (2009). *Military service members and veterans in higher education: What the new GI Bill may mean for postsecondary institutions*. American Council On Education.

"RioLounge." (2011). Rio Salado College. Retrieved July 31, 2011 from http://www.riosalado.edu/about/teaching-learning/student-life/riolounge/Pages/default.aspx

Roberts, C. J., & Hai-Jew, S. (2009). Issues of academic integrity: An online course for students addressing academic dishonesty. *MERLOT Journal of Online Learning and Teaching*, 5(2).

Roberts, J., Crittenden, L., & Crittenden, J. (2009). Students with disabilities & online learning: A national study of enrollment & perceived satisfaction with institutional accessibility compliance & services. *Proceedings of World Conference on Educational Multimedia, Hypermedia and Telecommunications 2008* (pp. 4419–4422). Presented at the Association for the Advancement of Computing in Education, Chesapeake, VA.

Robinson, C. C., & Hullinger, H. (2008). New benchmarks in higher education: Student engagement in online learning. *The Journal of Education for Business*, 84(2), 101–109.

Roscorla, T. (2011, April 18). 4 universities use social networks to engage community. *Converge*. Retrieved from http://www.convergemag.com/policy/4-Universities-Use-Social-Networks.html

Rovai, A. P., Ponton, M. K., & Baker, J. D. (2008). *Distance Learning in Higher Education: A Programmatic Approach to Planning, Design, Instruction, Evaluation, and Accreditation*. New York & London: Teachers College Press.

Russell, T. L. (1999). No significant difference phenomenon. *Educational Technology & Society*, 2, 3.

Saenz, V. B., Hurtado, S., Barrera, D., Wolf, D., & Yeung, F. (2007). *First in My Family: A Profile of First-Generation College Students at Four-Year Institutions Since 1971*. Los Angeles: Higher Education Research Institute.

Scagnoli, N. I. (2001). Student orientations for online programs. *Journal of Research on Technology in Education*, 34(1), 19–28.

Scheer, S. B., & Lockee, B. B. (2003). Addressing the wellness needs of online distance learners. *Open Learning: The Journal of Open and Distance Learning, 18*(2), 177–196.

Scrolling Towards Enrollment. (2009). Coralville, IA: Noel-Levitz.

Sener, J., & Baer, B. (2002). A gap analysis of online student services: Report on administrator and student surveys. http://www.marylandonline.org/about/sponsored_research/gap_analysis

SENSE: Survey of Entering Student Engagement. (2010). Center for Community College Student.

Shea, P. A. (2005). Serving students online: Enhancing their learning experience. *New Directions for Student Services* (Vol. 112, p. 15). San Francisco: Jossey-Bass.

Shea, P., & Armitage, S. (2002). *Beyond the Administrative Core: Creating Web-Based Student Services for Online Learners.* Boulder, CO: WCET-LAAP Project. Available: http://www.wcet.info/projects/laap/guidelines/overview.htm

Sheehan, M. C., & Pirani, J. A. (2009). Spreading the word: Messaging and communications in higher education. *EDUCAUSE Center for Applied Research (ECAR) Research Study, 2*(9).

Shelton, K. (2010). A quality scorecard for the administration of online education programs: A Delphi study. *Journal of Asynchronous Learning Networks, 14*(4).

Shelton, K., & Saltsman, G. (2005). *An Administrator's Guide to Online Education.* United States Distance Learning Association Series on Distance Learning. Greenwich, CT: Information Age Pub Inc.

Slover-Linett, C., & Stoner, M. (2010). *Succeeding with Social Media: Lessons from the First Survey of Social Media in Advancement.* Chicago: Slover Linett Strategies & Council for Advancement and Support of Education.

Slover-Linett, C., & Stoner, M. (2011). *Best Practices in Social Media.* Chicago: Slover Linett Strategies & Council for Advancement and Support of Education.

Smith, A. (2010). *Home Broadband 2010* (No. 11). Internet & American Life Project. Washington, DC: Pew Research Center.

Smith, S., & Caruso, J. B. (2010). *The ECAR Study of Undergraduate Students and Information Technology.* Boulder, CO: Educause.

Standards for Advising Distance Learners. (2010). NACADA. Retrieved from http://www.nacada.ksu.edu/Commissions/C23/documents/DistanceStandards.pdf

Standards for Distance Learning Library Services. (2008). Chicago: Association of College and Research Libraries: A Division of the American

Library Association. Retrieved from http://www.ala.org/ala/mgrps/divs/acrl/standards/guidelinesdistancelearning.cfm#exsum

Steele, G., & Thurmond, K. C. (2009). Academic advising in a virtual world. *New Directions for Higher Education* (Vol. 146). San Francisco: Jossey-Bass.

Stenehjem, D. (2011). Universal design for the web. *Website Accessibility for Online Learning.* CANNECT. Retrieved February 4, 2011, from http://projectone.cannect.org/universal-design/

Student Information Systems, Collection of Grades, Application for Degree, and Degree Audit Functions. (2007). Washington, DC: American Association of Collegiate Registrars and Admissions Officers.

Student Retention Practices and Strategies at Four-Year and Two-Year Institutions. (2009). Higher Ed Benchmarks. Coralville, IA: Noel-Levitz.

Taylor, B., & Holley, K. (2009). Providing academic and support services to students enrolled in online degree programs. *College Student Affairs Journal, 28*(1).

Thompson, M. M., & Irele, M. E. (2007). Evaluating distance education programs. *Handbook of Distance Education* (2nd ed.). Mahwah, NJ: Lawrence Erlbaum Associates.

Trends in Elearning: Tracking the Impact of Elearning at Community Colleges. (2010). Retrieved http://www.itcnetwork.org/images/stories/itcannualsurveymay2011final.pdf. Instructional Technology Council.

Tyler-Smith, K. (2006). Early attrition among first time eLearners: A review of factors that contribute to drop-out, withdrawal and non-completion rates of adult learners undertaking eLearning Programs. *Journal of Online Learning and Teaching.* Retrieved from http://jolt.merlot.org/Vol2_No2_TylerSmith.htm

Upcraft, M. L., & Terenzini, P. T. (1999). *Looking Beyond the Horizon: Trends Shaping Student Affairs.* Washington, DC: American College Personnel Association.

"The users perspective." (2011). *WebAIM Web Accessibility in Mind.* Utah State University, Center for Persons with Disabilities. Retrieved July 31, 2011 from http://webaim.org/articles/

Vogel, C. (2011, April 21). The spirit of sharing. *New York Times.* New York.

"WAI Resources on Introducing Web Accessibility." (2010, October 26). *World Wide Web Consortium (W3C).* Retrieved February 4, 2011, from http://www.w3.org/WAI/gettingstarted/Overview.html

Walker, B. (2007). *Bridging the Distance: How Social Interaction, Presence, Social Presence, and a Sense Of Community Influence Student Learning*

Experiences in an Online Virtual Environment (Dissertation). University of North Carolina at Greensboro.

Wall, V. (2011, January 23). Supporting Online Students.

Waters, J. K. (2011). Can tech transcend the textbook? *Campus Technology, 24*(7).

What Works in Student Retention. (2010). Washington, DC: American College Testing Program.

Whiting, J. (2008, April 28). WebAIM Blog. *508 and Higher Education.* Utah State University, Center for Persons with Disabilities. Retrieved February 5, 2011, from http://webaim.org/blog/508-and-higher-ed/

Whorley, J. F. (2010, February 24). Go figure: What net price calculator should your institution offer? *Campus Technology.*

Willging, P. A., & Johnson, S. D. (2004). Factors that influence students' decision to drop out of online courses. *Journal of Asynchronous Learning Networks, 8*(4).

Wilson, M. (2008). An investigation into the perceptions of first-time online undergraduate learners on orientation events. *Journal of Online Learning and Teaching, 4*(1).

Wojciechowski, A. (2005). Individual student characteristics: Can any be predictors of success in online classes. *Online Journal of Distance Learning Administration, 8*(2).

Xu, D., & Jaggars, S. S. (2011). *Online and Hybrid Course Enrollment and Performance in Washington State Community and Technical Colleges* (No. 31). Community College Research Center: Teachers College, Columbia University.

Young, J. (2008, November 20). Minnesota state colleges plan to offer one-fourth of credits online by 2015. *The Chronicle of Higher Education.*

Zickuhr, K. (2010). *Generations 2010.* Internet and American Life Project. Washington, DC: Pew Research Center.

INDEX

A

AACRAO. *See* American Association rof Collegiate Registrars and Admissions Officers

Academic Advising Highly Important to Students (Noel Levitz), 104, 105, 130, 197

Academic advising, online: challenges of, 104–105; description of, 102; drawbacks of, 106–107; importance of, 104; innovative practices in, 108–109; models for, 105–107; need for, 68; preparation for, 107; standards for, 103–104; strengths of, 104; student satisfaction with, 104–105

Academic challenge, 159

Academic Integrity and Student Verification Survey (WCET), 109, 111, 112

Academic Services Suite: advising and counseling in, 102–109; assessment and testing in, 109–113; bookstore in, 113–116; description of, 67–68; library in, 116–121; standards for, 211–214t; technical support in, 121–122; tutoring in, 123–127

Accelerated Learning Program, 30

Accelerated programs: admissions page content and, 87; adult enrollment in, 15

Accelerating the Academic Achievement of Students Referred to Developmental Education (Edgecombe), 26

Access Entitlement Principle, 116

Accessibility committees, 58–59, 61

Accessibility, of library services, 117

Accessibility, of technology: benchmarking tool for, 61; indicators of, 54–56; lawsuits involving, 48–49; policies for, 59–60; principles of, 50–52; solutions for, 57–61; students with disabilities and, 41, 42, 49–52; universal design and, 50–52

Accommodations, for students with disabilities, 42

Accountability, 199

ACHA. *See* American College Health Association

ACHIEVE scholarship, 5

Achieving the Dream, 14

ACPA. *See* American College Personnel Association

ACRL. *See* Association of College and Research Libraries

ACSCI. *See* Association of Computer-based Systems for Career Information

Active learning, 159

ADA. *See* Americans with Disabilities Act

Adding courses, 98

Administrative Suite: catalog in, 90–91; components of, 83; course schedule in, 91–93; description of, 67; financial aid/planning in, 93–97; online admissions in, 84–90; registration in, 97–99;

Administrative Suite (continued) standards for, 208–210*t*; student records and accounts in, 99–100

Administrative support: for accessibility solutions, 58; during prelaunch planning phase, 195; in WebAIM Model, 58

Admissions services, online: audience for, 86–87; content and presentation of, 85–86; importance of, 85, 89; innovative practices in, 89–90; interactivity of, 87–88; prospective students communication with, 89

Adult Learner: An Eduventures Perspective (Eduventures), 15, 16, 35, 190

Adult Learning Focused Institution (ALFI) initiative, 18

Adult learning theory, principles of, 18–20

Adult students: admissions page content for, 87; career changes of, 16; challenges of, 15; ease of use of website and, 190; enrollment trends of, 15; goals of, 20; growing enrollment of, 13–14, 15, 16; history of, 16–18; importance of student services to, 15–16; needs of, 19*t*; technology use of, 20–21; visits to college websites by, 15

Advising students. *See* Academic advising, online

Advocacy culture, 79

Advocacy, for students with disabilities, 62

Affective expression, 157

Age gaps, in social media use, 10

ALFI. *See* Adult Learning Focused Institution initiative

Ali, R., 48, 131, 180, 182, 183*t*, 197

Allen, I. E., xi, 2, 3, 4, 6, 10, 182

American Association of Collegiate Registrars and Admissions Officers (AACRAO), 83, 84, 97

American Association of Community Colleges, 16

American Association of Community Colleges Convention, 26

American College Health Association (ACHA), 148

American College Personnel Association (ACPA), 207

American Council of the Blind, 48

American Council on Education, 32–33

American Public University System, 3, 158

American Sign Language, 44–45

Americans with Disabilities Act (ADA): compliance with, 56–61; description of, 47–48; lawsuits involving, 48; revisions to, 49

Anderson, T., 157

Angelino, L. M., xii, 180

Appendices, 203

Aragon, S. R., 183*t*

Arbaugh, J. B., 157

Archer, W., 157

Arizona State University, 48, 54

Armitage, S., xiii, 65

Artificial intelligence, 72

"As Textbooks Go Digital, Campus Bookstores May Go Bookless" *(Chronicle of Higher Education)*, 113

Assessment phase, of planning, 195–196

Assessments, online: for career services, 140; description of, 109–112; honesty in, 110–113; plan for, 203; of readiness for online learning, 133–134; skeptics of, 109; verifying identities for, 109

Assistive technology standards, 53

Associated Students of Washington State University Online Degree Programs, 173–174

Association of College and Research Libraries (ACRL), 116

Association of Computer-based Systems for Career Information (ACSCI), 138, 139
Athabasca University, 22
Athey, S., 155
At-risk students: challenges of, 35; innovative practices regarding, 35–37; national attention on, 34–35
Attendance, at orientation, 131
Attrition rates, xii
Audience, for admissions home page, 86–87
Audio content: for career services, 143; private counselors and, 147; social isolation and, 156; versus text-only communication, 155; usability standards and, 52
Audit tools, 193–198

B

Baby boomers, 16
Baer, B., 196
Bailey, T., 25
Baker, J. D., 222
Bakia, M., 167, 200
Bambara, C. S., 155
Barham, P. D., 197
Barr, V., 145
Barrera, D., 24
Best Practice Strategies to Promote Academic Integrity, 111, 112
Best Practices for Electronically Offered Degree and Certificate Programs, 204
Betts, K., 137, 154, 169, 170
Beyond the Administrative Core FIPSE grant, 193, 194
Beyond the Administrative Core project, 73
Bill and Melinda Gates Foundation, 25–27, 35
Biometric software, 109
Blackboard: benchmarks for quality by, 207; increased use of, 7; for tutoring services, 125

Blaylock, B. K., 15, 16, 17
Blended courses: benefits of, 167; definition of, 5
Blind students, 41, 48
Blogs, for online counseling services, 146
Bookmarking pages, 75
Bookstores, 113–116
Boomers: characteristics of, 17–18; technology use of, 20–21
Boston, W., 157, 158, 180
Bozarth, J., 133, 134, 182, 197
Brescia, W., 130
Bresciani, M. J., 197, 199, 202, 223, 226
Bridgeport Education, 3
Broadband Internet connections, 21, 31
Brown University, 120
Bruyère, S., 49
Bucks County Community College, 136
Burgstahler, S., 55

C

Cabral, K., 183t
Calculators, online, 95, 96, 124
California State Polytechnic University, 34
California State University, Long Beach, 145
Campus Computing Survey, 10, 114, 116
Campus culture. See Institutional culture
Campus tours, 89
Capella University, 99, 106, 225
Career centers, online, 141
Career changes, 16
Career development courses, 142–143
Career service functional areas, 139–140
Career Services Benchmark Survey for Four-Year Colleges and Universities (NACE), 141

Career services, online: approaches to, 137–138; availability of, 68; career centers in, 141; innovative practices in, 143–144; interactivity of, 141–143; relationship of student and professional in, 138; standards for, 138–139; website design for, 139–140

Caruso, J. B., 9, 10

CAS. *See* Council for Advancement of Standards in Higher Education

CASE. *See* Council for Advancement and Support of Education

Casey-Powell, D., 80, 190

CashCourse, 32, 96

Catalog, online: described, 90; innovative practices in, 91

Catalyst Web Tool project, 122–123

CCRC. *See* Community College Research Center

CCSSE. *See* Community College Survey of Student Engagement

Center for Persons with Disabilities, 57

Center for the Study of Technology in Counseling and Career Development, 147

Center for Transforming Student Services (CENTSS), 193–198

"Center for Universal Design," 50

Central Piedmont Community College, 125

Chaloux, B., 96

Chan, A., 155, 156

Chaney, B. H., 225

Chapman, D. D., 133, 134, 182, 197

Cheating, 110–113, 151

Chen, C. H., 134

Chen, P., 160

Chen, P.S.D., 159, 160–161

Chen, X., 23

Choi, H. J., 182, 183*t*

Chou, C., 134

Chronicle of Higher Education, 113

CIRP. *See* Cooperative Institutional Research Program

Class Differences: Online Education in the United States, 2010, xi

Clubs, 173–175

Cognitive disabilities, 45

Cognitive presence, 158

CoI. *See* Community of Inquiry framework

Cole-Avent, G. A., 164

Collaborative learning, 159

Collaborative planning, 178

Collaborative tutoring, 126–127

College Board, 95

Collegesource.org, 90

Collegial culture, 79

Color-blind students, 52–53

Columbia University, 145–146

Commoncraft.com, 164

Communication: admissions pages and, 87–88, 89–90; Community of Inquiry framework and, 156–158; electronic means of, 7–8; in Generation 3 services, 75; online culture and, 158; personalization principle and, 155; during planning, 195–196; tone of, 154; types of, 153–155

Communications Suite: description of, 69; faculty-to-student communication, 167–170; institution-to-student communication, 170–172; multimedia and, 166; social media and, 161–166; standards for, 218–219*t*; student engagement and, 158–161; student-to-student communication and, 172–176; types of communication in, 153–158; virtual classrooms and, 167

Community College of Baltimore County, 30

Community College Open Textbook Collaborative, 115

Community College Research Center (CCRC), 28, 35

Community College Survey of Student Engagement (CCSSE), 159, 168–169

Community colleges: adult students in, 16; challenges of academic advising at, 104–105; first generation students in, 24–25; growth of online learning in, 3, 4; national attention on, 34; student populations in, 13–14

Community of Inquiry (CoI) framework, 156–158

Competitive advantage, 192

Completion by Design (Pennington & Milliron), 26–27

Compton, J. I., 17

Computers: versus mobile devices, 10; students with disabilities and, 44–46

Connecticut Distance Learning Consortium (CTDLC), 126

The Consortium of College Testing Centers, 110

"Constructing a Perceivable, Operable, Understandable, Robust Website," 52, 53, 54

Consumerism, 79

Content management systems, 197

Content, of website: for career services, 139–140; of health and wellness services, 149; for online admissions, 85–86

Convenient services, 70–72, 190

Conversation Prism (Solis & Thomas), 162

Cook, B. J., 33

Coombs, N., 40, 51

Cooperative Institutional Research Program (CIRP), 23–24

Copyright protections, 116

Cornell University, 146

Cost savings: for electronic textbooks, 115; of online student services, 72

Council for Adult and Experiential Learning (CAEL), 14, 18, 21

Council for Advancement and Support of Education (CASE), 170

Council for Advancement of Standards in Higher Education (CAS), 204, 206

Counseling services, online: examples of, 145–146; external resources in, 146–147; function of, 144; need for, 144–145; private counselors in, 147–148; standards for, 147–148

Counselors, 147–148

Course schedules, online: description of, 91–92; innovative practices in, 91, 92–93

Course searches, 91

Cox, E., 17

Crawley, A., 207

Creighton University, 32

Crittenden, J., 43

Crittenden, L., 43

Cross-functional teams, 195

CTDLC. *See* Connecticut Distance Learning Consortium

Curry, R. F., 197

D

Dale, P. A., 80, 207

Dare, L. A., 80, 81, 207

Davies, T. G., 155

Debt, postgraduate, 96

Decision making, 140

Degree audits, online, 92

Degree plans, online, 92

Degree programs, online, 3

Delhi Online Education website, 122

DePaul School for New Learning, 22

Design phase, of planning, 197

Desktop conferencing software, 7

Developmental advising: description of, 106; online versions of, 107

Developmental courses: *Completion by Design* format for, 26–27; first generation student enrollment in, 23; Gates' initiative and, 25–26; importance of, 26; innovative

Developmental courses (continued) practices in, 26, 29–30; interventions for, 26–27; lack of online options in, 27–28; need for, 25; online enrollment in, 27–28; online versus on-site completion of, 28; placement testing and, 109–110; for veterans, 33

Developmental culture, 79

Developmental phase, of planning, 197

DeVry, 3

Díaz, S. R., 157, 158, 180

Dietz-Uhler, B., 180

Diploma to Nowhere (Strong American Schools), 25

Director, project, 194–195

Disabilities, students with: accessible technology and, 41, 42; accommodations for, 42; admissions page content for, 87; advocating for, 62; benefits of online learning to, 38, 40; categories of, 43; challenges of, 41–42; description of, 39; discrimination against, 48; enrollment of, in online courses, 43; increased enrollment of, 40; innovative practices for, 44–46; laws and standards regarding, 46–61; support services for, 61–62; technology innovations and, 40

Discrimination, students with disabilities and, 47, 48

Distance education: components of, 11; critics of, 199–200; definition of, 6; history of, 1, 11

Distance Education at Degree-Granting Postsecondary Institutions: 2006–2007 (Parsad, Lewis, & Tice), 4

Distance Learning and Student Affairs: Defining the Issues (NASPA), 206

Distance Learning Program (DLP) Accessibility Indicators, 54–56

Diversity, in student population: versus graduation of diverse students, 13; growth in enrollment of, 13–14

DLP. *See* Distance Learning Program Accessibility Indicators

Doherty, W., 180, 183*t*

Dorman, S. M., 225

Drake, T. M., 80, 207

Drexel University, 136–137, 169–170

Dropping courses, 98

Drouin, M. A., 180, 183*t*

Dual purpose institutions: challenges of, 78; description of, 77; services offered online at, 188

Duke University, 95, 146

Dunlap, J. C., 130, 155, 156, 180, 182, 197

E

ECAR Study of Undergraduate Students and Information Technology (Smith & Caruso), 9

Economic downturn, 4

Eddy, J. M., 225

Edgecombe, N., 26

Educational Services for Distance Learners, 206

Educause, 164

Eduventures, 15, 16, 35, 190

Edwards, M., 182

"Eight-Step Implementation Model," 57, 59, 60, 61

Electronic book readers, 48

Electronic textbooks, 115–116

Email: changes in, 7–8; versus social media, 7–8; students with disabilities and, 40

Empire State College, 21–22

Engaged advising: description of, 106; online version of, 107

Enriching educational experiences, 159

Enrollment, in online learning: adult students' trends in, 15, 16; in developmental courses, 27–28; of diverse populations, 13–14; evaluation criteria and, 205; of first generation students, 24; growth in, 2–3, 16, 34; of low-income students, 31; of students with disabilities, 40, 43

Enrollment period, 140

Equitable design, 50

eReaders, 113, 114

E-Recruiting Practices and Trends (Noel Levitz), 189

Erickson, W., 49

"Essential Components of Web Accessibility," 51

Ethical and legal services, online: focus of, 150–151; innovative practices in, 151

Ethics, of private counselors, 147–148

Evaluation: approaches to, 201–203; description of, 201–202; elements of, 223*t*; importance of, 199–201; measurement instruments for, 222–226; of online versus on-site learning, 201; during planning phases, 195–196; to promote retention, 200–201; standards and guidelines for, 203–222

F

Facebook: admissions communication and, 89; for health and wellness services, 150; for institution-student communication, 170–171; for online career services, 144; for online counseling services, 146; popularity of, 162; for student-student communication, 175; varied uses of, 162

Faculty: accessibility indicators for, 55; communication in online courses, 167–170; of early online learning, 1; in online orientation, 131, 132, 133; responsibilities of, to prevent cheating, 112–113; social isolation of students and, 156; social network knowledge of,

164; as sole support for online learning, xi–xii, 11

Fairfield University, 146

Falk, C. F., 15, 16, 17

Feedback, 203, 225

Feghali, T., 105

Fike, D. S., 13, 25, 180

Fike, R., 13, 25, 180

Financial aid/planning, online: importance of, 96; innovative ideas in, 96–97; site content for, 93–97

Financial Literacy CashCourse, 96

First generation students: characteristics of, 24; community college enrollment and, 24–25; definition of, 23; unique needs of, 23

First in My Family: A Profile of First-Generation College Students at Four-Year Institutions Since 1971 (Cooperative Institutional Research Program), 23–24

First Year Experience program, 136–137

First-Generation Students in Postsecondary Education study (Chen), 23

Fisher, A., 180

Fisher, M., 180, 183*t*

Flexibility, of design, 50

Floyd, D. L., 80, 190

Focusing Your ERecruitment Efforts to Meet the Expectations of College-Bound Students (Noel Levitz), 85, 86, 87

Foothill-De Anza Community College District, 115

For-profit universities. *See* Private institutions

Forrester Research, 114

Fox, S., 39

Frissell, L., 183*t*

From Soldier to Student: Easing the Transition of Service Members on Campus (American Council on Education), 32–33

Fully online courses, 5
Fund for the Improvement of Postsecondary Education (FIPSE), xiii, 65

G

Gaining Online Accessible Learning Through Self-Study (GOALS), 61
Garrison, D. R., 157
Gates, B., 25–27
Generations, of online support services, 73–77
Gen-Xers: characteristics of, 17–18; technology use of, 20–21
Georgia Perimeter College, 32
GI Bill, 33
Gibson, A. M., 157, 158, 180
Glessner, L., 225
Goals, program, 202
Goldstein, D. F., 49
Gomez, J., 180
Gonyea, R., 160
Grade point averages, 124
Graduating students, diversity of, 13
Green, B. L., 225
Green, K. C., 3, 4, 5, 56, 62, 67, 105, 114, 116, 229
Gross, J.P.K., 180, 182, 197
Group cohesion, 157
Guidelines for Creating Online Student Services (WICHE), xiii
Guidelines for the Use of the Internet for Delivery of Career Counseling and Career Planning Services (NCDA), 138–139
Guidry, K. R., 159, 160–161
Gunderson, J., 50

H

Hai-Jew, S., 151
Hallal, S., 105
Han, A., 180
Harbour, C. P., 155
Hardware requirements, 121
Hartwick College, 147

Harvard University, 32
Health alerts, 150
Health and wellness services, online: challenges of, 68–69; innovative practices in, 150; principles for, 148–149; web content for, 149
Hearing disabilities: adaptations for, 44–45; usability standards and, 52
Heiberger, G., 164
Herbert, M., 180
Heyman, E., 180, 183*t*
High school graduation, 35
Higher Education Act Reform Amendments (2005), 93
Higher Education and Disability: Education Needs a Coordinated Approach to Improve Its Assistance to Schools in Supporting Students, 39
Higher Education Opportunity Act (HEOA; 2008), 6, 95, 204–206, 222
Hintz, S., 174, 175
Holder, B., 49, 180, 183*t*
Holley, K., 207
Holton, E. F., 18
Horizon Report, 114
Hossler, D., 180, 182, 197
Hsiung, R., 146
Huett, J. B., 180
Huett, K. C., 180
Hullinger, H., 159, 161
Hung, M. L., 134
Hurtado, S., 24
Hybrid courses, 5

I

I-BEST. *See* Integrated Basic Education and Skills Training
Ibrahima, P., 130
Ice, P., 157, 158, 180
Identity verification, 109
iGuide, 99
IHEP. *See* Institute for Higher Education Policy
Illinois State University, 145

Illinois Virtual Campus, 109–110
Implementation plans: for
accessibility solutions, 60; in
planning phases, 198
Improvement goals, 196
Inclusive Student Services Process
Model, 190–191
Information gathering, 57–58
Information literacy, 118
Information technology (IT)
departments, 81
Informed consent, 107
Institute for Higher Education Policy
(IHEP), 204, 207
Institutional culture, 78–80
Instructional designers, 55
Instructional Technology Council
(ITC), 3, 188
Integrated advising: description of,
106; online version of, 107
Integrated Basic Education and
Skills Training (I-BEST)
program, 29
Integrated support services, 169
Interactivity: evaluation criteria
and, 205; legal requirements for,
6; of online admissions services,
87–88; of online career services,
141–143; of online orientations,
132; social isolation and, 156;
social media and, 9; usability
standards and, 53
Internal websites, 63
Internet: Americans with Disabilities
Act and, 47; electronic textbooks
on, 116; popularity of, across age
groups, 20–21; use of, by students
with disabilities, 39, 40
Intuitive design, 50
Irele, M. E., 201
"Is Social Media Changing
Museums?" (New York Times), 8
IT departments. See Information
technology departments
ITC. See Instructional Technology
Council

J

Jaggars, S. S., 3, 28, 28, 31, 35, 36
Jencius, M., 140, 143
Johnson, E. S., 183t
Johnson, L., 10, 114
Johnson, S. D., 155
Jones, K., 167, 200
Junco, R., 164, 165, 166

K

Kalinowski, K. E., 180
Kansas State University, 151
Kaplan University, 3
Kendall, J. R., 80
Khan Academy, 124
Kim, Y., 33
Kindle electronic reader, 48
Kittelson, L., 107
Kleemann, G. L., 80, 207
Kleinglass, N., 207
Knowles, M. S., 18
Kolowich, S., 116
Kretovics, M., 8, 80, 207
Krylowicz, B., 145
Kuh, G., 159, 160

L

Laanan, F. S., 17
Lam, S. S., 108
Lambert, A. D., 159, 160–161
LaMonica, L., 133, 134, 182, 197
Lara-Alecio, R., 225
Learning Anytime Anyplace
Partnership (LAAP) program,
xiii, 65
Learning management systems
(LMSs): ADA compliance of, 56;
cheating deterrents and, 111;
definition of, 7; function of, 63;
for online career services, 142,
143; for online orientation, 133;
online tutoring through, 124;
students with disabilities and, 41
Lee, C., 49
Lee, M.J.W., 155, 156
Leeds, E., 131, 180, 182, 183t, 197

Legal services. *See* Ethical and legal services, online
LeGore, C., 207
Leong, P., 182
Lester, J., 162
Leung, C. M., 108
Levine, A., 10, 114
Levy, Y., 183*t*
Lewis, L., 4
Lezberg, A. K., 204
Library services, online: innovative practices in, 120–121; for open source content, 115; standards for, 116–118; websites for, 118–120
Link descriptions, 52
Liu, S., 118, 119, 120
Liu, S. Y., 180
Live chats: for admission information, 89; for tutoring, 125
Live orientations, 131, 135
LMS. *See* Learning management systems
Lock-down browsers, 111
Lockee, B. B., 149
Logins, 205
Loken, E., 164
Long Beach Community College, 131–132
Long Island University, 147
Low physical effort, 51
Lowery, J. W., 207
Low-income students: challenges of, 30–31; innovative practices for success of, 31–32; suggestions for success of, 31
Ludwig-Hardman, S., 130, 155, 156, 180, 182, 197
Lumina Foundation, 35

M

Madison Area Technical College, 98
Majors, college, 140
Making Web Sites an Effective Recruitment Asset (Noel-Levitz), 189–190
Managerial culture, 79

Managing Online Education Survey, 2010, 56, 62, 67, 80, 105
Mandatory Cognitive and Affective Testing and Placement of Students into College Courses, 109
Mandernach, B. J., 154, 155
Manning, K., 78
Mariger, H., 45, 46
Marylhurst University, 22
Massachusetts Institute of Technology (MIT), 115
Mayer, R. E., 155
McInnerney, J. M., 155
McKimmy, P., 182
McPherson, M., 155
McQuaid, J. W., 183*t*
Means, B., 167, 200
Med, P. D., 182
Mentors, 175
Mercer, R., 134
Merisotis, J., 207
Meyer, K. A., 191, 192
Military service personnel. *See* Veterans
Millennials: characteristics of, 17–18; technology use of, 20–21
Miller, M., 130
Miller, M. T., 134
Milliron, M. D., 13, 27
Minnesota State Colleges and Universities, 5–6, 193
Mission, program, 202
MIT. *See* Massachusetts Institute of Technology
Mobile technology trends, 9–10
Moller, L., 180
Moltz, D., 16
Monster.com, 140
Moore, S. I., 182
Mouse, computer, 53
Multimedia communication, 154–155, 166
Munoz, F. M., 78
Murphy, R., 167, 200
Murry, J., 130
Museums, 8

MyAccount systems, 76, 99–100
MyInstitution portal, 190

N

Nagel, D., 3
Nash, R. D., 130, 180, 182, 197
NASPA. *See* National Association
    of Student Personnel
    Administrators
National Academic Advising
    Association (NACADA),
    103–104
National Association for
    Developmental Education
    (NADE), 109
National Association of College
    Stores (NACS), 114
National Association of Colleges
    and Employers (NACE), 138,
    139, 141
National Association of Student
    Personnel Administrators
    (NASPA), 206
National Board for Certified
    Counselors (NBCC), 147
National Board of Certified
    Counselors, 144
National Career Development
    Association (NCDA), 138, 139
National Center of Educational
    Statistics (NCES), 16
National Center on Disability and
    Access to Education, 61
National College Testing Association
    (NCTA), 110
National Educators Association
    (NEA), 207
National Endowment for Financial
    Education, 32, 96
National Endowment for Financial
    Education (NEFE), 96–97
National Federation of the Blind,
    48–49
*National Online Learners Priorities
    Report* (Green), 14–15, 105, 127,
    183, 185, 224

National Survey of Student
    Engagement (NSSE), 159, 160,
    161
Natvig, D., xii, 180
Navigation, website: online
    admissions and, 85–86; students'
    preferences regarding, 192;
    usability standards and, 53
NBCC. *See* National Board for
    Certified Counselors
NCDA. *See* National Career
    Development Association
NCES. *See* National Center of
    Educational Statistics
NCTA. *See* National College Testing
    Association
NEA. *See* National Educators
    Association
Needs assessments, 196, 225
NEFE. *See* National Endowment for
    Financial Education
Neubauer, K., 182
New York Times, 8
Nichols, M., 180
Nistor, N., 182
Noel-Levitz, 85, 86, 87, 104, 105, 127,
    130, 185, 186, 189, 224
*Nondiscrimination on the Basis of
    Disability; Accessibility of Web
    Information and Services of State and
    Local Government Entities and Public
    Accommodations*, 47
Nontraditional adult students. *See*
    Adult students
North Carolina State University, 81,
    92–93
North Dakota State University, 125
NSSE. *See* National Survey of Student
    Engagement
Nunes, M. B., 155

O

Obama, B., 8, 34, 35
Oblinger, D., 17
Occupational Outlook Handbook,
    140

Office of Civil Rights (OCR), 48
The Ohio Learning Network, 3
The Ohio State University, 96, 150
O*NET Online, 140
Online calendars, 75, 76
Online courses: definition of, 5–6; growth in, 34; integrated support services and, 63–64; for orientation to online learning, 132; students with disabilities in, 43
Online Human Touch, 170
Online learning: admissions home page for, 86; appeal of, 64; critics of, 199–200; growth in, xi, 2–5, 14; history of, 1, 14; lack of services to support, xii–xi; student withdrawal from, 181–182; students' expectations of, 2; terminology related to, 5–7
Online Registration Services study (AACRAO), 97
Open communication, 157
Open content, 114, 115
Open Course Library, 115
Open University, 108
Operable online content, 53
Oregon State University, 172
Orientation, to online learning: content of, 134–136; formats for, 131–133; goal of, 130; importance of, 130–131, 137; innovative practices in, 136–137; interactivity of, 132; measuring readiness for online learning in, 133–134
Outcome-based assessments, 202–203, 225–226
Outcomes, 202, 203
Overland, M. A., 115
"Overview of the CENTSS Online Student Services Audit," 73
Own, Z. Y., 134
Ozoglu, M., 130, 182, 197

P

Pang, D.C.W., 108
Park, J., 182, 183t
Park University, 33–34
Parsad, B., 4
Password-protected portals, 75–76
Passwords, 205
Pelowski, S., 183t
Pennington, H., 27
Pennsylvania State University, 48–49, 95, 147, 172
Perceptible information, 51
Perez, T. E., 48
Perini, M., 162
Personal Services Suite: career services in, 137–144; description of, 68–69, 129; ethical/legal services in, 150–151; health and wellness services in, 148–150; online orientation in, 130–137; personnel counseling in, 144–148; standards for, 214–217t
Personalization principle, 155
Personalized services, 190
PEW Institute, 39
Pew Internet and American Life Project, Generations 2010 report, 20
Phipps, R., 207
Photo sharing, 143
Physical disabilities, 45
Pirani, J. A., 8
Placement services, 138
Placement testing, 109–110
Planning. See Strategic planning
Platforms, 6–7
Plus 50 Completion Strategy, 16
Ponton, M. K., 222
Pope, M. L., 134
Portable Document Format (pdf) files, 42
Portals, 84
Portfolios, 108
Post-9/11 Veterans Assistance Act (2009), 32

Practice of Internet Counseling (NBCC), 147
Pre-assessment surveys, 224
Prelaunch phase, of planning, 194–195
Prescriptive advising, 105–106
Principles of Effectiveness for Serving Adult Learners (CAEL), 18–20
Print textbooks, 115–116
Private institutions, 3
Proctoring services, 110
Program evaluators: accessibility indicators for, 55; measurement tools for, 226
Purdue University, 143–144
Puzziferro, M., 183*t*

Q
Quality Matters (QM), 168
Quality on the Line: Benchmarks for Success in Internet-Based Distance Education (Phipps & Merisotis), 207
Quality Scorecard for the Administration of Online Education Programs, 226
Quintessential Careers, 140

R
Radford, A. W., 32
Rainey, S., 140, 143
Rando, R., 145
Randolph-Macon College, 145
Readability, 46
Readiness assessments, 133–134
ReadyMinds, 144
Really Simple Syndication (RSS). *See* RSS
Regional accrediting commissions, 205, 222
Regional Network Groups, 144
Registration, online: innovative practices in, 98–99; need for, 97–98; services offered in, 97
Rehabilitation Act (1973), 47

Remediation. *See* Developmental courses
Rented textbooks, 114
Request for Proposal (RFP) process, 197
Retention, of online students: challenges of, 130; definition of, 180; evaluation to promote, 200–201; factors contributing to, 181–182; high-impact interventions for, 182, 185–186; innovative practices in, 186–187; interventions to improve, 184–185*t*; statistics on, 180; variables affecting, 183*t*
RFP process. *See* Request for Proposal process
Richardson, J., 157, 158, 180
Rio Salado Community College, 176
Roberts, C. J., 151
Roberts, J., 43
Roberts, T. S., 155
Robinson, C. C., 159, 161
Robust websites, 54
Roscorla, T., 171
Rovai, A. P., 222
Rowan University, 136
RSS (Really Simple Syndication), 77, 118, 150
Russell, T. L., 201
Rutgers University, 144

S
Saenz, V. B., 24
Saltsman, G., 194
San Diego City College, 107
San Diego State University, 145
San Jose State University, 143
Santa Clara University, 146
Scagnoli, N. I., 182
Schedules, class. *See* Course schedules, online
Scheer, S. B., 149
Scholarships, 94
Scroll bars, 85
Seaman, J., xi, 2, 3, 4, 6, 10, 182

Seamless services, 75
Second Life, 137; for faculty-student communication, 170; for online counseling services, 146
Section 504 and 508 (Rehabilitation Act), 47–48, 50, 56–61
Self-assessment tools, 124
Self-directed learning, 134
Self-paced orientation, 133
Self-paced tutoring, 124
Sener, J., 196
Senior operating officers, 229
Seton Hall University, 145
7 Things You Should Know About series (Educause), 164
Shea, P., xiii, 65
Shea, P. A., 65, 80, 83
Sheehan, M. C., 8
Shelton, K., 194, 207, 208, 212t, 226
Silent Generation, 20–21
Simmons, M., 134
Simple design, 50
Sinclair Community College: developmental courses at, 30; innovative practices at, 22; retention practices at, 186–187
SIS. See Student information system
Sloan Consortium, 2, 3, 4, 6
Slover-Linett, C., 170, 171
SmarterMeasure, 134, 224
Smarthinking, 126
Smith, A., 31
Smith, R., 10, 114
Smith, S., 9, 10
Social isolation: causes of, 156; initiatives for at-risk students regarding, 35, 36; remedies for, 156; risk for, 155
Social media: admissions information on, 88; adoption and implementation of, 164–165; age gap in, 10; barriers to, 171; benefits of, 162; college presence in, 88; for college searches, 88; as communication platform,

8, 161–166; examples of, 162–164; goals for, 171; for health and wellness services, 150; influence of, 8; innovative practices in, 171–172; for institution-student communication, 170–171; interactivity of, 9; management of, 171; for online career services, 142, 143; policy for, 165–166; potential of, 7; trends in, 9–10; use of, by students, 8–9
Social networking services, 162
Social presence, 157, 158
Software, career services, 139
Software requirements, 121
Software, tutoring, 125
South Seattle Community College, 29
South Texas College, 26, 28
Specific Review Standards (Quality Matters), 168
Spider Web: description of, xiii, 65–66; standards for, 208–221t
SSP. See Student Success Plan
St. Mary's College of Maryland, 145
St. Norbert College, 96
Standards for Distance Learning Library Services, 116–118
Stanford University, 96
State University of New York Learning Network, 3, 94, 122
Statement of Commitment by the Regional Accrediting Commissions for the Evaluation of Electronically Offered Degree and Certificate Programs, 204
Steele, G., 77, 197
Stenehjem, D., 42, 49
Stone, S., 10, 114
Stoner, M., 170
Stony Brook University, 147
Storify, 8
Strategic planning: collaboration in, 178–179; description of, 178–179; phased approach for, 194–198

Strong American Schools, 25
Student activities, 173–174
Student affairs departments: commitment of, 207; IT departments and, 81; mission of, 80; online support services and, 80–81; program evaluations and, 206–207
Student Communities Suite: description of, 69; standards for, 217–218*t*
Student engagement: communication and, 158–161; definition of, 158–159; library services and, 119–120; measures of, 159–160; online student activities and, 175; online student services and, 72–73; social networks and, 164
Student evaluations, 223–226
Student Information Systems, Collection of Grades, Application for Degree, and Degree Audit Function (AACRAO), 83
Student information systems (SISs), 71–72, 83–84
Student portals, 7
Student records/accounts, online, 99–100
Student Retention Practices and Strategies at Four-Year and Two-Year Institutions, 183, 186
Student satisfaction surveys, 224
Student service professionals, 11
Student Services for Online Learners Spider Web, xiii, 64–65
Student services, online. *See* Support services, online
Student Success Plan (SSP), 30
Student unions, 173
Student-faculty interaction, 159
Students: communication among, 172–176; demand for online learning from, 4; demographics of, in online learning, 14–15, 181; diversity of, in graduating

classes, 13; expectation of, regarding online learning, 2; faculty and institution communication with, 167–172; first impression of institution and, 189; responsibility of, to prevent cheating, 113; technical skills self-assessment of, 9; use of social media by, 8–9; withdrawal of, from online learning, 181–182
Study guides, 124
Subject matter experts, 197
Subjective assessments, 111–112
Support services: adult students and, 16; for at-risk students, 36–37; collaboration in, 1–2; faculty communication in, 168–169; importance of, 10–12; lack of, in online learning, xi–xii; need for, 64; for students with disabilities, 61–62
Support services, online: benefits of, 70–73; categories of, 67–70; in course content, 169; definition of, 10–11; development of, 73–77, 189–193; generations of, 73–77; goal of, 188; importance of, 10–12; institutional culture and, 78–80; institutional type and, 77–78; launch pads for, 63–64; planning tool for, 193–198; prevalence of, 187–188; scope of, 64–67; Spider Web for, 65–66; student affairs and, 80–81; students' ranking of, 185, 186
Supportive campus environment, 159
Survey of Community College Presidents (Green), 3
Swan, K., 157, 158, 180
Swanson, R. A., 18
Syllabus, 112–113, 132

T

Tangible culture, 79
Taylor, B., 207

Teaching presence, 158
Technical skills, 9
Technical support: for accessibility solutions, 60; availability of, 67; innovative practices in, 122–123; for online registration, 98; websites for, 121–122
Technology: accessibility indicators for, 54–56; adult students' use of, 20–21; growth of online learning and, 5; legal definitions of, 6; in new media, 7–10; students' expectations of, 2, 47–48; students with disabilities and, 40, 44–46; usability standards and, 52–54
Technology alerts, 122
Terenzini, P. T., 207
Textbooks, 113–116
Text-only communication, 153–154
Thomas, A. G., 80, 207
Thompson, M. M., 201
Thurmond, K. C., 77, 197
Tice, P., 4
Time limits, 53
Tolerance for error, 51
Tone, of communication, 154
Tours, campus, 89
Toyama, Y., 167, 200
Traditional courses, 6
Training, in accessibility solutions, 60
Transfer students, 87
Trends in Elearning: Tracking the Impact of Elearning at Community Colleges (Instructional Technology Council), 3, 4, 188
Trerise, S., 49
Trouble shooting, 122
Tsang, E.Y.M., 108
Tuition, 94–97
Tutorials, for online registration, 98
Tutoring, online: collaborative options, 126–127; evaluating need for, 68; in Generation 3 services, 75; goals of, 123; institution based options, 124–125; multimedia for, 166; perceived importance of, 127; platforms for, 123–124; selection of, 127; vendor options, 125–126
Twitter: admissions communication and, 89; for institution-student communication, 170–171; for online counseling services, 146; popularity of, 162; student engagement and, 164
2010 Campus Computing Survey (Green), 5
Tyler-Smith, K., 182, 197

U

ULifeline network, 146–147
UMassOnline, 3
Unabridged Student Counseling Virtual Pamphlet Collection (Hsiung), 146
Universal Design: benefits of, 51; description of, 50; principles of, 50–52
University of Alabama, 192, 193
University of Buffalo, 145
University of California, Berkeley, 91
University of California, San Diego, 96
University of Cincinnati, 146
University of Illinois, 89–90
University of Iowa, 120
University of Maryland University College, 174
University of Minnesota, 54–55, 124, 147
University of North Carolina, Chapel Hill, 120
University of Pennsylvania, 144
University of Phoenix, 3, 116
University of South Carolina, 54
University of South Dakota, 192, 193
University of Texas at Austin, 90, 166
University of Washington, 44, 54, 122
University of Wisconsin-Madison, 54
Upcraft, M. L., 207
U.S. Department of Education, xiii, 16, 48, 65, 95

U.S. Department of Justice, 47, 48, 49
U.S. Department of Labor, 140
U.S. News and World Report, 8
Usability standards, 52–54
"The User's Perspective," 45
Utah State University, 57

V

Valencia Community College, 108
Values, program, 204
VanLooy, S., 49
Veterans, 13–14, 16; definition of, 32; innovative practices regarding, 33–34; unique needs of, 33
Video conferences, 133, 142
Videos: admissions information and, 88, 90; for faculty professional development, 164; financial aid information on, 95; for orientation, 131, 133; versus text-only communication, 155
Virginia Tech University, 110, 148–149
Virtual classrooms, 142, 167
Virtual communities: examples of, 170; indicators of success in, 8; for student activities, 173–174; for support services, 169
Virtual culture, 78
Virtual World applications, 21
Vision, of online services, 196, 197
Visual disabilities: adaptations for, 44; usability standards and, 52–53
Vogel, C., 8
Voice Over Internet Protocol, 147

W

Walden University, 3
Walker, B., 155
Wall, V., 207
Wal-Mart Foundation, 33
Washington State University, 175
Waters, J. K., 114

WCET. *See* WICHE Cooperative for Educational Technologies
Web accessibility committees, 58–59, 61
Web Accessibility Initiative (WAI), 51
Web Content Accessibility Guidelines (WCAG), 50, 51
Web developers: on accessibility committees, 59; technical support by, 60
Web 2.0 technologies: versus email, 8; for personal counseling services, 146
WebAIM model, 57–61
Web-enhanced courses, 6
WebEx, 107
Website design: accessibility indicators for, 54–56; accessibility solutions for, 57–61; adult students and, 190; Americans with Disabilities Act and, 47, 56; for bookstores, 113–114; for career services, 139–140; ease of use and, 190, 192; in generations of online support services, 72–77; increased dynamics of, 71; for library services, 118–120; navigation and, 192; online admissions and, 84–89; student engagement and, 72–73; students' first impressions and, 189; students' preferences regarding, 192; for students with disabilities, 44, 45, 46, 48–49, 49; universal design principles and, 50–52; usability standards and, 52–54
Website visits, 15
What Works in Student Retention, 183, 185–186
Whiting, J., 50
Whorley, J. F., 95
WICHE Cooperative for Educational Technologies (WCET), xiii, 67, 111, 112, 193
Wiki, 143–144
Willging, P. A., 155

Williams, F. K., xii, 180
Wilson, J. L., 192
Wilson, M., 131, 182, 197
Wimba, 125, 137
Winfield, E., 145
Withdrawal, of students,
    181–182
Wojciechowski, A., 182
Wolf, D., 24
Worcester Polytechnic Institute, 90
Working students, 24, 25
World War II, 16
World Wide Web Consortium (W3C),
    51
Writing style, 154

X

Xu, D., 28, 28

Y

Yen, C. J., 180
Yeung, F., 24
Young, J., 5
YouTube, 166
Yu, T., 183t

Z

Zahib, I., 105
Zapata, L. P., 80, 207
Zickuhr, K., 21
Ziskin, M., 180, 182, 197